THE COMPLETE
STEP-BY-STEP GUIDE TO
HOME SEWING

THE COMPLETE
STEP-BY-STEP GUIDE TO
HOME SEWING

Introduced by Jeanne Argent

CHILTON BOOK COMPANY

RADNOR · PENNSYLVANIA

© Eaglemoss Publications Limited 1983, 1984, 1990

Published in the U.S. in 1990, by Chilton Book Company,
Radnor, Pennsylvania 19089

234567890   9876543210

This material previously appeared in the
partwork *Superstitch*

Printed in Hong Kong

Library of Congress Cataloging-in-Publication Data

The complete Step-by-Step Guide to Home Sewing
Introduced by Jeanne Argent
        p. cm.
    This material previously appeared in the partwork Superstitch –
T.p. verso.
    First published in Great Britain by Orbis Publishing Limited.
London, 1985 – T.p. verso
        ISBN 0-8019-8080-1:
        1. Machine Sewing   2. Home Furnishings.
TT713,C65 1990
646.2' 1 – dc20   89-27169
                                                        CIP

Contents

Introduction

Here is a book filled with hundreds of ideas to transform your home with up-to-the-minute 'designer look' furnishings and accessories. Just leafing through these photographs of attractive room settings will inspire you to get out the sewing machine and scissors. But this is not simply a collection of pretty pictures. Clear diagrams and text describe in step-by-step stages exactly how everything is made *and* how to get just the right finish. Projects range from those simple enough for an absolute beginner to more ambitious tasks. So there is something here for you – whatever your skill.

The sections on curtains, blinds and pelmets are very comprehensive, giving information on various effects you can achieve using either ready-made heading tape or hand-sewn headings. There is advice on the best types of fabric for each style and a guide to the quantities needed for the various different headings. Designer ideas, such as contrast borders, pleated or gathered frilled edges, tiebacks and draped valances, are included, and blinds and pelmets are finished off with scalloped or crenellated edges, fringes, tassels or bows.

Scatter cushions bring an impression of luxury and comfort to any room, softening the lines of chairs and sofas and adding a touch of colour or contrast. The simpler ones make ideal beginner projects since each is a small task in its own right. Home-sewn cushions also work out much cheaper than the purchased equivalent because they are often made from remnants and trimmed with offcuts of ribbon, lace and braid.

There is a lot of money to be saved too in making your own bedlinen, particularly in the nursery and children's section. The special 'fun' designs would cost a small fortune in the shops, but can be made inexpensively at home using simple sewing techniques.

Straightforward techniques are also used to make some attractive tablelinen, whether it be a cloth for the dining table with co-ordinated napkins, or a pretty fitted cover for a circular occasional table.

Good lighting is very important and the section on lampshades will give you ideas for making a variety of attractive shades: styles range from the plain drum shade to quite complicated fitted and lined shapes.

Loose covers will transform your chairs and sofas and can be used to unite an odd collection of furniture. Different seat covers will give your dining chairs a new lease of life, and new canvas can save an old deck chair from the scrap-heap. None of these jobs is difficult to tackle if you follow the instructions.

Fabric requirements are described throughout, enabling you to choose the right materials for each project, and there are handy tips on co-ordinating fabrics and mixing and matching textures. Guidance is given too on fastenings, fittings and fixings. The special 'professional touch' section included in many projects details some of the time-saving tips which can be employed to achieve a really professional finish. This is an excellent reference book – strong on inspiration and on sewing know-how.

Jeanne Argent

Jeanne Argent, 1985

PART 1

Curtains

The choice of curtain fabric and style is one of the most important decisions to make when furnishing a room. Windows are often the focal point of a scheme and curtaining must be chosen to suit the proportions of the window and style of furnishings in the room, not forgetting the practical needs such as insulation.

Curtain fabrics can be expensive and lining, interlining and some sort of heading all add to the cost. You can keep the expense down by making curtains yourself and the following chapters set out clearly and simply all the techniques for a wide range of styles.

For the beginner, the variety of heading tapes and curtain tracks available makes it quite straightforward to sew and hang basic styles of curtain. If, however, you wish to achieve a really luxurious and professional look, hand-made headings, locked-in linings and interlinings are also described in detail and valances, pelmets and tie-backs will add the finishing touches.

Choosing curtain fabrics

Traditional curtain fabrics are brocade, velvet, linen and cotton and nowadays there is a wide range of man-made fabrics developed for use in soft furnishing. Some manufacturers produce a range of matching or co-ordinating wallpapers and fabrics, the latter often in two weights suitable for curtains and upholstery. Do not confine yourself to the furnishing fabric departments – many dress-making fabrics can also be used successfully for curtains.

The main requirements when choosing fabric are that it drapes well, has stable colours and will not fade excessively in sunlight, wears well and will not shrink or stretch when washed or hung. The fabric label should guide you on these points but, if in doubt, consult the sales assistant. Check whether the fabric is washable or needs to be drycleaned as this will affect your choice of lining and interlining.

Curtain fabric guide

Acetate Man-made fibre, silky-looking fabrics, often combined with cotton or linen in brocades and open-weave effects. Drapes well but is not very strong. Usually washable, does not shrink.

Acrylic Synthetic fibre; used for lightweight yet strong and crease-resistant fabrics such as velvet and satin. Washable but some varieties may need drycleaning.

Cotton Natural fibre which is strong and wears well. Used for many types of fabric including glazed cotton, which has a shiny finish and resists dirt. Other varieties include velveteen, cotton satin, sateen and towelling. Washable.

Fibreglass Man-made fibre – flame resistant. Dryclean.

Hessian Natural fibre which is cheap and comes in a wide range of colours. The loose weave may tend to droop. Dryclean.

Milium Man-made fibre for aluminium-backed curtain lining with good insulation properties. Available in silver, white and cream. Dryclean.

Nylon Synthetic fibre used for fabrics of all weights and types. Varieties include nylon velvet and nets. Can fade, and may discolour in sunlight. Washable.

Polyester Synthetic fibre often blended with natural fibres – does not shrink or fade. Drapes well, very strong and used for its sheer and opaque qualities.

Rayon Also known as viscose. Man-made fibre fabric which includes taffeta, linen types and velvet. Drapes and wears well but tends to fray so care needed when making up. Hand wash.

Silk Natural fibre fabric in all weights and types. May fade in bright sunlight. Dryclean or hand wash with care.

Simple unlined curtains – the lightweight look

Unlined curtains involve a minimum of sewing and are the simplest type to make up. Join fabric widths, neaten side hems, add heading tape, sew bottom hems and you're there. Sheer fabrics – the kind that let in lots of light and give you privacy too – are highly suitable for making up by this quick method.

Unlined curtains are ideal for use in kitchens, bathrooms, playrooms or on any window where insulation and light exclusion are less important than a cheap and cheerful effect and easy laundering. Unlined curtains are also the simplest to make.

Double hems neaten edges and standard curtain tape attached to the top has pockets for the hooks which hang the curtain on the track. For curtains that do not need to be drawn back, a cased heading hung on elasticated wire or a length of dowelling is an even cheaper alternative.

Choosing and buying fabrics

All furnishing fabric departments include a wide range of plain and printed cottons ideal for unlined curtains. Many dressmaking fabrics are also suitable, although they may tend to fade more quickly.

There is also a wide choice of semi-transparent fabrics, usually in man-made fibres and often incorporating a woven thread pattern. Curtains made from these sheer fabrics usually remain drawn to provide privacy while letting in light and are also excellent for disguising a far from scenic view.

Instructions for measuring up for curtains are given on page 10 but bear in mind that some washable fabrics have a tendency to shrink: if in doubt buy an extra 10% of fabric length (10cm/4in for every metre/yard). Either wash the fabric before cutting out or make up with all the excess incorporated in the bottom hem. The curtain can then be let down after the first wash.

The sewing thread should match the fibre content of the fabric. A polyester thread is best for man-made fabrics. Sheers, man-made fabrics in particular, tend to slip when machining so tacking is essential. Fine pins and machine needles should be used and the tension set fairly loose. Use a scrap of spare fabric to test stitch size and tension before beginning. Fabrics which are very slippery or have an open weave can be machined by placing tissue paper between the machine base plate and fabric – to be torn away later.

Joining widths Curtain fabrics come in fairly standard widths. Try to buy the widest possible to avoid seams, but if necessary, join widths with a flat or French seam. See page 28 for matching patterns.

Selvedges, if they are woven more tightly than the rest of the fabric, should be trimmed off before seaming to prevent puckering. If selvedges are left, they should be clipped every 10cm/4in along the edge.

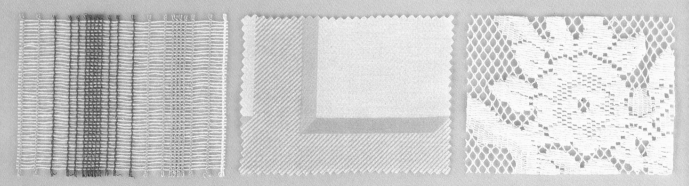

Above: In this bay window corner, full length sheer curtains soften the effect of plain roller blinds.
Left: The variety of fibres and weaving/ printing techniques makes for an abundant choice of sheer fabrics, from fine nets to heavier lace designs and open weaves.

Measuring up

The curtain track or pole can be either in the window recess (most net curtains are hung in this position) or outside the recess and just above the window frame.

If the track is *outside* the recess, it should extend, if possible, 15cm/6in on each side of the window frame so that the curtains can be pulled back from the glass area during the day for maximum light. The height of the track above the window will depend on the best visual effect for the curtain length you choose. Lightweight sheer fabrics hung *inside* a window recess can be supported by a thin pole or elasticated wire slotted through a casing at the top of the curtain. A pole can also look good outside the recess.

How much fabric do you need? This method of calculating the total amount of fabric needed should be used for all curtains, lined or unlined. You may find that a pocket calculator is helpful.

1 Measure the total width needed
2 Work out number of fabric widths required
3 Multiply fabric widths by length to arrive at a total amount.

For a six-step guide to calculating your fabric needs see far right.

Width Measure the width of your track or pole using a steel tape or wooden rule. Multiply this figure by 1½ to 3 times depending on the heading tape. Standard heading tape, such as Rufflette 'Standard', needs at least 1½ – 2 times the track width in fabric. Light sheers can use up to three times. To the total width required, add on 2.5cm/1in for each side hem on the curtains (5cm/2in for sheers) and add the overlap for each curtain if the track is in two overlapping halves. Divide this total figure by the fabric width chosen for number of fabric widths needed. Err on the generous side, rounding up to full widths as you will need 3cm/1¼in seam allowance for each width join.

Length Measure the curtain length (see diagrams below). Add 4cm/1½in for top heading hem (Standard heading tape) and 15cm/6in for bottom hem. For sheer fabrics double this bottom hem allowance and add 6cm/2¼in for top hem for cased heading.

Pattern repeats If your fabric has a definite pattern, you must make an allowance for matching. As a guideline, add one extra pattern repeat for every fabric width. Pattern matching is covered in detail on page 28.

Pattern matching is covered in detail on page 28.

Six-step guide to fabric calculation

Taking curtain track width and finished curtain length, follow this step-by-step method to arrive at the total quantity of fabric required.

1 Measure width of track
2 Multiply track width by 1½-2 (for Standard heading tape) or by up to 3 times for other heading tapes and add side hem allowances (double for sheers). Add overlap fabric allowance if applicable.
3 Divide this figure by the width of fabric to give number of fabric widths.
4 This will probably not work out to a whole number of widths, so round this figure up to the next full width.
5 Multiply the number of fabric widths by length of curtain with top hem and bottom hem allowances to give total fabric needed.
6 This total has now to be divided between the number of curtains (generally two).

sill length   just below sill length   floor length

How long should your curtains be?

This is a matter of personal choice, and depends on the size of the window, your style of furnishings and the visual effect you want but basically curtain lengths fall into three categories: sill length, just below sill length (15–20cm/6–8in) and floor length.

Making up the curtains

Preparing to cut

You need a large flat surface that will take the complete length of your curtain and a full width of the fabric. A large table is best, or clear an area of floor space to work on. If you work in cramped conditions, you're likely to make mistakes in measuring and cutting out. You'll need space for an ironing board too.

Cutting out

It's vitally important that you start with a straight cut across the width. If the fabric has a straight thread pattern (the weft) across the width, pull out a thread for a straight line, otherwise cut at a right angle to the selvedges. Line up the pattern repeat (if necessary) before cutting subsequent widths.

Joining widths

Seam widths of fabric together to make up the total width for each curtain. If the curtain contains full widths and a half, place the half width on the outer side of the curtain. Use a flat seam if the edges are selvedges or for raw edges that can be neatly finished off. To hide raw edges use fell or French seams.

Seams for joining widths

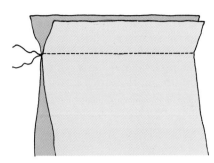

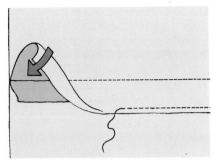

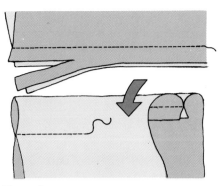

Flat seam
Right sides of fabric facing and edges matching, pin the two layers of fabric together and tack. Stitch 1.5cm/⅝in from edges. Remove tacking, press seam open. If the fabric edges are selvedges, clip seam allowance every 10cm/4in along the selvedge to prevent fabric puckering.

Fell seam
Right sides facing, make a flat seam of 1.5cm/⅝in. Press open. Trim one seam allowance in half. Fold other seam allowance over trimmed one and tack down to enclose raw edge. Top stitch through all layers. Remove tacking and press. One stitching line will show on right side of fabric.

French seam
Wrong sides facing, make a flat seam of 5mm/¼in. Trim to 3mm/⅛in. Press. Turn so right sides face and seam is on the fold. Tack the two layers together. Sew 1cm/½in down from first seam. Remove tacking. All raw edges are enclosed in seam and are to the reverse of the fabric. No stitching line shows on the right side of fabric.

Side hems

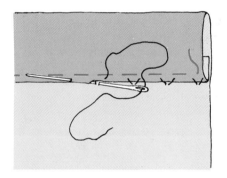

To neaten sides, turn 5mm/¼in of the hem allowance to wrong side and press. Fold remaining 2cm/¾in of hem allowance to wrong side. Tack. Stitch through all layers by machine or slipstitch. Remove all tacking. Slipstitch by passing the sewing needle through 1cm/½in of hem fold, picking up a single thread of the main fabric and then passing through 1cm/½in of fold again. Repeat down hem. Remove tacking. Sheer fabrics should be finished with a double side hem to look neat and prevent raw edges from showing through. Fold the 2.5cm/1in hem allowance to the wrong side and press. Fold over again to same size. Tack through all layers. Machine stitch or slipstitch in place.

PROFESSIONAL TOUCH

Hems for open weave fabrics

As with all sheer fabrics, side and bottom hems must be sewn with double turnings. You'll need to plan the placing of these hems so that the weave or pattern matches when the hem is turned under and also so that there's a maximum of solid pattern area available to sew through. In approximately the right position for the first turn of the hem, mark, with tailor's chalk or tacking, a vertical line between the pattern repeats (horizontal for bottom hems).
1 Mark again between the next line of pattern repeats.
2 Fold the fabric to the wrong side along the first marked line, and the pattern of the main fabric and turned under hem should match. Tack.

3 Turn the hem again along the second line. Tack and stitch. Remove tacking.
If the pattern is large, mark a suitable hem allowance and match pattern areas as best as possible. Use French seams to join widths taking care to match the pattern repeat as for hems.

Choosing the right heading tape

A heading tape is designed to take up the fullness of the curtain fabric in even gathers or pleats. Various styles of ready-made heading tapes are available, and the choice will depend on the gathered/pleated effect you personally find most pleasing. Standard tape gives an evenly gathered heading while deeper tapes are made to create various pleat effects – eg, Rufflette Regis produces very close deep pleats. Cartridge wider pleats and Tridis, fan-shaped triple pleats (see pages 22 and 23).

The synthetic fibre version of Standard tape is particularly suitable for sheers and lightweight fabrics. When you buy heading tape, check with the retailer how much fullness of fabric is required for the tape chosen. Rufflette Standard Tape for example requires a minimum of 1½ times track width, Regis 2½ times.

Attaching Standard heading tape

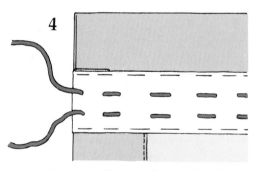

Measure finished width of curtain and add 4cm/1½in at either end for neatening. Cut a piece of heading tape to this length.
1 At the end where the curtains will overlap, pull 4cm/1½in of each cord free at the back of the tape.

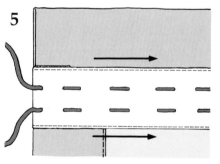

On the wrong side of the heading tape, tie the 4cm/1½in of free cords together securely with a knot.
2 Trim off the surplus tape to leave 1.5cm/⅝in beyond the knot and press this seam allowance to the wrong side of the tape.

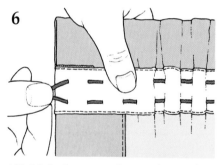

3 At the other end of the heading tape, gently ease out 4cm/1½in of cords on the right side. These cords will be used to pull the tape and fabric into gathers. Turn surplus tape to wrong side and press.

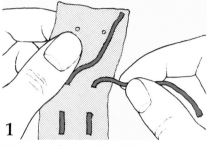

Turn 4cm/1½in at the head of the curtain to wrong side and press. Position the tape on the wrong side of curtain with top edge no more than 2.5cm/1in below the head.
4 Tack, tucking knot at centre side edge to wrong side.

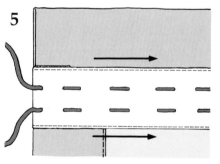

5 Machine stitch the heading tape to curtain. Do not stitch across the short end with the loose cords. Stitch both long edges in the same direction as this will prevent any puckering while sewing. Remove tacking.

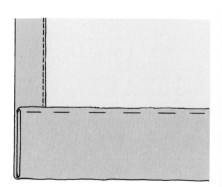

6 Hold the loose cords together and gently push tape up to gather the fabric until fully pleated.
Then ease out evenly until curtain is the right width.
Tie loose cords together. Insert tape hooks about every 8cm/3in.

Bottom hems

At bottom edge, turn 1cm/½in to wrong side and press. Turn balance of hem allowance to wrong side and pin. (For sheers see previous page.) Tack hem. Press complete curtain and hang on the track or pole for several days to allow fabric to 'drop'. Check level and height of hem and adjust if necessary. Slipstitch hem by hand and remove tacking. Sheer fabrics need a double hem, to hide raw edges, and look best with machined hems. Fold half the hem allowance to the wrong side and press. Fold the same amount again and tack hem (see diagram right). Hang for a few days. Check height and level and machine or slipstitch the hem. Remove tackings. Press.

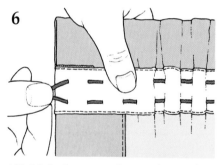

Choosing, making and caring for net curtains

Net curtains come in a wide range of plain, patterned and frilled sheer fabrics. Learn the most economical way of buying curtaining to suit the proportions of your window and keep unsightly joins to a minimum using these cutting and sewing techniques.

Net, lace and sheer curtains let in light while retaining privacy. They also filter harsh sunlight without totally obscuring the view, adding a fresh, decorative touch to the room scheme. Forget the old image of yellowing nets hanging limply from drooping wire – with recent developments in the design and manufacturing of sheer fabrics and hanging methods, there are now endless ways of styling them to create attractive window treatments.

Traditionally, net or lace curtains are hung permanently across the window recess, with heavier curtains on top. This gives scope for adding colourful trimmings, for using frilled or shaped curtaining, and for making use of modern curtain headings. Alternatively, try decorative lacy drapes over a simple roller blind, which is pulled down for warmth and privacy, or make a pretty sheer or net fabric into an Austrian blind, trimmed to echo the colours of top curtains.

Below: Modern net and sheer fabrics give you privacy with style.

Buying net curtain fabric

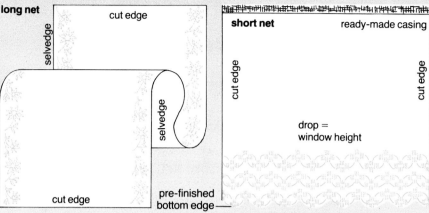

As seams in sheer curtains, particularly nets, tend to be very obvious against the light of a window, curtain net fabrics are sold in a wide variety of widths and drops to eliminate the need for seaming widths together.

Buying nets can be confusing – you can choose the fabric either in a suitable width (long nets) or with a suitable drop (short nets).

Long nets are sold in widths up to about 300cm/118in so that most curtains can be made from one piece of fabric, avoiding joins. The selvedges of the fabric form the side edges of the curtain. Measure the width of the window area to be covered and multiply this by 1½-3, according to the amount of fullness required, to calculate the width of curtain to buy.

Measure the height of the window area and add allowances for a top casing or turning, and a bottom hem, to calculate the length of curtaining to buy.

Short nets are ideal for windows that are wide rather than tall. They are manufactured so that the two edges of the fabric become the top and bottom of the curtain. One edge is pre-finished into a bottom hem, often with a frill, scallop or some other decorative finish, and the other edge has a casing to take either an elastic wire or a hanging rod. You therefore buy the *width* of fabric (called the drop) to fit the *height* of your window.

To determine the length of fabric to buy, multiply the width of the window area to be covered by 1½-3 times, according to how much fullness you require. The cut edges become the sides of the curtain and should be neatened with narrow double hems.

If you cannot buy the exact width that provides the drop of fabric that

Caring for and hanging net curtains

Some lace and sheer fabrics, particularly those in natural fibres such as cotton, can shrink by as much as 10% so buy sufficient fabric to allow for this if necessary. Wash and dry the fabric before cutting out so that any shrinkage has already occurred before making it up.

Check washing instructions when purchasing sheers as some of the more delicate fabrics can be damaged by machine washing. If in any doubt, wash gently by hand. If nylon nets turn yellow after a while try soaking them in a nylon whitener.

Net curtains are generally very light in weight so the method of hanging

does not have to be as bulky and strong as a standard type of curtain track. Nor do they need to be drawn back and forth as they are usually positioned permanently across the window.

Elasticated wire, with a small hook screwed in at each end, is the cheapest and most often used way to hang permanently positioned nets. This plastic-coated wire simply threads through the casing at the top of the curtain and, stretched taut, hooks to screw eyes inserted at either side of the window frame. It is suitable for small lightweight curtains but, unless put under very strong tension, tends to sag with large or

a selection of
sheer curtain fabrics

you need, buy the next size up and carefully unpick the top casing. Trim away any surplus fabric and remake the casing to the required depth so that the fabric is the exact drop required.

Stitching techniques for nets

Because of the transparency of nets, care must be taken in making hems and seams. Avoid seams where possible. If you have exceptionally large windows and cannot make a curtain from just one width of fabric, rather than joining fabric widths, make up two (or as many as necessary) separate curtains. Hang them next to each other and conceal the overlapping edges of the fabric in the folds of the curtain.

Hems should be double so that the raw edge of the fabric lies at the fold of the hem. If you have a deep hem on a patterned fabric and the pattern showing through the hem looks unsightly, insert a ribbon or a strip of fabric (the same width as the hem depth) into the hem so that only the solid colour shows through. The ribbon or fabric strip must have the same fibre content as the curtain, as should sewing thread and any heading tape used. See pages 11 and 17 for details of sewing hems and cased headings on sheer or net curtains.

Right: A length of lacy net transforms a bare window in a matter of minutes. Simply machine hem the ends and drape over a wooden pole and side brackets.

heavier curtains.

Curtain rods, designed for net or lightweight curtains that will not need to be drawn back and forth, also thread through the casing but – being in a rigid material – will not sag. Most of the rods designed for net curtains consist of two sections slotted together so that they are telescopic and easily adjustable to the exact size of the window. The rods simply sit on small hook-type fittings attached to the window frame. At least one manufacturer supplies the fittings backed with self-adhesive pads so they are easy to attach even to metal window frames.

Curtain track is required when net or lace curtains may need to be drawn back, perhaps to open French doors or to reveal large windows on a sunny day. Several tracks are specifically designed to be suitable for nets and lightweight curtains, and can be fixed to the wall or to the underside of a window recess. The curtains must have a taped – rather than a cased – heading so that hooks can be inserted to hang them on the track.

Heading for net curtains A cased heading is simple to make (see page 17) and gives a pretty gathered effect, but you may prefer to use a curtain heading tape for a more stylish finish. Some ordinary curtain tapes tend to be too heavy

for nets and even those that are lightweight must be used with proper curtain track. However, a translucent man-made fibre tape specifically designed for nets is now available. It draws the fabric into neat pencil pleats, but differs from other pencil pleating tapes in having bars on the back that simply thread on to an elasticated wire or narrow rod for hanging. Alternatively, the tape also has pockets which enable it to be hung with curtain hooks from a curtain track or decorative pole.

Attach the heading tape to the top of the curtain in the usual way, then pull up the two cords to form the pleating.

15

Cased headings

Not all curtains have to be hung from tracks. When positioning fixed curtains either inside a window recess or in front of the window, a quick and effective method is to use an elasticated wire, or a brass or wooden rod, slotted through a casing at the top of the curtain. This is particularly suitable for lightweight sheers which are not to be drawn back and forth, and are used to give permanent privacy at a window. When estimating fabric for this method, allow 12cm/5in for the heading (more if rod is thick).

Turn 6cm/2½in to wrong side on top of curtain and press. Fold over again 6cm/2½in. Tack. Sew along lower edge of hem and again 2.5cm/1in higher up. Remove tacking and press. This forms the casing. If the rod is thicker than 1cm/½in diameter, measure the diameter and add 1.5cm/⅝in to give a casing depth into which the rod will slip easily. Add 3.5cm/1¾in and double this total figure. Make up as above, but with a deeper casing. Insert rod or wire through the casing, easing the fabric into gathers.

The fabric between the top line of casing stitching and the curtain head forms a frill.

Left: These sheer curtains hang from a dowel rod slotted through a top casing. Below: A half curtain supported on elasticated wire through a narrow casing.
Opposite: Instructions for making a combined curtain/valance are given on page 18.

Creative ways to style net curtains

Use one of the many lovely net, lace, sheer or semi-sheer fabrics now in the shops to transform a bare window into a pretty and eye-catching room feature. Style the fabric into cross-over curtains, valanced curtains or a dramatic full-length drape

Make pretty curtains from net, lace, sheer or semi-sheer fabric to dress a window in a kitchen, bathroom, hall or landing where heavier, drawn curtains are not always necessary. Use them in other rooms, too, during the summer when heavy curtains benefit from being cleaned and 'rested' away from the strong sunshine which fades and ages them.

Many styles of ready-made net curtains are now available in the shops, but making your own is economical and enables you to achieve a perfect fit for windows that are not a standard size. You also have a wider choice of fabric and can add trimmings to match your room scheme. Details of buying and sewing sheer fabrics, making a cased heading and how to care for net curtaining are given on pages 13 to 17. This chapter gives design ideas and making up instructions for three decorative styles of window dressing using these delicate fabrics. Choose from curtains with a combined valance, cross-over draped curtains or a simple but eye-catching draped valance over a decorative curtain pole.

Combined curtain and valance

A valance and lightweight side curtains sewn in one eliminates the need for two rods or wires and ensures a neater, less bulky heading. The curtains are gathered and fixed at the top so they cannot be drawn back and forth. Instead, they look very pretty draped to the sides and held with fabric or brass tie-backs which are easily released.

A separate strip of fabric joins the curtain and valance and forms the cased heading so the curtains can be hung on a decorative pole, simple rod or wire (see page 16).

Measuring up and cutting out
Cut a strip of fabric for the casing the length of the pole or the width of the window (whichever is the longer) plus side hem allowances. The depth of the strip must accommodate the wire or pole plus 1cm/½in seam allowance on each long side. Neaten the short side edges with narrow double hems if necessary.

Measure up and cut out the curtains in the usual way allowing at least 1½ times the window width for fullness, and sew side and lower edge hems. Trim the top of each curtain so that it will just reach the hanging rod. Run a row of gathering stitches 1cm/½in below this edge and pull up each curtain to exactly half the width of the casing strip. Tie the gathering

threads securely and spread the gathers evenly over the width. The depth of the valance is a matter of personal taste and varies according to the proportion of the window. Add 3cm/1¼in seam allowance to the required depth and allow approximately twice the width of the window for the width of the valance. Neaten the side edges with a narrow double hem (1cm/½in and 1cm/½in). Hem the bottom edge in a similar way or add a lace or frilled edging, trimming away any excess hem allowance. Omit hems if using selvedges. Run a gathering thread along the top edge of the valance and pull up to the width of the casing strip.

Making up the curtains and valance

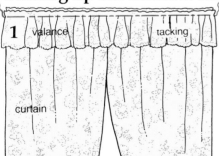

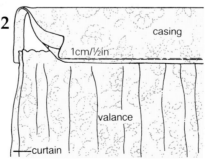

Lay the curtains out flat, right side up and with the two inside edges butted up together. Lay the valance across the two curtains, wrong side down, matching gathered edges.
1 Tack securely together along the top edge.

2 Turn 1cm/½in to the wrong side along all the edges of the casing strip and tack to hold. Fold the strip in half, lengthwise, wrong sides facing, and place over the top gathered edges of the curtain/valance, overlapping it by 1cm/½in

so that the raw edges are enclosed in the casing. Tack in place. Machine stitch the length of casing in place, sewing 5mm/⅜in from the edge through all layers – curtain, valance and both sides of the casing.

Remove all tacking, press well and thread on to a rod or wire to hang. Hold the curtains to the sides of the window with a simple tie-back. Choose from a length of silken cord (adding tassels to the ends), matching or contrasting ribbon or a length of delicately scalloped and embroidered broderie anglaise with the raw edge neatened. See pages 16, 17 and opposite for ideas.

Prettily draped cross-over curtains: the top edges can be overlapped either partially or completely.

Cross-over draped curtains

These are gathered up with the usual amount of fullness but are wide enough to overlap at the top so that while draped back to the sides of the window, forming attractive folds, they do not leave a large area of bare window.

The two curtains are sewn together at the top and hang on a single rod or wire, so they can't, of course, be drawn back and forth.

To maintain a straight lower edge on the curtain, the draped inside edge of each curtain requires a greater length of fabric than the straight outer edge. The hems are therefore angled.

Measuring up and cutting out

Allow at least 1½ times the window width for the width of *each* curtain.
1 Measure the length of the straight shorter outside edge from the hanging wire or rod to the window sill. To calculate the length of the longer inner edge, drape a tape measure from one end of the rod to a suitable tie-back point on the opposite side of the window and down to the window sill. Add the

1 measuring finished length of longer draped edges

same allowance for the top casing and bottom hem to each of these measurements.

Cut both curtains to the longer length then lay right sides together and mark off the shorter length along one side. Cut diagonally across from this point to the opposite lower corner to angle the hem. This ensures that one curtain slopes in the reverse direction to the other.

Neaten side and lower edges with

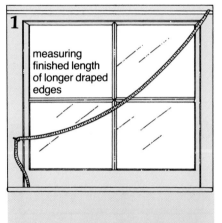

2 curtains tacked together at top

short outer edge

long inner edge

narrow double hems, adding a frill to the longer inside edges if required (see page 48).
2 With right sides upwards, lay one curtain on top of the other and tack the straight top edges together. Complete the heading, treating the two curtains as one, either adding a heading tape or making a casing. Hang the curtains and drape them back to the sides, holding them with fabric tie-backs or decorative curtain holders.

19

All-in-one valance and side curtains

The dramatic effect of this draped valance falling into side curtains is simply achieved by securing a long length of reversible lacy curtaining over a decorative curtain pole. This creative style of window dressing is pretty rather than practical and ideal as a replacement for heavier curtains during the summer.

Measuring up

To calculate the amount of fabric required, drape a tape measure (or a piece of string) from one end of the pole to the other, allowing it to droop in the curve you want for the valance. Add this measurement to the length needed for the side curtains (twice the height from floor to pole) plus hem allowances on both sides. This gives the length of fabric required.

If you are using a patterned fabric with a one-way design, the curtain will have to be cut in two so that the pattern will be upright on both sides. Add enough extra fabric to join two pieces together with a narrow French seam. The design should be level on both side curtains, so that the same part of the pattern lies at the lower edge on each, and you may also need to allow extra fabric for this.

Making up

As this type of curtain is not drawn across the window, one width of fabric is normally sufficient, and therefore side hems are unnecessary. Cut a fabric with a one way pattern in half across the width and join the top edges of the two halves with a narrow French seam so that the pattern will be upright on both side curtains. Neaten the lower edges with a narrow double hem, a pretty satin binding or with a lace or frilled edging.

Measure the length of the drop from each end and, with tailor's chalk, draw two lines across the width of the fabric to mark the central area allowed for the valance drape. Lay the fabric over the pole with the curtains falling behind and the valance in front of the pole. Adjust the fabric so that the two curtains hang well, then adjust and pin folds at both ends of the valance so that it falls in a pleasing way. Take down the curtains/valance carefully and secure the folds at each end of the valance with a few hand stitches. Remove pins and re-hang to check the final effect, adjusting if necessary.

To prevent the fabric slipping off the pole, cut two 5cm/2in pieces of 'stick and sew' Velcro fastening. Stitch the sew-on halves of the Velcro to the ends of the valance on the wrong side, at a point where the fabric has been folded several times so that they will not show.

Replace the curtains/valance on the curtain pole and stick the self-adhesive halves of the Velcro to the pole to correspond with the sewn on halves. Add extra Velcro if the valance shows a tendency to slip.

Below: Lengths of border-patterned Terylene net create a strikingly pretty window dressing.

Curtain heading tapes and detachable linings

All curtains, with the exception of sheers and curtains with a deliberately delicate look, gain from a lining. Adding a lining will cost you more in money and effort, but the curtains will hang better, look more professional and provide valuable insulation.

Curtains shut out the dark, protect the sleeper from the dawn and give privacy. A lining acts as a barrier between the curtain and window and fulfils several vital functions:
– it cuts down light penetration through the curtain fabric (especially important in bedrooms)
– it provides insulation, helping to cut down on draughts and cold air from the windows
– it weighs down the curtain, giving it more 'body' and a better hang
– it protects the curtain fabric from the damaging effects of sunlight, and to some extent from dirt and dust

– a detachable lining can be removed for separate laundering
– on really draughty windows where one lining is not enough, an inter-lining of a fine blanket-like material sewn to the curtain fabric before the lining is attached gives a further layer of insulation. Interlinings are dealt with on page 32.
The fabric generally sold as curtain lining' is 100% cotton. The weave is close and dense to cut out light and draughts. Thermal curtain-lining fabric, which has a special coating on one side, is a little more expensive to buy, but provides extra insulation.

Choosing the lining method
There are several ways to line curtains. Which method you choose depends on the size of the curtain and the weight of the fabric and, of course, your personal preference.
Detachable linings are suitable if the curtain and lining fabric have different laundering requirements, or if you want to add a lining to an existing unlined curtain. The curtain and lining are completely separate and just held together at the top by virtue of sharing the same curtain hooks.
Sewn-in linings are suitable for small or lightweight curtains. They are joined to the curtain down the side hems and across the top. They are covered in the next chapter.
Locked-in linings are suitable for large or weighty curtains. In addition to being attached to the curtain across the top and down the sides, the lining is invisibly lock-stitched to the curtain fabric at regular intervals from top to bottom over the whole curtain. Locked-in linings are dealt with on pages 30-31.

Below: The lining in these curtains gives them extra body and a good hang.

Creating a heading for your curtain

The easiest way to create a decorative heading is to use a ready-made curtain heading tape. This has cords running through it to pull both tape and fabric up into gathers or pleats, and pockets for hanging hooks.

The basic heading styles are:
1 Even gathering
2 Pencil pleating
3 Triple pleating
4 Cylindrical pleating

There are other tapes which create different visual effects, but they are less widely available. If you do use tapes other than the four styles above, follow the manufacturers' instructions for the amount of tape and fabric needed and attaching method. Hand-made headings – hard work but very professional-looking – are dealt with on pages 34-37.

How much fabric?

The type of heading you use determines the amount of fabric needed for both curtains and lining, so choosing a heading should be your first consideration. A gathered heading needs only 1½ times the track width of fabric, although up to 3 times can be used for sheers. Pencil pleats need 2¼ to 2½ times and triple and cylindrical pleats twice the track width.

How much tape?

You need as much tape as the finished flat width of each curtain plus an extra amount for accurate placing of the pleats and neatening. Check with the shop assistant how much you need – for triple pleating allow 30cm/12in extra per curtain.

Which heading?

The type of heading you choose depends on the look you want. Each style of heading tape shown is suitable for any weight of fabric, but there are some general guidelines to follow.

For short curtains the shallower tapes such as 'Rufflette' brand gathered tape, pencil pleating, triple pleating and cylindrical pleating look best. A deep heading tape might look top-heavy on a short curtain.

Pencil pleating

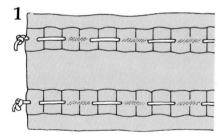

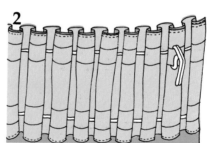

For each curtain, cut a piece of tape to the curtain width plus at least 7cm/2¾in for neatening edges.
1 At the edge of the tape which will be at the centre, pull 4cm/1½in of cords free and knot. Trim surplus tape to within 5mm/¼in of knots and turn edge to wrong side. (The right side of the tape has pockets.) At the other end, pull 5cm/2in of cords free and turn tape to wrong side. Place wrong side of tape to wrong side of curtain 3mm/⅛in down from the top edge with the tape the correct way up. (Rufflette brand tape has a yellow line at the bottom.) If you are not sure which way up the tape should be, insert hooks and check the hang on your track. Tack the tape to the curtain 3mm/⅛in in from each long edge and, from the wrong side of the curtain, machine the tape each side in the same direction. Machine both short edges, taking care not to stitch across loose cords. Hold cords, pull up fabric to maximum pleating, then ease to correct width.
2 Knot the cords to secure, and insert hooks at either end and at about 8cm/3in intervals along the tape. (With Rufflette Regis, use R40 hooks) If you want the curtain to cover the track, add hooks to the bottom row of pockets. If you want it to hang below, use the top row.

Triple pleating

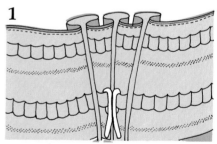

At the edge of the tape which will be at the centre, cut across the first pleat to free the cords. Knot each cord and trim surplus tape to 5mm/¼in. If the curtain tracks overlap turn 4cm/1½in of tape to the wrong side of this centre edge. If the curtains are to butt up, turn 9cm/3½in. The amount of tape turned back on the centre edge governs the pleat position. Neaten this edge and cut tape to fit curtain width allowing at least 6cm/2¼in at the outer edge for neatening. Free 5cm/2in of the cords from outer edge, free from tape with scissors point. Trim off surplus tape to within 5mm/¼in of cords and fold to

For long curtains extra-deep versions of pencil and triple pleating give the best proportioned look, but standard depth tapes can also be used if preferred. With sheer fabrics, even a simple gathered tape gives a neat heading on long curtains.

Fabric choice and laundering

Curtain tapes are suitable for any weight or type of fabric and are washable and dry cleanable, so you should launder curtains according to the washing instructions of your curtain fabric. Use the lowest heat when ironing synthetic fibre tapes.

Which curtain track?

Which curtain track you use depends on whether you want the curtain to conceal it (as in most plastic tracking), or to be suspended below. Poles fall into this second category.

Some tapes such as Rufflette brand gathered (Standard), pencil pleating (Regis), triple pleating (Tridis) and cylindrical pleating (Cartridge) have hook pockets positioned so that they can be used with either type of hanging. Deep triple pleating (Deep Tridis) and deeper pencil pleating (Deep Regis) are manufactured in two versions, one for covering the track, the other for a suspended heading.

How to attach a heading tape

The easiest tape to sew to a curtain head is gathered tape (see page 12).

Above: The photographs show,
1 gathered heading (Rufflette Standard),
2 pencil pleating (Rufflette Regis),
3 triple pleating (Rufflette Tridis) and
4 cylindrical pleating (Rufflette Cartridge).

For pencil, triple or cylindrical pleating tape, turn a minimum hem allowance of 6mm/¼in at the top of curtain to the wrong side and press. When attaching tape; be careful to knot the cords on the correct end of the curtain, depending on whether it is to be hung on the left or on the right. The cord ends are knotted and turned to the wrong side on the centre edges of each curtain. Never cut off surplus cords at outer edges.

Cylindrical pleating

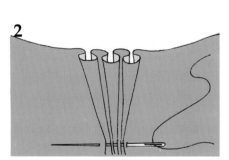

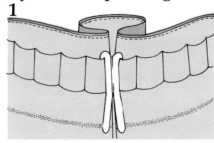

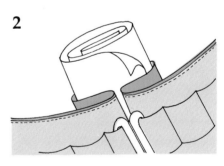

wrong side.
Sew in place as for pencil pleating. Pull the cords and push up the tape and fabric to form the first set of pleats. Move along, forming pleats and tie a slip knot with the cords.
1 This style of tape needs a two-pronged hook (Rufflette R10). One hook is inserted behind each pleat set, each prong into an adjacent pocket. Add a hook at both the centre and outer edge. Use the bottom pockets for covering the track, the top for suspending the curtain.
2 To keep the pleats tight, a small neat tack can be sewn through the base of the front of each pleat.

At the edge of the tape which will be at the centre, cut across the first pleat to free the cords. Knot each cord and cut tape to within 5mm/¼in of knots.
If your two curtain tracks overlap, turn 2.5cm/1in to wrong side of this centre edge. If the curtains are to butt up, turn 5cm/2in to neaten. Cut the tape to fit the curtain width allowing at least 6cm/2¼in at the outer edge for neatening. Free 5cm/2in of the cords from outer edge, picking cords out with a scissor point if they are not visible. Trim tape to within 5mm/¼in of cords. Attach tape as for pencil pleating.

Hold the cords and push the tape up into pleats, keeping each pleat tight. Tie a slip knot to secure cords.
1 The same hooks are used as for the triple pleating, one for each pleat and one at each end, placed in the bottom row of pockets for covering the track or the top row for suspending.
2 For extra pleat definition, each pleat can be stuffed with rolled-up tissue paper.

Making a detachable lining

Detachable linings are the simplest of all to make. These completely separate linings are attached to the main curtains by sharing the same curtain hooks.

The main advantage of a detachable lining is that the curtain and lining can be laundered separately. This could be useful if the fabric and lining have different laundering requirements – in some cases the lining may be dry cleanable only (as with thermal lining material) and the curtain fabric washable, or vice-versa.

Even if both the curtain and lining are washable, the combined weight of both sewn together often makes the curtain a very heavy and bulky item to wash by hand. If the curtain is large it may be too bulky to fit in a domestic

washing machine. A detachable lining which can be separated from the curtain reduces this bulk.

A special heading tape is available for detachable linings. It is designed to be used in conjunction with a heading tape on the curtain sharing the same hooks. Some curtain tracks have combined hooks and gliders with an additional ring for hooking on a lining.

Detachable linings use less fabric than sewn-in linings since, whichever type of heading is on the curtain, only 1½ times the track width in lining is necessary.

This type of lining can easily be added to existing unlined curtains.

Measure up and cut out the main fabric and lining, using the same

Above: A strip of contrast fabric sewn to the inner edge and bottom of each curtain accentuates the draped shape. Instructions for making contrast fabric borders are given on pages 48-49. The pleated tie-back is shown opposite.

basic method as for unlined curtains (see page 10), but allowing sufficient fabric width for the heading of your choice.

Make up the main curtain in exactly the same way as for an unlined curtain, attaching the heading tape of your choice.

Make up the lining as for an unlined curtain, but leave the top as a raw edge and attach lining heading tape to this raw edge as described in the instructions (right).

Attaching lining heading tape

1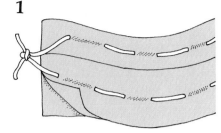

2

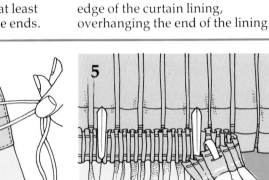

1cm/½in

3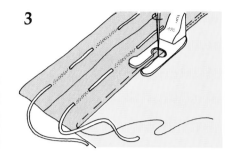

This tape (Rufflette brand) is made up of two 'skirts', one skirt fitting each side of the top of the lining fabric.
The right side of the tape is the corded side.
Remember to make a left and right-hand version for a pair of curtains.
Cut a length of lining tape to the width of the curtain plus at least 10cm/4in for neatening the ends.

1 At the end of the tape that will be at the centre, pull the two cords free and secure with a knot. Trim off surplus tape up to the knot.
2 Ease the two skirts apart and slip the top of the lining between the skirts, with the corded side on the right side of the lining.
Place the knotted end at the centre edge of the curtain lining, overhanging the end of the lining

by 1cm/½in.
Turn 5mm/¼in and then remaining 5mm/¼in at knotted end of tape to wrong side of lining. Pin tape in place.
At outer edge of tape, pull 4cm/1½in of each cord free and trim surplus tape so that it overhangs lining by 1cm/½in. Neaten with a double hem 5mm/¼in and 5mm/¼in to wrong side of lining, leaving the

4

5

6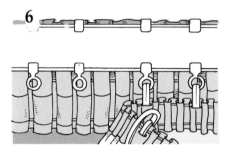

loose cords free for gathering up. Tack tape in place.
3 Stitch tape in place, close to the bottom edge and down both sides, being sure not to catch the loose ends of the cords into the stitching. Remove tacking.
4 Hold the two cord ends and gently pull the cords at the same time as pushing up the fabric and

tape until the fabric is fully gathered. Now ease out the gathers until the lining is the required fullness for the curtain.
5 Insert curtain hooks, spacing evenly at about every 8cm/3in through slits on top of the lining tape. With wrong side of lining and wrong side of curtain facing, fit the hooks through the pockets on the

curtain heading tape, so that both lining and curtain hang from the same hooks.
6 For curtain tracks that have combined hook/gliders with rings for lining hooks, the lining tape should be fitted with hooks which then fit through the rings under the main curtain hooks.

DESIGN EXTRA

Pleated curtain tie-back

This is a quick and simple way to make a professional looking pleated tie-back using curtain heading tape. The most suitable style of tape to use is pencil pleating, either Rufflette Regis (7.5cm/3in deep) or Deep Regis (13.8cm/5½in).
Measure round the full bulk of the pulled back curtain and lining. Cut fabric to 2½ times this length plus 3cm/1¼in and to same depth as the heading tape plus 3cm/1¼in. Cut tape the same

length.
All round the fabric, turn 1cm/½in to wrong side and tack.
Centre tape on wrong side of fabric. Neaten the short ends of the tape as for a curtain head. Stitch tape in place and pull up to pleat.
To hold the two ends of the tie-back together, sew a ring to each end on the wrong sides. Slot the rings onto a hook screwed into the wall, positioned so that the tie-back holds the curtain in a generous drape.

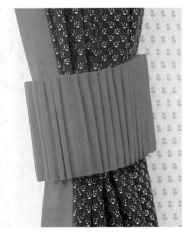

Sewn-in curtain linings for a permanent finish

If your curtain fabric and lining can be laundered together, the sewn-in method of curtain lining is ideal. Its advantage is that it gives you a neat finish down the side hems and across the top. The hem of the lining is left free from the curtain for the best possible hang.

With this method, curtains and lining are attached by being sewn together down the side hems and across the top. Both long and short curtains can be lined like this.

Before reading this chapter read through pages 10-12 and 21-23 for basic curtain making techniques.

Long, heavy curtains are best lined by the locked-in method which secures curtain and lining with vertical lines of stitching (see pages 30-31).

Measuring up and cutting out

Calculate the amount of fabric needed for each curtain using the same basic method as for unlined curtains, but allowing sufficient fabric width for the heading of your choice. Measure up for the lining fabric in exactly the same way as for the curtain fabric, but cut the lining fabric to 1cm/½in less than the *finished* width of curtain, and do not add the hem allowance at the top. The top hem allowance on the curtain is 4cm/1½in for gathered heading tape and a minimum of 6mm/¼in for other heading tapes (including gathered tape when used as a suspended heading).

Right: A pleated frill on these bedroom curtains gives them a soft, but not too feminine, designer touch.

Making a sewn-in curtain lining

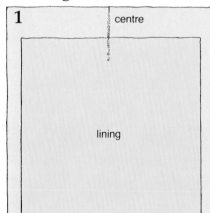

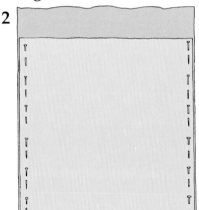

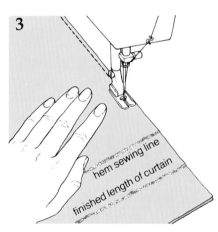

With flat seams, join the curtain fabric widths together to make up each curtain, and join the lining fabric widths to make up each lining. Fell or French seams are not necessary since the edges of the flat seam will be hidden between the lining and the curtain.

1 Mark the centre point on the wrong side of both the curtain fabric and the lining with tailor's chalk.

2 Position lining on curtain fabric, right sides facing with top of lining 4cm/1½in (or hem allowance) below the curtain fabric. Pin the raw edges together down both sides. You will find that the curtain fabric is wider than the lining, so allow the curtain fabric to form a few gentle folds in order to match the raw edges exactly.

Measuring from the top of the lining fabric (ie, the top of the finished curtain), mark the curtain length required with tailor's chalk on to both the lining and the curtain fabric. Also mark the position of the hem. The hem allowance for the bottom edge is generally 15cm/6in, 1cm/½in being turned under first, followed by 14cm/5½in.

3 Sew both side seams with a 1cm/½in seam, sewing from the top of the lining to within 10cm/4in of the hem sewing line.

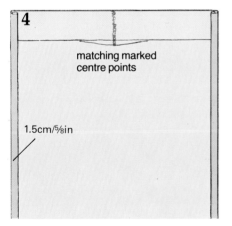
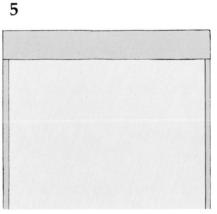
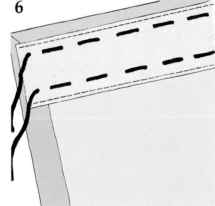

4 Turn curtain fabric and lining through to the right side. Press lining and curtain fabric flat, matching the centre marked points on lining and fabric. The curtain fabric overlaps on the lining side by 1.5cm/⅝in down each side edge.
5 Turn curtain fabric to the lining side at the top of the curtain, folding along the top edge of the lining.
6 Attach heading tape to the top of

the curtain, covering the raw edge. Turn up a double hem on the bottom of the curtain fabric. Tack in place.
For extra neatness and less bulk on the corners you can mitre each corner.
Turn up a double hem to the wrong side on the lining fabric, so that the lining hangs about 2cm/¾in above hem level of curtain fabric. The depth of the lining hem should be

the same as, or less than, the curtain fabric hem, so you will have to trim off the surplus lining fabric to make the hem to the correct depth. Tack hem in place.
Pull up the heading tape to make the curtains the correct width for the window. Hang the curtains in place for several days to give the fabric time to 'drop'. Adjust the hems if necessary and then slipstitch.

Mock mitres on hem corners

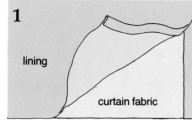

1

lining

curtain fabric

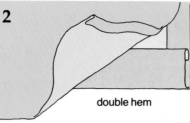

2

double hem

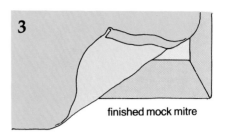

3

finished mock mitre

A mitred corner makes a neat finish on a curtain hem. A true mitre should be a 45° angle, but with curtains, the bottom hem is deeper than the side hems and a mock mitre is by far the simplest method.

To make this mock mitred corner you have to cheat with the angle

of the mitre. Only one side of the corner (the deeper bottom hem side) is mitred, and this is not at a 45° angle.

The lining and the curtain fabric are sewn together to within 10cm/4in of the hem sewing line (see page 26).

1 Turn in and press the

remaining side hern allowance on the curtain fabric.

2 Turn up a double hem at the bottom.

3 Fold the bottom hem allowance under at an angle on the corner until its top edge touches the side hem allowance. Sew in place with slipstitches.

Matching patterned fabrics

When working with patterned fabric, take care to match the pattern correctly along each seam. On the selvedge edge of the fabric, measure the distance between one pattern and the next identical one. This is called the 'pattern repeat' and you will often see it quoted on furnishing fabric details. You need to know the length of the pattern repeat when you are measuring up for curtains as you must buy extra fabric for matching the pattern. Unless you are making curtains for a very narrow window, each curtain will be made up of more than one width of fabric. With a patterned fabric, the pattern must be matched at each seam and also at the centre of a pair of curtains where they join when closed.

1 Before cutting your first piece of curtain fabric, make sure the end is cut exactly straight (at right angles to the sides.) With tailor's chalk mark a line across the width to

indicate the top hem allowance. For the best effect, you need to show the complete pattern, or a representative proportion of it, along the top edge of the curtain. If your tailor's chalk line intersects the pattern at a visually unbalanced point (perhaps cutting through a flower pattern so that the heads would be turned to the wrong side for hem allowance and stalks left at the top of the curtain) then alter the top hem allowance. Re-position the tailor's chalk line and cut off any surplus fabric to leave just the hem allowance.

2 Cut this first piece of fabric to the required length (drop of curtain plus top and bottom hems) and lay right side up on a large table or on the floor. Lay out the rest of the fabric, right side upwards, and match the pattern to the first cut piece.

Cut the second piece of fabric so that you have two identical pieces.

Right: Even if you are making up curtains in a small overall pattern like this design, it's important to match the pattern when cutting out the fabric widths and when seaming them together.

Continue in this way until you have cut all the required fabric pieces.

To seam two pieces together

Mark the centre of each pattern repeat on the fabric selvedges (or the cut side edges) with a pin. Lay the two pieces of fabric, right sides facing, matching the pins in the selvedge edges, and pin along the seamline. Turn the fabric to the right side and check that the pattern is matching exactly – make adjustments if necessary.

Tack along the seamline. Remove all pins and then turn the fabric to the right side and check again that the pattern is matching. Sew the seam and remove tacking.

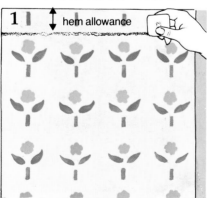

1

hem allowance

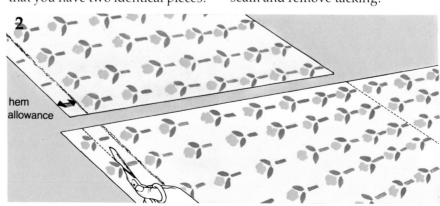

2

hem allowance

Pleated perfection

A pleated curtain frill gives a soft designer look to curtains used in any room.

Cut the curtain lining as for a sewn-in lining, but to the same width as the curtain fabric.

To calculate the fabric needed for the pleated frill, double the finished frill width (say 6cm/2¼in) and add 5cm/2in (ie total width of 17cm/6½in). For length allow three times the finished curtain drop and add 3cm/1¼in. Wrong sides facing, fold the fabric in half along its length. Make pleats in either box pleat style (below left) or side pleat style (below right), by marking the pleat spacings with tailor's chalk down the frill fabric and folding and tacking in place.

Neaten the top short edge with a 5mm/¼in and 1cm/½in double hem.
1 Place frill to right side of curtain, matching raw edges and with neatened short edge to finished top of curtain. Cut off any left-over trim at hemline and neaten the edge. Tack in place.
2 Lay lining fabric right sides facing to curtain fabric, matching raw edges and sew both side hems taking 2.5cm/1in seams. Continue making up as for sewn-in linings.

If you have a ruffler attachment for your machine, you can use this to make side pleats quickly from a single fabric thickness. Use half the frill width, and neaten the frill edge with a double hem.

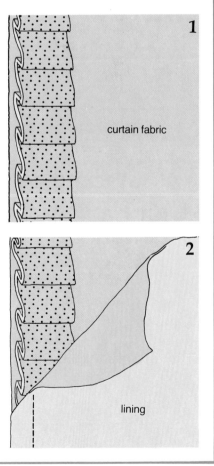

box pleats

side pleats

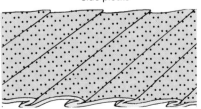

Locked-in and decorative linings and interlining

Locked-in linings give a really professional look to large curtains and help them to hang beautifully.
Add interlining for an even more luxurious touch or a thermal lining for extra insulation. Alternatively, turn the lining itself into a decorative feature.

Curtain linings no longer have to be dull beige sateen. They are now available in a wide range of colours and even thermal lining, coated with a layer of insulating material, can be silvery white or rich cream, as well as beige.

Locked-in linings help to give large curtains a really professional finish. For ultra-elegant curtains, add inter-

Above: Wide curtains often suffer from bunched up linings but with the lining locked-in they hang beautifully.

lining as well. This helps curtains to look luxuriously thick and to drape well, and will insulate windows almost as effectively as double glazing.

There is no real reason why a closely-woven dress print or furnishing cotton should not be used as a lining. The extra expense is justified by the decorative effect. Reveal the lining by making it into a decorative border or simply drape the curtain back attractively. Follow one of these two ways of showing off decorative linings for an attractive window treatment.

Curtains with locked-in linings

Locking is a means of joining curtain fabric and lining together at intervals down the length. Held against the lining in this way, the fabric of large, wide or heavy curtains drapes well and falls in graceful folds. Lining also protects the fabric from direct sunlight and dust, and provides more effective insulation.

Cutting out

Measure and cut out curtain fabric as for unlined curtains (see page 10), allowing sufficient width for the heading and adding 4cm/1½in top hem, 10cm/4in bottom hem, 4cm/1½in for each side hem and 3cm/1¼in for each seam joining fabric widths, if necessary. Cut lining to the same width, joining widths if necessary, but to the *finished* curtain length.

Right: Locking in the lining.

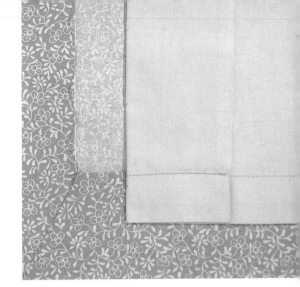

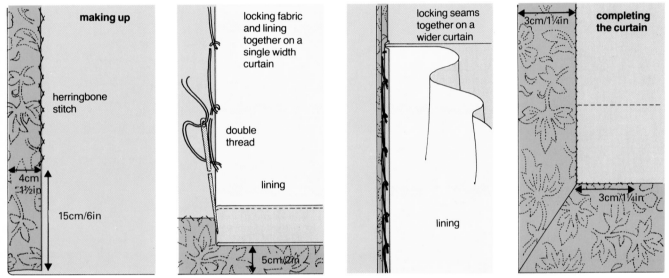

Making up

Press a 4cm/1½in turning to the wrong side down each side of the curtain, making sure it is straight with the grain.

Herringbone stitch down these edges using a large stitch and picking up just a thread on the main fabric so the stitches will not show on the right side. End stitching about 15cm/6in above lower edge to allow for hem.

Turn up and press a 10cm/4in bottom hem, making sure it is absolutely straight. Fold into a mock mitre in the corners (see page 28). Fold in 2cm/¾in along the top edge of hem, then tack and slipstitch down taking care not to make stitches noticeable on the right side of curtain.

Make a hem along the bottom edge of lining, turning 1.5cm/⅝in then 3.5cm/1⅜in to the wrong side, and machine or hand stitch.

Locking together

Lay curtain fabric out flat, right side down, on a large table or the floor.

Place the lining on top, wrong side down, with the lower edge 5cm/2in above lower edge of curtain.

On a single width curtain fold back one third of the lining, aligning top and bottom edges to make sure the fold is straight and smoothing it down with your fingertips.

Using double thread and working from right to left, pick up two threads on the lining and then the same on the curtain fabric. Leave a loop of thread running along for about 10cm/4in, then again pick up a thread or two in the lining and fabric, bringing the needle out into the loop of thread like a large blanket stitch. Continue working along the length of the curtain in this way, leaving the thread fairly loose so that it does not pull on the fabric.

Fold the lining back over the fabric and smooth flat, then fold back a third of the lining on the other long side and stitch in the same way.

On a wider curtain, the seams should be locked together and further lines of locking stitches made at approximately 40cm/16in intervals (dividing each width into thirds). Begin at the seam nearest to the centre of the curtain, folding back the lining and stitching as above, and work outwards from this. When locking two seams together, stitch through the seam allowances only so no stitches have to be made on the main fabric of curtain or lining.

Completing the curtain

Trim the lining width so the edges are even with the curtain edges then turn in 3cm/1in down each side of lining. Tack the lining down without stretching it, then neatly slipstitch it to the folded-in edge of the curtain. Remove tacking, then slipstitch lining around each lower corner for about 3cm/1¼in leaving the remaining hemmed edges free. Measure the required length from bottom to top at intervals and turn in the top hem. Press and tack down, then attach the heading tape, covering the raw edge in the usual way.

Curtains with interlining and linings

An interlining adds a luxurious, almost padded effect to curtains, as well as providing effective window insulation. Most curtain fabrics can be interlined except, of course, sheers and nets.

The most popular interlining is a brushed cotton, which resembles a thin fluffy blanket. A domette is a finer, fluffy fabric suitable for interlining more delicate curtaining. There are also synthetic versions which drape very well but do not help to block out the light.

Interlined curtains are an extension of curtains with locked-in linings, so read those instructions first.

Cutting out

Cut out and join widths of curtain fabric and lining. Cut out interlining to the same size as curtain fabric.

Making up

To join widths of interlining, butt the edges together, or very slightly overlap them, and oversew or herringbone stitch to hold. You can join with a zigzag machine stitch, but take care not to stretch the interlining in doing this.

Spread the interlining out flat on a table or the floor and lay the curtain fabric, wrong side down, on top, smoothing it out evenly all over. Fold back the fabric and lock it to the interlining, as for locking in linings. Stitch two rows of locking on each width of fabric and a row on each seam.

When the locking is complete, smooth down the fabric over the interlining and tack the two together all round the edge.

Turn the curtain over so that the interlining is uppermost, fold in a 4cm/1½in turning down each side and herringbone down. Fold up a 10cm/4in single thickness bottom hem, mitring corners, and herringbone this to the interlining.

Adding lining

Do not make a hem on the lining but lay it right side up on the interlined side of curtain with side and bottom edges together. Lock the lining to the interlining and complete curtain as before except along the lower edge of lining, which should be turned in and slipstitched down as for the side edges.

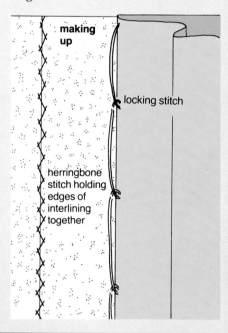

a selection of curtain linings and interlinings

Curtains with lining borders

A very attractive way of showing off a decorative lining is to use it to form a border down each side of the curtain. This does not involve any extra work when making up curtains by the sewn-in lining method, as it is simply a reversal of the normal procedure of wrapping the fabric on to the lining side.

Whether it is plain or patterned, toning or contrasting, choose your lining carefully so that it highlights the curtain fabric. Use a pretty print to enliven plain curtains, or frame a geometric or floral pattern with a plain border in a strong colour.

Making up

Follow the instructions on pages 26-27 for curtains with sewn-in linings, but cut the *lining* rather than the curtain fabric to the larger size. For a 5cm/2in border down each side of the curtain, cut the lining 10cm/4in wider than the curtain fabric. Make up the curtains in the normal way but press them so that a strip of lining forms a border down each side edge before completing top edge and finishing the bottom hem.

Diagonal draping

Turn simple curtains into an unusual and decorative room feature by using a pretty or eye-catching fabric rather than a plain lining fabric and draping back the curtain corners to reveal it. Choose the lining to complement your curtains and perhaps to bring a splash of colour or an interesting pattern into the room. Adapt the idea to give a fresh new look to existing but rather dull curtains or economise by using old but attractive curtains as the lining fabric for a new pair.

The method of making up is extremely simple but the two fabrics must be compatible, needing the same type of cleaning and care, and both must be pre-shrunk as you will not have a hem to let down. You will need the same amount of lining as curtain fabric.

Making up
Measure up (see page 10) and cut curtain fabric and lining to exactly the same size, joining widths if necessary.

Place the curtain fabric and lining right sides together and stitch round three sides, leaving the top edge open. Clip off corners of seam allowance, turn right side out and press well. Turn the top edge over to the lining side and lay the curtain heading tape in position, covering raw edges. Machine stitch in place.

Gather up the top to required width and hang the curtains, then sew a small brass ring to the sides or lower corners. Fold back the curtain edges to reveal the lining and mark the appropriate position on the wall behind each curtain for a hook. Screw in a small brass hook at each side and hook the ring over this to hold curtain in place. At night, simply slip the ring off the hook so the windows can be completely covered.

Below: A stunning flower print adds an eye-catching touch to plain curtains. The higher the rings are placed, the more lining is revealed.

Hand-made pleated headings for professional-looking curtains

Give curtains a really special, custom-made look with hand-stitched, pinch-pleat headings. Follow the professional method of making triple or goblet pleats, rather than using tape, to create fuller, more graceful curtains with perfectly-positioned pleats.

When you have splashed out on a luxurious and expensive fabric to make really special curtains, add the ultimate professional finish with a hand-stitched heading.

Although more time-consuming than using commercial heading tape, making pinch pleats by hand enables you to choose the exact depth of pleat that suits the proportions of your curtains or of a printed fabric design.

By being able to put more fullness in the pleats and spacing them more closely, you can make fuller curtains which will hang more gracefully. Hand-made curtains also have a softer appearance as there are no lines of machine stitching running across the top. And adding this exclusive finish may cost less than ready-made tape.

Left: Curtains with goblet pleated headings fall into graceful folds.

Types of pinch pleating

Triple pleats are the most popular form of pinch pleated heading, but goblet pleats provide an unusual variation and are even easier to make. Being one of the few styles of curtain heading that – as yet – it is not possible to create with commercial heading tape, goblet pleating invariably adds a very unusual, custom-made finish to your curtains.

The pinch pleat method can also be adapted to make a valance with clusters of pleats (they can be groups of four or five pleats – not necessarily three) spaced irregularly or more widely than usual, to echo vertical window divisions or just to add an individual touch.

Buying materials

The only items needed to make curtains with hand-stitched headings – apart from the curtain fabric, lining and possibly interlining – are some stiffening and hooks. White, buckram-type stiffenings made specifically for curtain headings in suitable widths are widely available. Select a width about 2cm/¾in greater than the required depth of pleat. Choose either steel pin hooks that simply slip behind the pleat stitching or traditional brass sew-on hooks.

You will need
Curtain fabric
Matching thread
Lining fabric
Interlining if used
Curtain buckram slightly deeper than required heading pleats, twice width of flat curtain
Pronged steel hooks or sew-on hooks and strong thread (1 hook for each pleat plus 4 for edges)

Measuring up and preparing the curtains

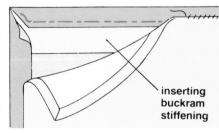

inserting buckram stiffening

Measure up as described on page 10, adding 14cm/5½in to the finished length for top and bottom hems.

For triple pleats, the width of each curtain should be two and a half times the width of half the curtain rail, which allows 10-17cm/4½-6in for each pleat, depending on the spaces between, and creates luxuriously full curtains.

For goblet pleats, twice the width is sufficient. Allow 4cm/1½in for each side hem, and 3cm/1¼in for each seam joining fabric widths, if necessary.

Cut out the curtains, joining widths as necessary. Cut lining to finished size of curtains and lock to prepared curtains (see page 31) but without stitching over heading area.

Inserting buckram stiffening Fold back top edge of lining and slip buckram underneath turnings of curtain fabric, trimming to fit, so that edges of buckram lie level with top and sides of curtain. Tack stiffening securely in place and re-position lining on top, smoothing it down.

Turn in top raw edge of lining to lie about 1cm/½in below top edge of curtain and slipstitch down taking care not to let stitches go through front of curtain.

curtain buckrams, lining and hooks

Calculating pleat sizes

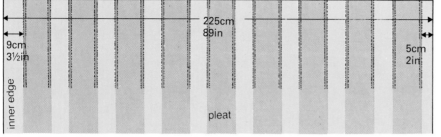

To ensure a perfect finish, spend some time calculating the size and spacing.

Number of pleats
Measure the required finished width of each curtain (half rail length) and, at each end, subtract 5cm/2in or the width of any overlap or return. Assuming a rough average figure of a triple pleat every 10cm/4in of finished curtain, calculate the number of pleats that will fit this width, with a pleat positioned at either end.

Example

Width of finished curtain (half track length)	90cm/35½in
Overlap at inner edge	9cm/3½in
Flat area at outer edge	5cm/2in
Distance between first and last pleat	76cm/30in
Number of pleats	9

Size of each pleat
From the width of the *flat* curtain, subtract the size of the *finished* curtain (including overlap) to calculate the amount of fabric left over for pleats. Divide this measurement by the required number of pleats to find the amount of fabric allowed for *each* pleat.

Example

Width of flat curtain	225cm/89
Width of finished curtain	90cm/35½
Difference to be taken up in pleats	135cm/53
Number of pleats	9
Fabric for each pleat = 135 ÷ 9 =	15cm/6in

Size of each space
To calculate the exact size of the spaces between pleats, divide the finished curtain width (less the return, overlap or 5cm/2in at each end) by the number of pleats less one.

Example

Width of finished curtain	90cm/35½
Less 5cm one end and 9cm overlap other end	76cm/30i
Number of pleats less one	8
Size of each space = 76cm ÷ 8 =	9.5cm/3¾

Making a goblet pleated heading

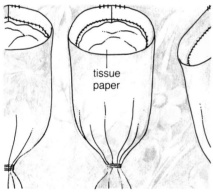

tissue paper

An unusual variation of pinch pleats, goblet pleats have the advantage of requiring slightly less width of fabric than triple pleats.

Calculating pleat sizes
Allowing 9-13cm/3½-5in for each goblet pleat and about the same amount for each space, calculate exact sizes as above.

If your flat curtain is exactly twice the finished size and there is no overlap or return, simply divide the flat width by an even number of pleats and spaces, for example, a 120cm/48in curtain would have twelve 10cm/4in pleats/spaces; that is six pleats, five whole spaces and a half space at either end.

Forming the goblet pleats
Mark out and stitch each pleat as for triple pleated headings (Step 1) as far as stitching from top edge to bottom of stiffening at each pleat. Instead of forming three pleats, pinch together the base of each pleat (folding the fabric into three or

Making a triple pleated heading

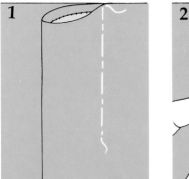 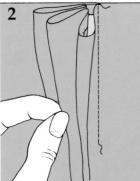 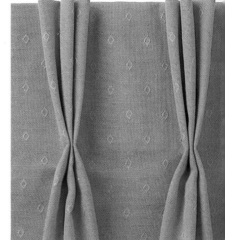

Calculate the exact size of spaces and pleats (see left) and then, using tailor's chalk and a ruler or set square, draw vertical lines to mark their position along the top edge of the curtains.

1 Bring together the two lines marking the first pleat, wrong sides of curtain facing, to form a single large pleat. Tack and stitch (by machine or by hand) from top edge of curtain to lower edge of stiffening, making sure that stitching is at a true right angle to curtain edge.

Repeat for each pleat: each curtain should then be the required finished width (half track length).

2 Hold the centre fold of each pleat between thumb and forefinger just above lower edge of stiffening, and push pleat inwards towards the stitching line, forming three small, evenly sized pleats. Catch the pleats together with a few small handstitches just above lower edge of stiffening.

3 At the top edge of curtain, catch the triple pleats together at the back and also anchor the back edge of the a few unobtrusive hand stitches using matching thread.

four small pleats) and catch the folds together with a few hand stitches at the base only.

To form the goblet shape, round out the top of each pleat and catch to the top edge of curtain about 1cm/½in out, on either side, from the first stitching line. To ensure that the goblet shape stays nicely rounded, lightly stuff each pleat with a piece of crumpled tissue paper. (Don't forget to remove this when cleaning curtains.)

Attaching hooks

If curtains are to hang just below a decorative wooden pole, attach the curtain hooks as close to the top edge as possible without protruding. If the curtain heading is to cover the rail, position the hooks lower down, according to depth of rail and style of gliders.

If using sew on hooks, attach one at each end of each curtain and one behind each pleat, stitching on very securely with strong button thread. If using pronged hooks, insert behind the stitching at each pleat. Insert the corner hooks by making two vertical rows of stitching at each end of curtains and inserting a hook between the rows.

PROFESSIONAL TOUCH

'Dressing' curtains

All curtains, whether or not their headings are made by hand, will drape more effectively if they are properly 'dressed'. To do this, hang the curtains half drawn open. Starting from the top, run your fingers down the curtain emphasizing each natural fold made by the heading. If necessary, a gentle tug on the lower hem edge, level with a heading pleat, will help the fabric fall into a natural pleat. Start from the outer edge and work along each curtain, drawing back the curtain as you create the draping.

If the curtain heading hangs below a decorative pole, push each space between pleats backwards. If the curtain covers the track, pull the space areas of fabric forwards.

When the curtains are fully drawn back into perfectly-draped folds, tie three lengths of cord or strips of soft fabric around each curtain and leave for as long as possible – at least overnight or preferably two or three days – to 'train' the pleats.

When the cords are removed, the curtains will retain the beautifully draped effect and will 'hang' well for quite some time, but repeat when re-hanging curtains after cleaning.

Traditional fabric pelmets

Custom-made to suit the proportions of your window and the styling of your room, traditional pelmets can be expensive to buy. With modern materials, however, they are simple to make yourself, cost very little, and add the same distinctive finish to your windows.

Pelmets are horizontal panels of stiffened fabric which, positioned at the top of curtains, cover curtain track and balance the proportions of a window. They are particularly attractive on tall windows and are also effective when used to link together adjoining sets of windows.

Below: The border from a printed curtain fabric is ideal for a straight pelmet.

Covered in a furnishing fabric to complement your curtains and shaped to suit the style of your décor, a pelmet never fails to add a distinctive touch to a room.

The material traditionally used to stiffen fabric pelmets is buckram interfacing, a woven fabric which has been treated to become rigid. More modern alternatives include self-adhesive non-woven materials, such as Rufflette Pelmform. This has a peel-off backing paper printed with several different pelmet silhouettes to follow when cutting out and with a grid to simplify drawing out your own design. One type of Pelmform is velour-backed thus eliminating the need for lining. These stiffenings can be bought by the metre from furnishing fabric departments.

Almost any furnishing fabric, except very open weaves and sheers, can be used to cover the pelmet. If using buckram, back your chosen fabric with bump interlining or an iron-on interfacing for a smooth finish.

Attach your pelmet to the pelmet board with touch-and-close fastener – Sew 'n' stick Velcro is ideal. This makes adding decorative braid (traditionally applied to cover tack-heads) purely a matter of choice.

Hanging a pelmet

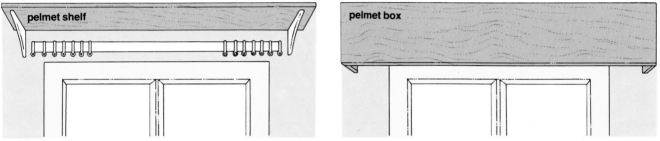

Pelmets must be attached to a firm support, called a pelmet board.

A pelmet shelf – simply a wooden shelf about 10-15cm/4-6in deep permanently attached to the wall just above the curtain track and/or architrave – is adequate for most windows. It should extend about 6cm/2½in beyond each end of the track.

A pelmet box, which also has narrow front and side box-style sections, gives the extra rigidity which may be needed for wide or particularly deep pelmets.

On deeply recessed windows, the pelmet board can be just a simple flat panel fixed across the top of the window area, level with the wall. When putting up a new pelmet shelf or box, bear in mind that, as the top edge of the pelmet will lie level with the top edge of the pelmet board, this will form the top edge of the window area. Consider therefore, the height and depth of the pelmet in relation to the window and to the height of the ceiling, not forgetting that the pelmet must be low enough to cover curtain track, before positioning a pelmet board.

Once screwed to the wall, a pelmet board becomes a permanent fixture which will probably outlast several pelmets. A pelmet, on the other hand, should be easy to remove for cleaning, while decorating, or to be replaced by a new one. Touch-and-close fastener, such as Velcro, is therefore ideal for attaching it. Tack or glue the hooked half of the Velcro all along the top edge of the front and sides (or returns) of the pelmet board (or use the self-adhesive half of Sew 'n' stick Velcro) and stitch the other half to the pelmet lining while making up.

Choosing fabric and a shape for your pelmet

Whatever the room scheme, pelmets can be pretty and decorative, classic and elegant, or stylishly simple to complement it. Choose a firmly-woven fabric to match, contrast or co-ordinate with your curtains and echo the style of the fabric design in the pelmet shape you choose – a prettily scalloped shape, for example, would not suit a sharp geometric print. You can, if using Pelmform, follow one of the shapes printed on the backing paper. Alternatively, draw up your own design, perhaps copying or adapting one of the styles illustrated here, devising your own shape, opting for a simple rectangle, or following the outlines of motifs printed on the fabric.

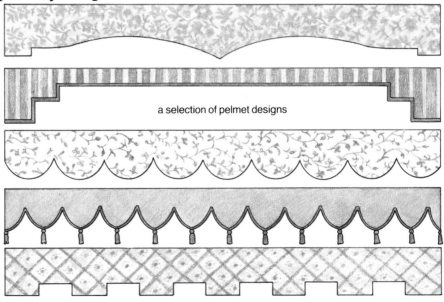

a selection of pelmet designs

Making a fabric pelmet

Put up a pelmet board, selecting the most suitable method of making a pelmet. This varies according to the type of stiffening used.

You will need

Buckram or Pelmform for stiffening
Fabric to match or contrast with curtains
Lining fabric (unless using one-sided Pelmform)
Interlining such as bump (if using buckram)
Paper to make a template (wallpaper is useful because of its length)
Velcro fastening
Decorative braid and fabric adhesive if desired

Making a template

Measure the length of the pelmet board including returns (short side ends) and cut a straight strip of paper to this length and slightly deeper than the widest section of your chosen pelmet shape. Fold the paper in half crosswise and mark the central point with a crease, and also crease the position of the corners.

Open out the paper and draw the intended shape on it, working from the centre out to the corner folds, and measuring accurately to make sure that any repeated shapes are of equal size and spacing. The returns can be shaped or left plain as desired. Fold the paper in half again and cut the shape from the doubled paper to ensure both sides are the same. Trim the top edge if necessary to make the template the exact size and shape of your finished pelmet, and check its proportions against your windows, adjusting if necessary.

Cutting out

Using the template, cut out the pelmet shape from buckram or Pelmform. Both are available in narrow widths so that the length can be cut from one piece without

Making up with traditional buckram

The traditional method of making a buckram pelmet involves a lot of hand sewing which takes time but gives a very professional finish. If your machine has a zip or piping foot, use the quick method.

Traditional method Place bump interlining centrally on the wrong side of the main fabric, and lock stitch together at intervals (see page 31). Place the buckram centrally on top of the bump interlining. Clipping into the border of fabric around curves or at corners, and trimming away excess where necessary, fold the fabric edges on to the wrong side of the buckram.

If using iron-on buckram, which is glue-impregnated, dampen the edges and stick down the fabric turnings by ironing in place. Otherwise slipstitch the edges of the fabric to the buckram.
Turn in the raw edges of the lining to make it 5mm/¼in smaller all round than the pelmet, clipping and trimming as necessary; press. Stitch the soft half of a strip of Velcro to right side along top edge of lining. Position the lining centrally on the wrong side of the buckram and slipstitch all round to hold.

Quick method Lock interlining to the fabric as above (or use iron-on

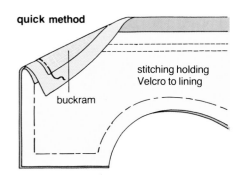

quick method

stitching holding Velcro to lining

buckram

interfacing). Smoothing out the fabric, tack buckram to interlined side. Stitch the soft half of the Velcro 4cm/1½in down from the top edge of the lining strip. Lay fabric and lining right sides together and tack securely all round edge of

Making up with self-adhesive stiffening

Backings such as Rufflette Pelmform may cost a little more than buckram but are available in different widths for economy and are extremely simple to use. They are particularly helpful if you wish to follow one of the ready printed designs to shape the pelmet edge. Choose between velour backed or double-sided adhesive styles.

Ready-backed type The back of this type of stiffening is coated in a velour-style finish to make lining unnecessary and the front is self-adhesive.

Using your template, cut out the pelmet shape you require. If

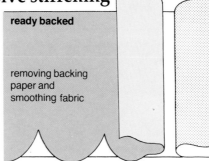

ready backed

removing backing paper and smoothing fabric

following one of the printed outlines for the lower edge, place the centre of your template either in the exact centre of a scallop or at the point between two shapes.
Ease the backing paper away from

the centre of the pelmet shape and cut it across the width. Peel back the paper for a little way on either side of the cut and place the wrong side of your fabric centrally on the exposed area of adhesive. Continue peeling back the paper while smoothing the fabric onto the stiffening adhesive, working from centre outwards so fabric remains absolutely smooth and wrinkle-free.

Press the backing and fabric firmly together and then, using sharp scissors, trim the fabric edges in line with the backing. Stick or tack the coarser hooked side of Velcro to the

Right: Trimming emphasizes the unusual shaping of a plain fabric pelmet.

much wastage; joins are not advisable as they tend to create ridges and will reduce the rigidity of the pelmet.

If using buckram, cut out the same shape in bump, for interlining, butting the edges together and herringbone stitching to join widths. Cut out fabric and lining 2.5cm/1in larger all round than the template. Plain fabrics can sometimes be cut along the length to avoid joins but if your fabric has a one-way design or a definite nap, you may need to join widths with narrow flat seams to make up a strip large enough for the pelmet. To avoid a centre seam, join extra fabric to either side of a central panel. Press seams open.

buckram. Trim lining level with top edge of buckram.

Using a zipper or piping foot, machine stitch as close to the edge of the buckram as possible around sides and lower edge.

Trim the seam to 1.5cm/⅝in, clip into curves and angles and across corners, then turn right side out. Press well, creasing the edges and smoothing the seam towards the lining side rather than the right side.

Press the top edge of fabric over the lining, turn in the raw edge, trimming if necessary, and slipstitch to lining just above the Velcro strip.

pelmet board. The velour backing clings to this without needing the other half of Velcro. Although not generally necessary except as a decorative effect, or on fabrics that have a marked tendency to fray, it may be advisable to stick a decorative braid around the cut edges for a neater finish.

Double-sided adhesive type This does need lining but it gives a more professional finish.

Cut the lining and the stiffening to the finished shape. Stitch the soft half of Velcro along the top edge on the lining, 2.5cm/1in down. Stick the main fabric onto right side

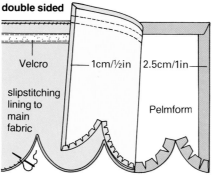

double sided

Velcro

slipstitching lining to main fabric

1cm/½in   2.5cm/1in

Pelmform

of stiffening as above but leaving a 2.5cm/1in turning all round. Clip into the turning around curves and into angles.

Press a 1cm/½in turning to the wrong side all round lining piece.

Removing the backing paper as you work, fold the fabric edges onto the wrong side of the pelmet, smoothing down so that they adhere.

Working from the centre outwards, stick wrong side of lining to wrong side of pelmet, overlapping the fabric edges. Slipstitch round lining to secure in place.

Add any braid trimmings required, slipstitching in place.

Attach hooked half of Velcro to pelmet board to correspond with soft half and press pelmet in place to hang. Do not use Pelmform for silk fabrics.

41

Curtain valances to frame your windows

Elegant and formal or frilly and charming, a curtain valance adds a decorative feature to your window. The wide choice of easy-to-make styles can be fitted on a pole, shelf or curtain track and only the hand-pleated headings require much sewing skill.

Curtain valances are often confused with pelmets, but in fact a pelmet is a rigid fitting, either in wood or fabric-covered wood, whereas a valance is a soft fabric drape. Both are used to disguise the tops of curtains and the curtain track, as well as enhancing the proportions of the window or adding a decorative feature.

The curtain valances shown here can be hung on tracks, poles, rods or a simple shelf-style fitting, above an existing curtain.

Style and proportion

If possible, hang the curtains before finally deciding on the style and depth of the valance.

The style will depend on the fabric the curtains are made from and on the way the room is furnished. A gathered valance made from a fresh, printed cotton will give a pretty, country look, while a valance of regular or grouped pleats will provide a more formal touch for heavier fabrics. A draped valance can be used for either look depending on the lightness of the fabric and on the surrounding furnishings.

The depth of the valance depends on the proportions of the window and personal taste. It can be used to improve the look of a window. For example, a deep valance will lower a tall narrow window, or help to obscure an unsightly view, while a shorter valance allows in the maximum of light through a small or shaded window.

There are no hard and fast rules that set the size of valance in relation to the curtain. If you start with the valance being one sixth of the curtain drop, this gives a point from which to

Left: Bound edges and a fabric-covered batten add style to a gathered valance.

work. Bear in mind that the valance must cover the track on which it is hung, the curtain track and the heading of the curtains.

Valance fittings

There are four main methods for fitting curtain valances: rod or tube, wooden pole, shelf or track.

Rod or tube fitting If the valance is hanging within a recess, or if the side view is not critical, it can be made with a simple cased heading and threaded on to a narrow rod, tube or curtain wire, fixed with brackets or hooks at each end.

Wooden curtain pole fitting The valance can be hung from the rings of a wooden curtain pole with decorative ends and brackets. The pole should be approximately 12cm/5in longer than the curtain track and project far enough from the wall to allow for the curtains. The actual measurement of this projection will be determined by the depth of the brackets used.

Curtain track fittings A simple curtain track is suitable for a valance if it is fitted with extended brackets to clear the curtains; alternatively fittings are available to clip the valance track straight on to the curtain track brackets.

The valance track must extend forward from the wall at least 4cm/1½in in front of the curtain track so that it does not interrupt the free movement of the curtains.

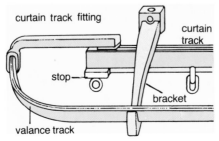

curtain track fitting

curtain track

stop

bracket

valance track

It is not practical to fix valance track above decorative curtain poles that extend away from the wall.

If both curtain and valance are to hang within a window recess, the valance track is the same width as the curtain track. Otherwise it should be longer and of the pliable type so that the ends can be bent back towards the wall to form sides or returns.

The valance is fitted to the track in the same way as a curtain, using curtain tape and hooks.

Shelf fittings If you cannot find a suitable track, pole or rod, fix a simple shelf supported by angle iron brackets above the curtain track. It should be 12cm/4¾in longer than the curtain track (unless in a recess) and protrude from the wall for 4cm/1½in more. Either attach the valance to the front and side edges of the shelf with upholstery tacks, gluing a decorative braid on top to hide the tack heads, or screw eyes round the shelf and attach the valance on to these with curtain hooks. The latter method allows the valance to be taken down for washing.

Measuring up

To find the depth most suitable for your valance, measure one sixth of the curtain drop and cut a strip of paper to this depth and as wide as your curtains. Carefully pin the paper to the top of the curtains in the correct position covering both tracks. Stand well back from the window and check the proportion of the valance in relation to the length of the curtains.

If it looks too deep, unpin the paper and trim off some of the depth. Re-pin and check again, repeating until you find the correct depth.

If the paper valance looks too shallow, make a new paper pattern with plenty of depth, and trim off until the correct proportion is reached. Remember that ultimately this is a matter of personal taste.

The depth of the fabric needed will be the paper pattern depth plus 2cm/¾in for the lower seam allowance, and a top seam allowance which varies according to the type of heading. The width of the fabric required depends on the type of heading used and fullness required.

If you have to join fabric strips to make up the width, join with 1.5cm/⅝in flat seams, neaten and press.

43

Making a valance with a taped heading

This style of valance is made as if it were a very short curtain (see pages 10-12 and 21-23). Choose the appropriate curtain tape to give a gathered, pencil pleated or triple pleated heading. Position the tape so that the valance will completely cover the track but still clear the ceiling. A standard gathering tape can be positioned 2cm/1in down from the top edge so that it creates a small upstanding frill along the top.

The valance can be made with just a single thickness of fabric like an unlined curtain or it can be given more body with an iron-on interfacing, in which case it should be lined for a neat finish. A valance with a triple-pleated heading particularly benefits from being interlined and lined.

The depth of fabric required will be as described plus a top seam allowance

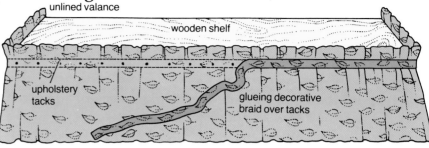

of 4cm/1½in. The width will depend on the manufacturer's recommendation for the type of heading tape used.

An unlined valance

Measure up, cut out and join the fabric. Neaten the side and lower edges as for cased heading valances. Turn in the seam allowance along the top edge and pin the curtain tape into position to

cover the raw edge. Turn in the raw ends of the tape – but not the pulling up cords – and tack and stitch it in place.

Pull up the cords until the valance is the correct width and tie the ends to secure. Even out the pleats or gathers, insert curtain hooks and hang the valance in the same way as a curtain.

If you are using a wooden shelf fitment, line up the curtain tape

Making a valance with a hand-pleated heading

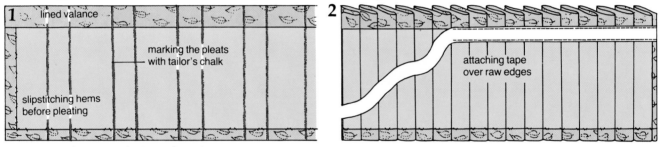

A pleated valance looks best if made with a stiffened fabric – interfaced and lined as the interlined valance with heading tape.

With a strip of paper, work out the size and type of pleat that will suit your valance and fit evenly into its length. Cut a piece of fabric of

sufficient depth and width (join pieces if necessary) to make the valance. Three times the finished width required, plus seam allowances, will be sufficient for continuous knife or box pleats. Allow 4cm/1½in for the top seam allowance.

Make up the valance in the same way as the lined version with curtain tape but, after folding over top seam allowance, do not add tape.

1 Following the pleat size from your experimental paper strip, mark out the valance into even divisions

Making a valance with cased heading

This is the easiest valance to make and hang as the supporting rod, tube or wire is simply threaded through the cased heading.

Measure the depth as described and add 6cm/2½in top seam allowance to enclose a rod up to 2cm in diameter between two rows of stitching.

For the width of fabric required allow one and a half to two times the length of the rod or pole.

Cut out your fabric to the required measurements, joining widths if necessary with 1.5cm/⅝in flat seam or French seam.

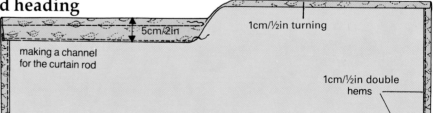

1 Turn a double hem (5mm/¼in and then 1cm/½in) to the wrong side down each side edge and stitch. Turn a double hem (1cm/½in and 1cm/½in) along the lower edge and stitch. (Alternatively, trim off lower seam allowance and bind edge with a contrasting binding.)

2 On the top edge, turn the seam allowance to the wrong side, then turn in the raw edge by 1cm/½in and stitch. Make another row of stitching 4cm/1½in above this one to form a channel through which the rod is threaded.

Press well and add any trimmings

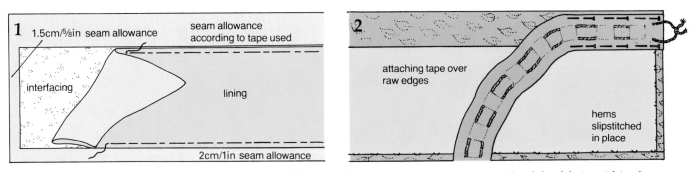

1 1.5cm/⅝in seam allowance

seam allowance according to tape used

interfacing

lining

2cm/1in seam allowance

2 attaching tape over raw edges

hems slipstitched in place

with the facing edges of the shelf and attach the valance with upholstery tacks. Cover the tack heads with a decorative braid or a fabric-covered batten glued in place.

A lined valance

An interfacing such as iron-on Vilene can be added to give your fabric more body and a crisper look. There are several weights available – select the weight that, together with your fabric, will give the desired thickness.

A lining is necessary to give a neat finish and also protects the valance from sunlight.

Cut out the valance as for an unlined one, and cut the lining and interlining to the exact finished measurements without seam allowances. If necessary, join fabric widths and lining widths.

1 Position the interfacing to the wrong side of the fabric within the seamlines. Following the manufacturer's instructions for heat setting, dry iron the interfacing on to the fabric.

Lay lining on top of interfacing right side upwards and tack in place.

2 Turn in double hems along side and lower edges as for the cased valance, slipstitching down to the lining. Finish the top edge with heading tape.

using tailor's chalk on the wrong side. Fold and press the pleats, one by one, and tack in position.

2 Place a length of plain tape about 2.5cm/1in wide, on the wrong side of the valance to cover the raw edge (as with the heading tape) and sew in place.

You can hand sew the tape if you do not want the stitching lines to show on the right side, but you must be sure to stitch through all but the front layer of fabric in order to secure the pleats in place.

If necessary, neatly catchstitch the top edges of the pleats together on the right side.

Sew rings or hooks to the tape to attach the valance to its support.

before threading on to the rod. This method can be adapted for a simple gathered heading attached around a shelf fitting. Instead of adding the second row of stitching along the top edge, insert two rows of gathering stitches and pull up to the appropriate size. Nail it around the edge of the shelf and cover the nail heads with braid or a neatened bias strip of fabric. Turning in the ends of the braid to neaten, use fabric adhesive to glue in place.

Right: Rufflette Tridis tape gives regular triple pleating; hand-made pleats can be grouped or spaced out.

Draped valance with cascades

Complex swagged valances can be time consuming to make, but this simple draped valance with its cascades on each side gives an equally sumptuous effect for relatively little time and effort.

Choose a lining that is colour matched or use the same fabric for both valance and lining as it will tend to show. If you wish to use a sheer fabric for an unlined valance, omit any seam allowances and bind edges.

The valance is draped over a pair of wooden or metal brackets – such as the type used with curtain poles. Position the brackets just above and slightly outside each end of the curtain track.

Measuring up

To calculate the amount of fabric needed, use a tape measure (or a length of string) and drape it over the two brackets allowing it to drop into a gentle swag between them to hide the curtain track and headings. Allow it to hang down at either side of the window frame to measure the depth of cascade required.

Measure the total length of the tape or string (A–A) to give you the total width of fabric needed, adding 3cm/1¼in for seam allowances. Measure the drop of the swag between the two brackets (B–B) and also the distance in a straight line between the two brackets (C–C).

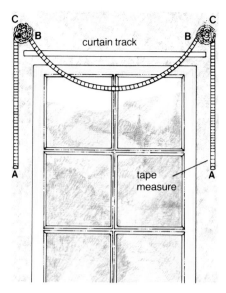

Making up the draped valance

Cut a piece of fabric the width from A to A plus 3cm/1¼in, joining widths if necessary, with a depth of 120cm/47¼in.

1 With tailor's chalk, mark the distance B–B centrally on one long side of the fabric. Draw diagonal lines to join B to A on each side and cut the fabric along these two lines. Now cut a piece of lining fabric to exactly the same size and shape. Tack the lining fabric and valance fabric together right sides facing. Sew the lining and valance fabric together all round, taking a 1.5cm/⅝in seam and leaving a 20cm/7in gap for turning through. Trim the seam to 1cm/½in and clip off each corner close to the stitching line. Turn to the right side and slipstitch the opening closed. Press.

On the lining side, mark the distance between the two C points centrally on the longest side.

2 Join points C and B with chalk lines, then sew a length of standard heading tape along each line. Knot the ends of the cord at the B edge, leaving them loose for pulling up on the C edge.

Pull up the cords in the heading tape to gather the fabric and then lay the gathers over the brackets. Adjust the cascades if necessary. If the fabric shows a tendency to slip, tie the ends of the heading tape cords around the brackets so that they don't show.

Right: The valance can be draped over brass curtain holders or wooden brackets.

Decorative curtain borders for a stylish finish

Add a decorative edging when making up new curtains or to highlight an old pair. Choose a style which suits the room – a frilled edge for a pretty finish, a piped edge for elegance or a bold contrast border or appliqué motif for a striking feature.

Below: Bear in mind the proportions of your curtains when choosing the width and position of a border and use bold colour contrasts for a dramatic effect.

Give curtains a designer style finish by adding a frill or piping to the edges or by applying a fabric border or appliqué motifs. These can easily be incorporated when making up new curtains, but the ideas can be adapted to brighten up an old pair if you unpick hems and sewn-in linings as necessary.

Cut out the curtain fabric and join widths if necessary, following instructions given on pages 10-11 and 26-28. For curtains with sewn-in linings, cut the lining to the *same width* as the curtain fabric.

Take 1.5cm/⅝in seam allowances throughout unless otherwise stated. Bear in mind the proportion of your curtains when deciding which edges are to be decorated. The most usual position is down the inner edge where the curtains meet, but outer and hem edges can be bordered too.

Making a gathered frill

A frill, whether applied to lined or unlined curtains, can be either a single or double thickness of fabric. Double thickness is generally preferable so that the right side of the fabric will show on both sides of the frill, but a single thickness is more suitable if the fabric is bulky.

To calculate the length of fabric for a frill, multiply the length of the edge to be frilled by one and a half to two times. The finished width of the frill should be about 10cm/4in for an average-sized curtain.

For a double-thickness frill cut fabric to the required length (joining strips if necessary), and to double the finished width of the frill plus 3cm/1¼in for seam allowances. Fold the fabric in half along its length, wrong sides facing, and run two rows of gathering threads along the raw edge of the frill, just inside the seam allowance and stitching through both layers of fabric. If you are using a machine, gather in sections no longer than 1m/1yd to make it easier to pull up the threads without breaking.

For a single-thickness frill cut fabric to the required length (joining strips if necessary), and to the width of the finished frill plus 3cm/1¼in for seam and hem allowance. Neaten one long edge with a double hem, 5mm and 1cm/¼in and ⅜in. Run two rows of gathering threads along the other long edge, within the seam allowance.

Applying the frill

Gathered frills can be applied to both lined and unlined curtains.
Unlined curtains Pull up the gathering threads until the frill fits between the top and bottom hem lines of the curtain fabric. With right sides and raw edges together, tack frill to curtain fabric. Sew frill in place with a 1.5cm/⅝in seam and zigzag raw edges together to neaten. Press frill out from curtain. This method is also used for curtains with detachable linings.
Lined curtains Pull up the gathering threads until the frill fits between the top and bottom hem lines of the curtain fabric. With right sides and raw edges together, tack the frill to the curtain fabric. Place the lining and curtain fabric right sides together, sandwiching the frill, and sew side seams with 1.5cm/⅝in seams. Trim the seam allowances and turn right side out so that the frill protrudes from the seam.
Complete curtains in the usual way.

Making fabric borders

A ready-made printed border is the easiest kind to apply. They are available in different widths and a wide variety of colours and designs to match or complement a particular range of wallpapers and fabrics.
You can make your own borders from furnishing fabrics to match or contrast with your curtains. Choose fabrics of similar weight as the curtains to ensure they hang well.
Borders can be applied to the edges of both lined and unlined curtains. Decide which edges of the curtain are to be trimmed and the width of the border in proportion to the curtain.

Making the border strips

Cut strips of fabric the length of each border plus 2cm/1in seam allowances all round. Try to cut each section in one continuous strip – if you join strips match the pattern, if there is one, as necessary.
With tailor's chalk, mark the finished side edges and the top and bottom hem foldlines on to the right side of each curtain.
Press the seam allowance to the wrong side on both long edges.

Applying the border

Tack the border to the right side of the curtain fabric, one edge close to the side chalk line. Turn under the short edges to lie along top and bottom hem lines.
If the borders continue around the bottom of the curtain, form a mitre at the corner where they join. Fold the ends at a 45° angle and press. Cut away the excess fabric, leaving a small seam allowance. Slipstitch the mitred edges together or, with right sides together, machine along foldline and open out.
Machine topstitch the borders on to the curtains, then make up the curtains in the usual way.

Making an appliqué border

For a really original touch, appliqué can be used to form a border around a curtain. The motifs can be applied to both lined or unlined curtains before making up. It is best to choose one or two simple motifs to repeat along the edge to form the border.

Making the appliqué motif

To check that the design is in proportion to the curtain, pin a paper pattern on to the curtain fabric to judge the size and position. When you are satisfied with the pattern make an accurate template of the motif. Position it on the right side of the curtain fabric and draw round the template as often as necessary until the appliqué has been accurately marked out.
Use the template to cut out the appliqué shapes from the border fabric. Choose a fabric which matches the weight of the curtain fabric if possible, but if a lightweight fabric is chosen back the motifs with iron-on Vilene.

Applying the motifs

Place each motif within its chalk outline and tack to the curtain. Use a close zigzag stitch to machine over the raw edges of each motif.
If you do not have a swing needle

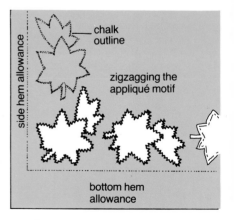

machine, sew round the raw edges with a close buttonhole stitch.
When the appliqué is complete, make up curtains in the usual way.

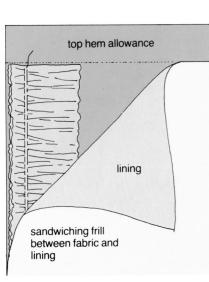

top hem allowance

lining

sandwiching frill
between fabric and
lining

*Right: A gathered curtain frill
emphasizes a pretty fresh cotton print.
Highlight a matching frill with piping
in an accent colour or choose a
contrasting fabric. Echo the frill on
tie-backs, cushions or a bedspread.*

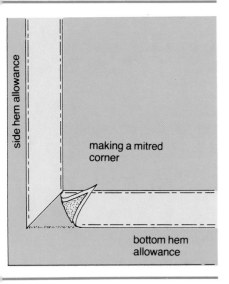

side hem allowance

making a mitred
corner

bottom hem
allowance

Making a piped edge

Piping down the inside and possibly even the outside edges of curtains provides a subtle accent of colour. The piping is inserted between two layers of fabric so this trimming is not suitable for unlined curtains or those with detachable linings.

Making the piping

Cut piping cord to the exact finished length of each edge to be piped. Cut bias strips of fabric wide enough to cover the cord plus 3cm/1¼in seam allowance. Join bias strips to 3cm/1¼in longer than edge to be piped. Wrap the fabric strips, right sides outwards, around the cord and tack the two layers together as close to the cord as possible. Using the zipper foot on your sewing machine, stitch close to the cord. Remove tacking. Alternatively, you can use purchased ready-made piping.

Applying the piping

Tack piping to the right side of the curtain fabric, raw edges together. Place the lining and curtain fabric right sides together, sandwiching the piping between. Tack through all layers close to the piping cord, then machine stitch with a zipper foot.

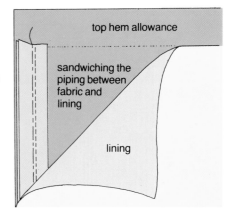

top hem allowance

sandwiching the
piping between
fabric and
lining

lining

Turn the curtain and lining through to the right side, so that the piping protrudes from the seamline. Make up curtains in the usual way.

Curtain tiebacks for a designer look

Tiebacks can be both pretty and practical. Choose a simple curved band or add piping, pleats or flounces for decoration. They make plain curtains more interesting, hold full ones back from a window or door or tie back the hangings round a four-poster bed.

They're only small, and often sadly forgotten, but curtain tiebacks are very useful and can give a new lease of life to a pair of dull or old curtains. A remnant of fabric is all that is needed – choose it to match the curtains, or to tone or contrast.

Make the tiebacks perfectly plain, or pipe them, add a ruffle, pleats or scallops; make them straight or gently curved.

As an alternative to using fabric, a length of chunky dressing gown cord makes a graceful, elegant tieback for full-length velvet curtains. Other ideas can come from furnishing braids, dress trims and ribbons.

You will need

Fabric Most light, closely woven furnishing fabrics are suitable. Don't try to use heavy brocades or velvet as they will not make up successfully – the fabric is too bulky. Both sides of the tieback can be of furnishing fabric, but if you haven't got enough, or the fabric is expensive or bulky, you can use a toning lining fabric for the backing.

Interfacing Use pelmet buckram or firm Vilene interfacing.

4 small curtain rings and two hooks for fixing to wall
Sewing thread
Paper for making patterns

Measuring up

To calculate where to place the tieback and how long and wide it should be, loop a tape measure around the curtain about two-thirds down from the top and arrange the curtain into the curve or folds you want. Note the measurement on the tape measure as this gives the length of the finished tieback. While the tape measure is still in place, make a small pencil mark on the wall to indicate the position for fixing the hook.

For sill-length curtains, the depth of the tieback should be no more than 10cm/4in, but for longer curtains it may be enlarged proportionally. Instructions given here are for 10cm/4in depth tiebacks. Seams throughout are 1.5cm/⅝in unless otherwise stated.

Right: This attractive square bay window is ideal for four separate curtains. The tiebacks hold them back during the day to allow in plenty of light.

Making a straight-edged tieback

This is very simple to make up and any of the variations shown overleaf can be added.

Cut a paper pattern to the length required × 10cm/4in deep. Pin the pattern to a double thickness of fabric and cut out (or cut out once in fabric and once in lining), allowing an extra 1.5cm/⅝in all round for seams.

Pin the pattern to a single thickness of interfacing and cut out without any seam allowance.

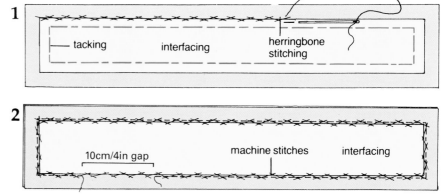

1
tacking   interfacing   herringbone stitching

2
10cm/4in gap   machine stitches   interfacing

1 Lay the interfacing centrally on the wrong side of one piece of fabric. Tack together. Herringbone stitch all round the edges of the interfacing to catch to fabric. Work the herringbone stitch from left to right, first taking a small stitch horizontally in the tieback fabric and then diagonally opposite and lower down on the interfacing. The stitches should not show on the right side of the tieback fabric.

2 Place the two tieback pieces right sides facing and tack together all round, leaving a 10cm/4in gap for turning through to the right side. Machine with the interfacing uppermost, being careful to sew close to, but not over, the edge of the interfacing.
Trim the seams and clip diagonally across the corners. Remove tacking. Turn through to right side and slipstitch the open edges together to close. Press.

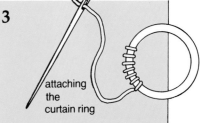

attaching the curtain ring

3 Sew a curtain ring to the middle of each short edge. Working on the wrong side of the fabric, overcast the ring just inside the edge so that most of the ring protrudes.

Making a shaped tieback

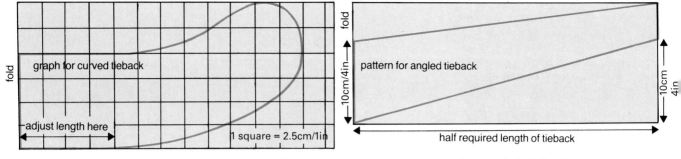

graph for curved tieback

fold

adjust length here

1 square = 2.5cm/1in

fold

10cm/4in

pattern for angled tieback

half required length of tieback

10cm/4in

A curved tieback gives an elegant shape that echoes the graceful lines of a draped curtain.

Cut a piece of paper to the length of the tieback × 15cm/6in deep and fold in half widthways. Divide into 2.5cm/1in squares and scale up the diagram shown to draw in the curve.

Cut out the paper pattern, open out flat, and cut out twice in fabric, with an additional 1.5cm/⅝in all round for the seam allowance. Cut out once in interfacing.

Continue to make up as for the straight-edged tieback.

An angled tieback gives a stream-lined shape that is easy to emphasise with trimmings.

Cut a piece of paper to the length of the tieback × 15cm/6in.

Fold the paper in half widthways and mark a point 10cm/4in up on each short side. Join points to diagonally opposite corners as shown to make the tieback shape. Make up as for a straight tieback.

Trimming tiebacks

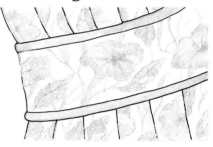

A plain tieback looks very smart but it also lends itself to additional trimmings that create a softer, crisper or more feminine look.

Piped edges Piping in the seam line emphasises shape and can provide a contrast colour. Either cover the piping cord with bias strips cut from the same fabric as the tieback or use purchased bias binding, 2.5cm/1in wide. Cover the cord and apply to the right side of one piece of the tieback, raw edges together. Continue making up the tieback as before, but sandwiching the piping between the two layers of fabric. Use a zipper foot to sew the seam, stitching as close to the piping as possible.

Left: Cut tieback patterns in paper and adjust their proportions to suit your curtains. These curved tiebacks were narrowed down to allow for the addition of a deep frill.

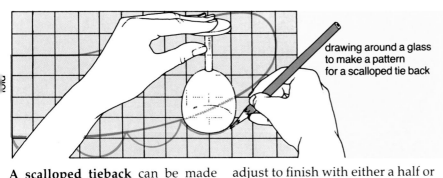

drawing around a glass to make a pattern for a scalloped tie back

A scalloped tieback can be made straight or curved.

Draw up a pattern for the basic shape of tieback you require but on deeper paper. Using a suitable size curve – an egg-cup or the rim of a small wine glass – draw a series of even-sized scallop shapes along the lower edge of the paper pattern. Start with a full scallop at the fold and, when you reach the end, adjust to finish with either a half or a complete scallop.

Cut out the paper pattern and open out flat. Cut out twice in fabric with an additional 1.5cm/⅝in all round for the seam allowance. Cut out once in interfacing without a seam allowance.

Continue to make up the tieback as before, sewing carefully around the scallop shapes and snipping into the curves – taking care not to snip the stitching – before turning through to the right side.

As an alternative, you can zigzag the edges of the scallops with a contrasting coloured sewing thread. Cut out the fabric as for the scalloped edge and attach the interfacing. Right sides facing, sew the two pieces together along the top and two side edges only. Turn to the right side and press.

On the scalloped edge, trim the seam allowance so that the fabric and interfacing edges match. Tack the two scalloped edges together around the edge of each scallop. Using a contrast coloured sewing thread and a close machine zigzag stitch, machine very carefully around the curve of each scallop, so that the zigzag stitch covers the raw edges of the fabric.

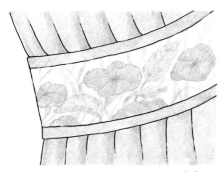

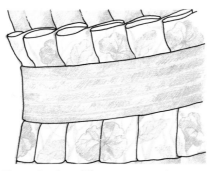

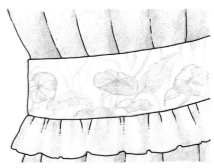

Bound edges Binding all round the edges gives the chance to introduce a contrast colour, or to pick up a plain colour from a patterned fabric. Again, you can use bias strips cut from the fabric or purchased bias binding. Cut out the fabric and interfacing to the shape you require, without any seam allowance.

Wrong sides facing, sandwich the interfacing between the two pieces of fabric, and tack together around the edges. Round off any corners slightly to make it easier to apply the binding. Attach bias strips or bias binding, slipstitching in place on the wrong side.

Pleated edges These are most suitable for straight-edged tiebacks. Cut from fabric two pleating strip pieces 11cm/4½in wide × three times the length of the tieback plus 3cm/1¼in.

Right sides facing, fold each pleating strip in half lengthways and sew across each short end. Turn right side out and press. Press in knife pleats, 1.5cm/⅝in wide, all facing in the same direction, along the total length of each pleating strip.

Lay the two pleated strips, one along either long edge, on the right side of one tieback piece, raw edges matching and 1.5cm/⅝in in from the short edge at each end. Adjust pleat depth slightly if the length is not quite accurate. Tack in place. Continue to make up as for the straight-edged tieback.

Frilled edges Open the pattern flat, and cut two pieces in fabric with an extra 1.5cm/⅝in seam allowance all round. Measure along the bottom edge of the tieback and cut enough 7.5cm/3in wide pieces of fabric to give a frill piece double this measurement when they are joined. Turn a double hem (5mm/¼in and then 1cm/½in) to the wrong side along one long edge of the frill piece and along the two short edges. Sew two lines of gathering threads along the remaining raw edge, 1cm/½in and 1.5cm/⅝in from the edge. Place the frill on one tieback piece, right sides facing and with raw edges together. Pin each end of the frill 1.5cm/⅝in in from the side edges of the tieback, and pull up the gathering threads until the frill, when evenly gathered, fits along the edge of the tieback. Tack in place. Continue to make up the tieback as for the straight version, being careful not to catch the free ends of the frill in the side seams.

53

Practical café curtains

These curtains were traditionally used in French cafés to cover the lower half of the window. They are easy and economical to make in a variety of styles – simply gather the top with a taped heading or cut a scalloped edge which can be plain or pleated.

Traditional café curtains cover only the lower half of a window, giving privacy without too much loss of light. They hang from brass or wooden poles, known as café rods, and because of their rather informal look they are most often used in kitchens and bathrooms. They can be unlined to give maximum light but, as with any curtain, a lining does protect the fabric and give added insulation.

Several variations on the traditional single curtain across the lower part of the window are shown below right. You can add a curtain valance at the top of the window. You can combine a single lower curtain with a pair of short upper curtains which can be opened to let in daylight and drawn together at night. Alternatively both lower and upper curtains can be pairs. Café curtains often have a simple gathered top, but perhaps the most distinctive style is the scalloped top, either plain or with triple pleating between the scallops. This chapter concentrates on how to make up this highly decorative variation.

For either style, fix the support brackets and place the pole in position so that the exact drop of the curtain can be measured before cutting out.

The pole for the lower curtain is positioned at least halfway up the window, coinciding with a window bar if there is one at about the required level. The finished curtain should be sill length.

For a valance or top curtains, the pole can be fixed either just above the window frame or within the recess. The top curtains should overlap the lower curtain by about 10cm/4in.

Choosing fabrics

The plain scalloped style of café curtain should be made in a furnishing fabric with a reasonable amount of body or it will not hang well. The other styles, however, do not neces-

Right: Disguise an uninspiring view with a pretty café curtain made with a cased heading and a frilled hem.

sarily need to be made in curtaining at all – choose a printed dress cotton, fresh gingham, cotton lace or a sheer fabric such as voile to complement the style of the room.

Simple gathered café curtain

This can be made in the same way as ordinary curtains with a simple cased heading and threaded on to a narrow rod or a curtain wire. (See pages 10-12 and 17 for making up instructions.) Alternatively, use a curtain heading tape to gather or pleat the top, insert hooks and hang it from the rings of a wooden or brass curtain pole. (See pages 21-23 and 26-28 for lined and unlined versions.)

Scalloped café curtain

An attractive scalloped edge shows to full advantage on a café curtain. It can also be a very economical use of fabric as the curtain is virtually flat – at the most slightly undulating – rather than gathered. If a fuller look is required, pleats can be formed between each scallop.

Curtain rings or hooks are sewn on to the strips between scallops to hang the curtain. Alternatively, crocodile clips are available which hook into the curtain rings and clip to the top of the curtain.

You will need to make a paper pattern for the scalloped edge before cutting out the curtain. The scallop size given overleaf will suit most average windows but it can be adjusted for a particularly large or small curtain. If you want to line the curtain, cut both fabric and lining and join using the sewn-in lining method (see page 26). Tack the top edge of the lining level with the foldline of the curtain top before sewing the scalloped top.

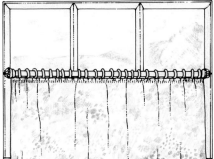

simple gathered café curtain

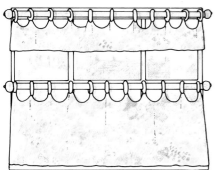

café curtain with valance

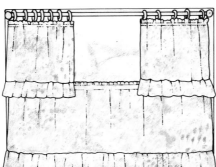

café curtain with pair of upper curtains

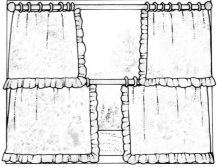

both upper and lower curtains in pairs

Making a plain scalloped curtain

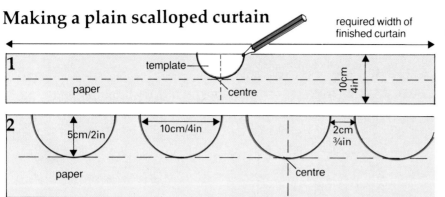

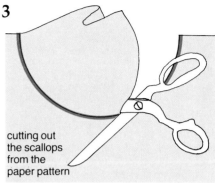

cutting out
the scallops
from the
paper pattern

The scalloped top gives style to a flat curtain. Because there is no fullness, choose a furnishing fabric with a fair amount of body rather than a soft or sheer material.

Cutting the pattern An exact semi-circle makes a scallop that is visually pleasing. Use a pair of compasses or a suitable size saucer to draw a circle 10cm/4in in diameter on to thin card. Cut out the circle then cut it across the diameter to make a semi-circular template. Measure the width of the window fairly generously as the curtain will be flat but not absolutely taut. Cut a strip of paper to the required width of

the finished curtain by 10cm/4in deep. Fold in half along the length and width to find the centre.
1 Place the template in the centre of the strip as shown – between the top edge and the centre line – and draw round it to mark the centre scallop.
2 Leaving a 2cm/1in space between each one, and working from the centre to one edge, lightly pencil in further scallops. Ideally, the last scallop will finish about 2cm/1in from the edge but, if you end up with a half scallop, either increase the width of the paper pattern (which will give your curtain a

softer less flat effect) or adjust the spacing between scallops and redraw the pattern. Repeat from the centre to the other end.
To work out the number of scallops and the spacing between them mathematically, take 2cm/1in (the ideal for the space) from the finished curtain width (to allow for a space at both ends) then divide this measurement by 12cm/5in (ie the size of one scallop plus one space). This will give you the number of scallops that will fit the width. If it is not a whole number, adjust the space between scallops until it is.

Making a pleated scalloped curtain

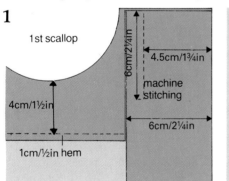

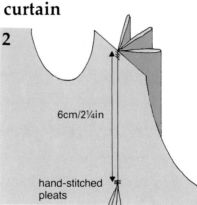

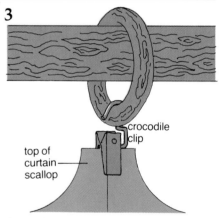

With this style a triple pleat is formed between each scallop to give the curtain more fullness.

Cutting the pattern Work out the number of scallops to fit across the width either by making a rough paper pattern or by calculating mathematically as for the plain scalloped curtain.
Having worked out the number of scallops required, make up a new paper pattern, leaving 12cm/5in between each scallop for the pleats. Although you will increase the fabric width you still have the same number of scallops as for the plain scalloped curtain.

Cutting out and making up Use the paper pattern to cut out the width of the curtain fabric, adding hem and seam allowances and joining widths if necessary, as for the plain version.
1 To form the pleats, fold the fabric between each scallop in half and, starting 4.5cm/2in from the fold, stitch down for about 6cm/2in from the top edge.
2 Make two folds within this pleat to form a triple pleat and tack in place.
Neatly hand stitch the pleats at the front at a point 6cm/2in from the top edge and at the back on the top edge to hold in place. Remove tacks.

Complete the hem along the lower edge as for the plain scalloped curtain.
3 Stitch a curtain ring or hook to the corners of each space between scallops or behind each set of pleats, depending on how much support your fabric needs. Alternatively, hang the curtain with crocodile clips which do not require stitching.

Right: A pleated scalloped curtain is bright and practical for the recess of a kitchen window. With an all-over print, the fabric can be used horizontally and cut in one piece.

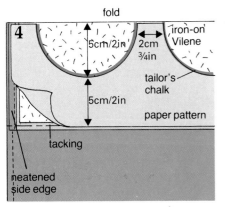

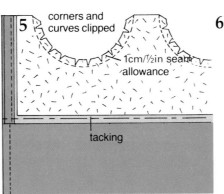

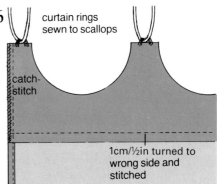

With these measurements, draw scallops along the whole strip.
3 When the paper pattern is completely drawn up, cut away the scallops.
Cutting out and making up Cut the curtain to the pattern width plus 3cm/1¼in seam allowances. If more than one width of fabric is needed allow 1cm/½in seam allowances, join selvedges and press seams open. Cut to the finished length plus a 5cm/2in bottom hem allowance and 10cm/4in for the top turning.
Neaten side edges by turning in 5mm/¼in and 1cm/½in and stitch.

Along the top edge of curtain, turn 10cm/4in of fabric to the right side and tack down. Cut a strip of iron-on Vilene 2cm/1in less than the curtain width and 9cm/3½in deep and iron on to the turned-over flap next to the fold and within the side seams.
4 Place the paper pattern on the flap with the straight edge of the scallops to the fold and draw round the scallop shapes with tailor's chalk. Remove pattern and machine stitch round each scallop following chalk lines.
5 Leaving 1cm/½in seam allowances, cut away each scallop.

Clip across corners and into seam allowances around each curve, remove tacks and turn flap to the wrong side of curtain, carefully turning out each scallop.
6 Turn 1cm/½in to the wrong side along bottom edge of flap and stitch. Catchstitch side edges together.
Sew a curtain pole ring centrally on the wrong side of each space between scallops. Complete the curtain by turning up and stitching the lower hem.

Shower curtains – meet splash with dash

Keep splashes in check with a practical shower curtain. Choose a stylishly simple version or combine it with a fabric or towelling curtain for an elegant and luxurious effect. Eyelets and rings make hanging the curtain quick and simple.

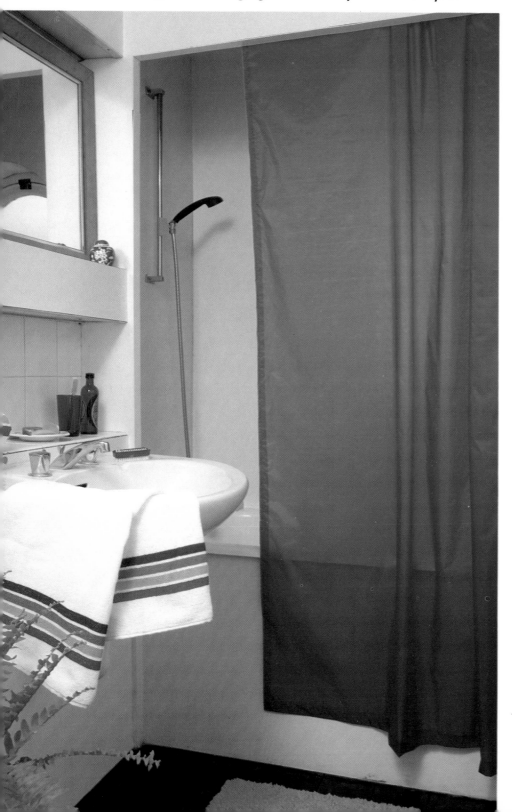

A curtain provides an inexpensive but effective method of keeping the splashes in check while having a shower. The shower curtain must have a waterproof surface and be long enough to tuck inside the bath or shower tray so that splashes of water are diverted by the curtain down the plug hole.

Shower curtains usually hang from a simple rail – you can buy shower rails from chain and hardware stores. There are expanding rails with suction ends which don't need to be screwed into the wall or through tiles and flexible rails which can be angled to fit around two or three sides of the shower.

The shower curtain is attached by means of large plastic rings which you simply thread on to the shower rail and clip together through eyelet holes made along the top edge of the shower curtain.

Inserting eyelets is very simple. You will need a large size of eyelet – 1cm/½in diameter – and a pair of eyelet pliers, or a kit which includes eyelets and a small hammer to insert them. The kit is much cheaper than the eyelet pliers.

You can of course hang the curtain by attaching a synthetic curtain heading tape and hooking this with curtain hooks on to the shower rail rings.

A basic shower curtain is made from a single unlined thickness of water-repellent rot-proof fabric, but to give your bathroom a more luxurious look, add an outer curtain that hangs over the outside of the bath. This can be made from normal curtaining fabric which, as it is protected by the inner curtain, can be trimmed and frilled to suit bathroom furnishings. The fabric side of the curtain must be completely detachable from the plastic or nylon side for laundering, so both plastic and fabric are made up as single thickness curtains and just joined together by sharing the same hooks on the rail. If your shower curtain hooks/rings will not take the bulk of two curtains or if you wish to gather the fabric curtain, use the curtain-tape method described on page 60 for hanging the curtains. Otherwise, simply make up two basic curtains, one fabric, one plastic.

Left: Waterproof rip-stop nylon, ideal for shower curtains, is available in strong, stylish colours.

Measuring up

Ready-made shower curtains are designed to fit along an average sized bath or around a shower and are about 180cm/70in square. This is a good standard size but, of course, not everyone's circumstances are standard. It is important that the curtain is of adequate size for the bath or shower, so measure up carefully before buying the fabric.

Shower curtains do not need to be gathered when pulled around the shower as gathering bunches up the curtain, trapping moisture and preventing the fabric drying off effectively. The outer curtain should not get wet so it can be gathered for a more draped effect.

The width Measure the curtain rail for the width of your shower curtain. The waterproof curtain should not be more than 1¼ times the measurement of the rail, but a perfectly flat shower curtain is quite adequate. Add 3cm/1¼in to each side for double side hems. Unless you are making a narrow shower curtain for a built-in shower unit, you will find that the fabrics generally available are not wide enough to make a shower curtain from a single width. Add 3cm/1¼in for each join in the fabric width.

The length Measure from the shower rail down to a point at least 20cm/8in inside the bath or almost to the floor in the shower tray. Add 6cm/2½in for a bottom double hem and 6cm/2½in for the top double hem to take the eyelets.

Choosing the fabric

The fabric for an unlined shower curtain, or for the shower side of a lined curtain, must be waterproof and unlikely to rot. Various synthetic materials such as 100% nylon, 100% pvc and 100% vinyl are available, usually in 130cm/51in widths, in patterned or plain colours. Rip-stop nylon, available from kite and sail shops, is also suitable and comes in a better range of bright colours.

Do not use pins on the fabric if they are likely to leave permanent holes. Hold the layers together with paper clips and use a wedge-pointed needle in the sewing machine.

These synthetic fabrics are not machine washable and should be wiped down with a soft cloth and non-abrasive cleaner.

Once a shower curtain is wet from use, it must be left as flat as possible to dry off. If it is drawn back and bunched up when wet, mildew can easily form and this is almost impossible to remove.

For a lined shower curtain, the fabric facing out into the bathroom does not need to be waterproof and can be chosen to co-ordinate with wallpaper, window curtains or other furnishings.

Towelling (but not the stretch variety) is an excellent choice, as it absorbs moisture but dries out quickly. The same colour towelling can be used for accessories such as bathrobes, towels and bath mat to give a co-ordinated effect which is essential in a small bathroom.

If you are using towelling, add at least 10% to your measurements and pre-wash the towelling before making up, to allow for its natural shrinkage.

A basic shower curtain

In the instructions below the 'right' side of the shower curtain is that which faces into the bathroom; the 'wrong' side faces into the bath or shower.

You will need
Waterproof fabric
Nylon or polyester thread
Eyelet kit or eyelet and pliers
Chinagraph pencil
Rail and rings

Cutting out and making up
Measure up as above and cut out including seam and hem allowances. Join widths if necessary with French seams (see page 11). If it is necessary to join widths of fabric the joins should be evenly spaced for the best visual effect. For example, if you are joining two pieces, join the two full widths and then cut off any excess from both sides so that the join is in the exact centre of the curtain.

On both side edges of the curtain, turn a double hem (1.5cm/⅝in and 1.5cm/⅝in) to the wrong side. Machine stitch in place close to the fold.

On the top edge, turn 3cm/1¼in then 3cm/1¼in as a double hem to the wrong side and machine stitch close to the lower folded edge.

Positioning the eyelets
To position the eyelets along the top hem, mark the fabric evenly about every 15cm/6in along the width of the curtain and about 1cm/½in down from the top edge. A chinagraph pencil makes a clear mark on plastic fabric and can be removed later with a soapy cloth. Check that you have sufficient shower curtain rings for the number of marks. If you do not have enough and are unable to buy any more to match, adjust the spacing evenly to tally with the number of rings. Follow the instructions supplied with the eyelet pliers or kit to make the holes and insert the eyelets.

Hanging the curtain
Hang the shower curtain by threading the rings/hooks on to the rail and clipping them through the eyelets.

Turn a double hem, 3cm/1¼in and 3cm/1¼in, along the bottom edge to the wrong side, and machine stitch in place close to the fold.

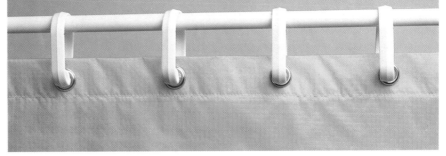

Rings clipping through eyelets of shower curtain heading.

Fabric curtain with waterproof lining

Make up the fabric curtain and the waterproof lining as two entirely separate curtains. They share the same hooks or rings which hold them together and so the fabric curtain can be laundered separately while the plastic lining is simply wiped clean. Eyelets along the top hem are the best method for hanging the waterproof lining. Use a synthetic curtain heading tape, in the standard design with a single row of pockets, to gather up the fabric curtain. The wrong sides of both fabric and lining face each other.

You will need
Sufficient fabric for the style of curtain

Synthetic curtain tape
Split rings
Waterproof fabric for the lining
Eyelets and pliers
Suitable threads
Rail and hanging rings

Making up
Make up a basic shower curtain in a waterproof fabric as described on the previous page but with the hems and seams to the *wrong* side of the fabric – the right side faces into the bath or shower.
Make up the fabric curtain in the same way as a single unlined curtain (see pages 10-12), adding synthetic tape along the top edge.

Give pretty curtains a waterproof backing.

Hanging the curtain
Shower rings are too thick to pass directly through the pockets on the tape so gather the curtain slightly to fit the bath length, then insert a split ring to correspond with each eyelet on the ungathered plastic curtain.
Thread each shower rail hook or ring through a split ring and an eyelet to hang the two curtains together.
Check the brass split rings for discoloration from time to time and replace them if they threaten to mark the fabric. Alternatively, coat them with a clear varnish (nail varnish will do) to prevent rusting.

60

PART 2

Blinds

There are several styles of blind and a variety of decorative treatments, making them suitable for all kinds of room decoration. Use a simple roller blind on its own in a kitchen or bathroom or where the fullness of a curtain would be obstructive – or in conjunction with curtains to give a choice of window treatments. For a more dressed look choose from elegantly folded Roman blinds or the feminine frills of an Austrian or ruched festoon blind.

Depending on the fabric used, a blind can exclude light completely or allow light to filter through, giving a translucent effect. Roman blinds, which must be lined, are also useful for insulation.

Blinds can be fitted into the window recess or across it and accurate measuring up is essential. Apart from the ruched styles they use much less fabric than curtains and are, therefore, an economical way of covering windows.

Choosing fabric for blinds

Closely-woven fabrics which do not have a tendency to fray are most suitable for roller blinds. Lightweight or flimsy fabrics will crease on the roller unless they are dipped, painted or sprayed with fabric stiffener. This has the added advantage of allowing the fabric to be sponged clean. Pvc or pvc-coated fabrics are particularly suitable for bathrooms or kitchens as long as they are not too heavy and bulky fabrics in general should be avoided as they will not roll up successfully.

Some soft furnishing departments sell made-to-measure roller blind fabric which is spongeable, fade-resistant and does not fray. The patterns are designed specifically for use on a blind.

Austrian and ruched festoon blinds should be made up in a fabric which drapes well and which is not too stiff to gather up in swags across the width. Suitable fabrics include moiré, soft cottons, slubbed satin, dupion and sheer voile.

Roman blinds must be lined and an aluminium backed lining such as Milium will give added insulation. Choose a firm, closely woven fabric such as linen types or chintz. The fabric must not be too stiff or the blind will not fall in even pleats.

Making a roller blind

Roller blinds are an attractive alternative to curtains, and need a fraction of the amount of fabric. They can be used as sunshades or to block out an ugly view and are simple to make from a kit. You can buy pre-stiffened blind fabric or stiffen a furnishing fabric yourself.

Blinds serve the same function as curtains, but they can also be used to cut out bright sunlight. When not in use they roll up out of the way, but their main advantage over curtains must be that they are so economical to make.

You need buy only the amount of fabric to cover the window area, plus a minimal amount top and bottom – there is no extra needed for pleats and gathers as in curtains and no need for lining fabric (although of course, lining fabric and fullness do make curtains better insulators.)
Roller blinds are useful at windows with radiators or furniture underneath them because they cover only the glass and need not hang below the sill. They look crisper and sharper than curtains and complement the clean lines of a modern room.

The blinds are quick and easy to put together. The straight bottom edge is the simplest to make, but the bottom of the blind can also be finished with decorative scallops or zigzag cuts. Alternative finishes are dealt with in the following chapter.

Right: A roller blind is ideal if you have furniture just beneath the window.

Decide whether you are going to hang your blind inside or outside the window recess – blinds are generally hung inside the recess.
1 Measure the width of the recess. If you are hanging the blind outside the recess, add 6cm/2¼in to allow for overlap. Buy a roller blind kit. They come in a range of standard sizes and, unless the width you need is a standard size, buy the next size up and cut the roller to fit. A 275cm/109in width is about the widest roller on sale.
2 Lay out the pieces of the roller kit to check you have everything you need. In most kits there is a wooden roller with a spring fitted at one end, an end cap and pin for the other end, two brackets, a wooden batten for the bottom of the blind,

tacks, cord, a cord holder and a pull. Check the roller kit instructions for the positioning of each bracket. Normally two different brackets are supplied in each kit. The slotted bracket, which takes the spring end of the blind, usually goes on the left-hand side, unless you have chosen a non-reversible fabric. In this case, the roller can be fitted so that the fabric rolls over the front of it with the right side of the fabric showing on the roller, rather than under the roller and down the back in the usual way.
If the fabric is non-reversible, fit the slotted bracket to the right-hand side of the recess for this alternative rolling up method.
If fixing your blind to the inside of the recess, position the brackets as close to the sides of the recess as

possible so that the maximum area is covered by the blind. Screw in the brackets tightly, making sure they are absolutely level.

If fixing it to the outside of the recess, the brackets should be at least 3cm/1¼in from the recess edge and at least 5cm/2in above it to prevent light from the window showing round the top and sides of the blind.

Cutting the roller to size

Measure the distance between the brackets with a steel or wooden rule and saw the roller to this width, making an allowance for the end cap, which you still have to fit.
Fix the end cap and pin to the sawn end of the roller, following instructions supplied with the kit. The roller is now ready to take the fabric.

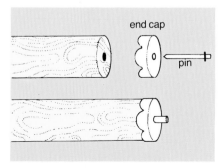

end cap

pin

Choosing and preparing the fabric

Use either commercially pre-stiffened fabric or a furnishing fabric, which you can stiffen at home.

Pre-stiffened roller blind fabric has been commercially treated to make it stiff, fray-resistant and, in some cases, spongeable and fade-resistant too. The fabric can be bought by the metre, in widths up to about 2m/2¼yd. Patterns without one-way designs can be used either vertically or horizontally to get the most economical use from the fabric.

Furnishing fabric as blind material
There are several do-it-yourself stiffening agents for roller blinds on the market. Choose a medium-weight fabric – too thin and it will not stiffen satisfactorily and will crease when rolled up – too thick and it will not roll up evenly. Many fabrics shrink slightly when stiffened, so treat the fabric before cutting it to size. Follow the instructions for stiffening provided with the product, testing a sample piece of fabric first to see if it is colour fast and can be stiffened.

Measuring up for the fabric
Measure the full width of your roller (excluding the protruding pin ends) and deduct 1cm/½in to arrive at the finished fabric width. Measure from the brackets down to the window sill, or to just below the sill for a blind hung outside the recess. Add 18cm/7in to allow for fixing round the roller and for a casing at the bottom for the wooden batten, to arrive at the fabric length. Pre-stiffened fabric will not fray when cut, and home-stiffened fabric should not do so either, so no

Cutting out and making up the blind

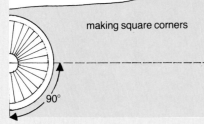

making square corners

90°

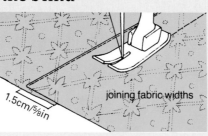

1.5cm/⅝in

joining fabric widths

Work on a flat surface to prevent the fabric from creasing.
Cut the pre-stiffened or home-stiffened fabric to size using a

sharp cutting knife or scalpel and a steel ruler or straight-edge tool as a cutting guide.
Square corners Each one must be an

exact right angle, or the blind will always roll up unevenly and hang badly. Use a protractor or a carpenter's try square to mark exact 90° angles before cutting out.
Joining fabric widths The same method of joining widths can be used for both types of fabric. Overlap the two pieces of fabric by 1.5cm/⅝in and topstitch down both edges to secure.
Neatening fabric edges Pre-stiffened fabric is fray resistant and the

Fitting the batten

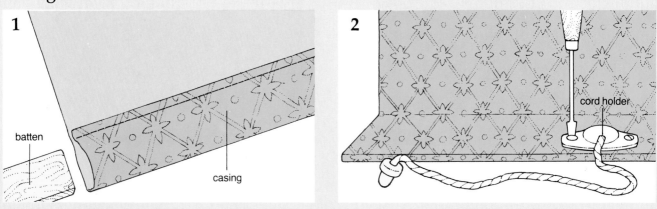

batten

casing

cord holder

Saw batten to 1cm/½in less than the width of the blind.
Turn a single hem about 4cm/1½in deep to wrong side along bottom edge. Check that the batten will slide easily into this space, and make the casing deeper if necessary.
1 Machine stitch close to the edge of the casing edge. On pre-stiffened fabric a zigzag stitch is preferable if your machine does this.
Slip the batten into the casing and sew up both ends with tiny overcast

stitches.
If you do not have a sewing machine, cut the batten to size and fold the fabric to make the casing. Spread both sides of the batten with a fabric glue. Position it carefully inside the fold and weight down with heavy objects, such as books or kitchen weights, until the glue has dried.
You need to position the batten differently if the blind is to have a decorative bottom finish. (These are dealt with in the following chapter.)

To attach cord holder and cord
Push one end of cord through the hole in the cord holder, and knot behind it to secure.
2 Position cord holder at the centre of the batten casing, and screw in through the material. Generally the cord holder is fixed to the front of the blind, but you can screw it to the back to hide it from view.
Attach cord pull to end of cord.

allowance needs to be made for side and bottom hems.

If fabric has to be joined to make up the width of the blind, allow 1.5cm/⅝in seam allowance on each piece of fabric. Position the joins at equal intervals for the best appearance. **Patterned blinds** that have joins or are to hang close to one another, such as three blinds at a bay window, should be pattern matched (see page 28). When you measure up for the fabric make an allowance for the pattern repeats so that you can match them.

edges will not need neatening. Furnishing fabric should be fray-resistant once it has been stiffened, but if it does have a tendency to fray, zigzag the edges on a sewing machine. Never turn under a side hem, as this will give you an uneven thickness of fabric on the ends of the roller.

Right: Roller blinds team successfully with curtains; the two can be made up in complementary or matching fabrics.

Fixing the fabric to the roller

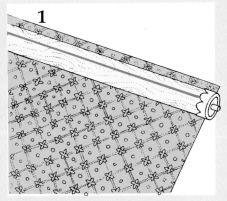

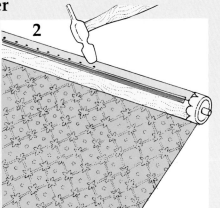

1 Lay the fabric flat, right-side upwards, and place the roller on the fabric at the top.

If you are making a blind in a non-reversible fabric and you have chosen the method of rolling the fabric over the roller rather than under it, you must lay the fabric *wrong* side upwards.

Lift the edge of the fabric over on to the roller, lining up with one of the horizontal marks on it. If your roller has no horizontal lines, clamp it in a carpenter's vice, or ask someone to

hold it very still for you, and mark a straight line at right angles to the ends along the length of the roller. Fix the edge of the fabric temporarily along this line with a length of sticky tape.

2 Hammer the small tacks provided with the kit through the edge of the fabric into the roller, spacing them evenly along it. Peel off the sticky tape.

(If you own or can borrow a staple gun, you'll find stapling the fabric to the roller is easier.)

Hanging the blind

Roll the fabric up tightly around the roller and fit it into the brackets. Pull the blind down to its full extent. You should now find that the tension is correct and when you give the cord a very gentle tug, the blind should roll up. If the tension is not correct, the blind will be sluggish and jerky as it rolls up or it may not roll up at all. Try again. Lift the extended blind out of the brackets and roll the fabric up round the roller. Put the blind back in the brackets and pull down again. Repeat until you get the correct tension, but be careful not to over-tension the blind or the spring may break.

65

Decorating roller blinds

*Cut the lower edge of a blind into scallops, zigzags or a
variety of wave shapes so that it remains
a decorative feature of the room, even when pulled up. Add
a braid trim to match your furnishings and
finish the pull cord with a wooden acorn or a tassel.*

Roller blinds are economical to make and practical to use but if you feel they leave windows looking rather bare when rolled up, add a decorative edging. Trim the lower edge of the blind into a dramatic wave shape, or cut a repeated shape such as scallops, inverted scallops or zigzags – choosing a style to suit the furnishings of the room.

Braid or lace trimmings can be added either to a straight edged blind or, if the fabric is likely to fray, to a cut, shaped edge.

On scalloped, zigzag and wave edged blinds, position the batten that straightens the lower edge of the blind above and well clear of any shaping or trimming. When the blind is pulled up, the shaping will still be visible, adding an attractive touch to the window.

There are two ways of making the batten casing and either can be used with any style of decorative edging given here.

The tuck method of making a blind casing leaves no surface stitching showing but is only suitable for plain fabrics and patterns without an obvious design as it interrupts the pattern.

The topstitched casing method leaves the main drop of fabric uninterrupted and requires less fabric but does involve a double row of stitching across the width of the blind. Make the batten casing but do not insert the batten until the lower edge is complete.

When planning a shaped edge, do not be tempted to draw the shaping directly on to the blind fabric as a mistake in measuring or drawing out could leave an ugly mark. Work out the proportions of the shaping, make up a paper pattern, then draw round this to transfer the exact pattern to the blind fabric.

If you are not confident of being able to draw a curve, you will find a flexible curve a worthwhile investment. This is a length of flexible plastic which is easy to bend into smooth, neat curves and retains its shape until re-positioned.

Preparing materials

Details of measuring up, materials required and basic making up instructions for roller blinds are given on pages 62-65. Add an extra 5cm/2in to the length of fabric to cut for a blind with a shaped edge.

Attach the brackets of the roller blind kit to the window and trim the wooden roller to fit. Cut the fabric 1cm/½in narrower than the roller and zigzag the edges to prevent fraying, if necessary.

A stiffened material called Pelmform, described on page 39, has a variety of shapes printed on it for use when making pelmets some of which are also suitable for decorative blind edges.

Making a scalloped blind

This method is also suitable for blinds edged with inverted scallops, zigzags and wave shapes.

Prepare and cut out the fabric then make a batten casing following one of the two methods below. The blind will only roll up as far as the batten so adjust the depth of scallop to suit the proportions of the window.

The tucked casing is suitable for plain or semi-patterned fabrics. Measure 13cm/5in up from the lower edge of blind fabric and mark on the side edges. Measure 9cm/3½in up from these points and mark again.

Fold the fabric across the width, right sides facing, to bring the two sets of marks together. Finger press the fold (an iron may damage stiffened fabric), then stitch across the width of the fabric 4.5cm/1¾in below the fold (between marks on either side), forming a tuck on the

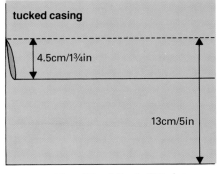

wrong side of the blind. Stitch across one end of the tuck to complete the casing and finger press tuck downwards.

The topstitched casing involves stitching a separate strip of fabric to the wrong side of the blind to form the casing and so does not interrupt the pattern.

Cut a strip 9cm/3½in deep from the bottom edge of the blind and zigzag the edges if they are likely to fray.

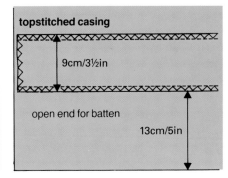

Lay the blind fabric wrong side uppermost and position the casing strip, also wrong side up, across the width 13cm/5in up from the lower edge.

Hold in place with adhesive tape or paper clips, as pins may leave permanent marks in the blind. Topstitch down both long edges and across one short edge, leaving the remaining short edge open to insert the batten later.

Planning the scallop pattern

For a scalloped edge (or one with any other repeated shape) to look its best, the width of the scallops has to be carefully calculated so that an exact number fit across the lower edge of the blind. A measurement of between 12cm/4½in and 14cm/5½in at the widest point of each scallop is a reasonable average size but you will be able to judge whether the proportion is correct after making the pattern and laying it against the blind.

To calculate the number of scallops that you need, divide the blind width by an estimated scallop width.

For example, if your blind is 132cm (or imperial equivalent) wide and you would like scallops about 14cm wide, divide 132 by 14. This gives 9.4 as the number of scallops. Obviously, a part scallop looks unbalanced so take the nearest whole number i.e. 9, and divide the width of the blind by this number to give the *exact* width of each scallop. In the example, 132 divided by 9 gives a scallop size of 14.7cm.

Left: Shallow inverted scallops, neatened and defined by a narrow trimming, add interest to a simple blind and echo the shaped edge of a pretty net curtain.

Cutting out the pattern

Cut a strip of paper 13cm/5in deep by the width of your blind and mark it out into sections *half* the calculated scallop width.

Fold the paper *concertina fashion* along the marked sections. On the unfolded edge at one end of the paper, make a mark 6cm/2¼in up from the bottom. Using a flexible curve for absolute accuracy, draw half a scallop curving from the bottom folded corner to the mark. Cut along the curve through all thicknesses of the paper and open the paper out. You will now have a paper pattern of even scallops to fit the width of your blind.

Note: If you are making a wide blind and the bulk of the folded paper is too much to cut through, cut two strips, each exactly half the blind width. Cut each into scallops, and then join the two pieces with adhesive tape to make a pattern to fit the complete blind width.

Shaping the blind edge

Lay the pattern on the wrong side of the blind, with the shaped edge close to the lower edge of the blind, and hold in place with adhesive tape.

With a sharp tailor's chalk pencil, carefully draw round the shaped

cutting the pattern

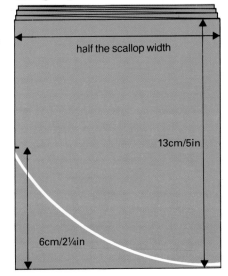

edge of the pattern. Remove the pattern and check that the outline is smooth and even.

Cut the fabric along the shaping line with a scalpel, DIY cutting knife or a special rotary cutting wheel (sold as a dressmaking/craft aid). Zigzag stitch around the shaping if it is liable to fray.

Insert the batten into the casing and hand stitch or machine stitch the remaining open edge to close. Attach the cord holder and cord to the back of the batten, attach the blind to the wooden roller, and hang it at the window.

Shaping variations

Follow the method of making up a scalloped blind, but choose one of the variations below for the shaping.

Inverted scallops

Calculate the width of these and prepare the pattern as for the scallop edged blind.

Having folded the paper concertina fashion to half a scallop width, mark 4cm/1½in (or your required scallop depth) up on the folded edge of the top piece of paper. Draw half an inverted scallop (like a shallow rainbow) from this point to the lower unfolded corner. Cut through all thicknesses and unfold to make the pattern.

Zigzags

Estimate the number and width of zigzags that will fit across the blind, using the same calculation method as for scallops – 10cm/4in wide is an average size. Half the width is a good guide to estimating the height of zigzags, but alter proportions to suit your blind.

Fold a strip of paper concertina fashion to half the width of a zigzag, as for scallops, but mark the top unfolded edge the required

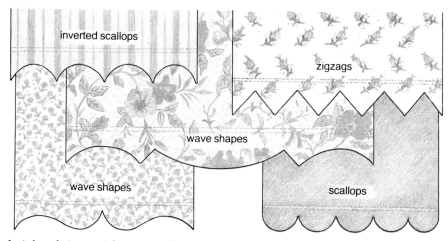

height of zigzag (about 5cm/2in) from the bottom. Rule a straight line from this mark down to the bottom corner on the folded side.

Cut along the line through all layers and unfold to make the pattern.

Wave shapes

These differ from repeated shapes such as scallops and zigzags as one shape covers half the width of the blind and is reversed to cover the other half.

Cut a strip of paper 12cm/4¾in deep by the width of the blind and fold in half, short ends together.

For a deep wave shape, draw a line across the full width of the folded paper 6cm/2¼in up from the bottom edge. For a shallower shape, draw the line about 4cm/1½in up from the bottom edge. Draw two or three evenly spaced vertical lines and use these and the horizontal line as a guide, when you are designing your required shape. A flexible curve makes this easy to do.

Cut out the shape through both layers of paper, unfold and check that the shape is visually pleasing, altering if necessary, before using as the pattern.

Adding a decorative trimming

In addition to, or instead of, cutting the bottom of your blind into a decorative shape, glue a pretty braid trimming – with or without fringing, tassels or bobbles – to the blind edges.

Use any type of braid trim along the bottom of a straight edged roller blind, but to attach braid around a curved shape, you must use bias cut braid or a flexible woven braid that will bend around the curves without puckering.

If the ends of the braid are liable to fray, either neaten with a zigzag stitch or turn a small amount of braid to the wrong side at each end and glue.

Use a fabric adhesive such as Copydex and follow the manufacturer's instructions to simply glue the braid along the edge of the blind.

A beautiful fabric print, which might be lost in the folds of a curtain, shows to perfection on a roller blind. The elegant wave shaped cut edge increases the stylish effect.

Austrian blinds

*A pretty fabric teased into soft swags and gentle gathers makes
an Austrian blind a charming alternative,
or addition, to curtains. It looks impressively complicated but
is easy to make by simply adding
tape, rings and cord to an unlined curtain.*

An Austrian blind – not to be confused with the ruched festoon blind described in the next chapter – gives a designer look to any room.
When completely lowered it looks like an unlined gathered curtain. The blind is pulled up by cords which are attached to rings and tapes running vertically up the back of the blind. Three types of tape can be used:

Plain woven tape (non-stretch) which has no pockets or bars. Rings have to be sewn on. Buy this about 2cm/¾in wide.
Dainty tape made by Rufflette. A lightweight, narrow curtain heading tape that is ideal for the vertical tapes on Austrian blinds. It has regular pockets for the rings to slot into, which also makes the job of spacing the rings much easier.
Austrian blind tape supplied in Rufflette's Austrian Blind Kit. This tape has regularly spaced bars for holding the cord so rings are not required.
The spacing of the rings and the ac-

Measuring up for an Austrian blind

To calculate how much fabric to buy, first measure your window.
For the width – as a general guide you will need 2-2½ times the window measurement. Check the instructions for the curtain heading tape you are using at the top of the blind, and be sure to allow enough fabric width to form the heading pleats. For all but the narrowest of windows, you will have to use more than one width of fabric.

For the drop – take the window height measurement and allow an extra 20cm/7¾in for hems. Add an allowance for pattern matching the width of fabric, if necessary. Multiply this total drop measurement by the number of fabric widths needed to arrive at the amount of fabric you need.
You will need extra fabric for a frill along the bottom edge, or if you add bows (see Design Extra on page 73).

The amount of tape needed depends on the size of blind you are making – (see above for the types of tape available). The total width of the fabric is divided into sections by vertical lines of tape spaced about 40cm/15¾in apart. You will need sufficient tape to run from top to bottom of the blind along each vertical division and down each side of the blind fabric.

Joining and hemming the fabric

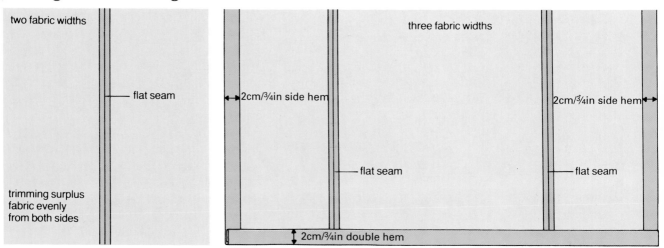

For most windows you will have to join at least two pieces of fabric to make up the width of the blind.
For two fabric widths Join widths together with a flat seam of 1.5cm/⅝in and then trim seam allowance to 5mm/¼in. Cut any surplus fabric evenly from both widths.
For three fabric widths, position a complete width in the centre, and join the widths together with flat seams of 1.5cm/⅝in. Trim the seam allowance to 5mm/¼in. Cut any surplus fabric evenly from both side widths. Down each side edge of the blind, turn a 2cm/¾in hem to wrong side and tack in place. Do not make this hem if you are adding side frills. For a plain bottom edge, turn a double hem (2cm and 2cm/¾in and ¾in) to wrong side and sew in place. Do not make this hem if you

are adding a bottom frill.
If you are adding a frill, make up and sew it in place (see Design Extra on page 73).

Right: A prettily trimmed frill emphasises the luxurious festooned effect of an Austrian blind. Piping and binding pick up the print colouring and a row of extravagantly styled bows adds a final flourish.

tion of pulling up the cords raises the blind into swags and gathers which form the characteristic appearance of an Austrian blind.

The swags and gathers raise up from the bottom, so the higher you pull up the blind, the more gathers are formed. Once you have raised the blind into the most visually pleasing position, you keep it in place by securing the cords around a cleat on the window frame.

An Austrian blind can be used at a window in addition to normal curtains, to give an extra soft look. Many people prefer to have both so that the blind can be left in a swagged position for decorative effect and the curtains can be drawn for privacy.

Because of its soft, frilly look, an Austrian blind can be used very effectively to make a feature of a plain window. You can use sheer fabric and most light furnishing fabrics, leaving the blind quite plain or adding a frilled bottom edge – trimmed and piped if you wish. You could also add frills down the side edges, or a set of bows to jolly up the top of the blind.

You will need
Fabric (as calculated opposite)
Matching sewing thread

Wooden batten 2.5cm/1in×5cm/2in ×width of your window
Curtain track and fittings of the same width as the batten
You will also need (unless you have purchased Rufflette's Austrian Blind Kit in which the items *below* are included):
Tape (as calculated opposite)
Small metal curtain rings (also known as split rings)
Non-stretch cord (about double the amount of tape required)
Screw eyes (one per length of tape)
Curtain heading tape to fit the total fabric width
1 cleat

Tapes, rings and cords

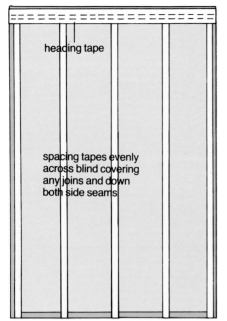

heading tape

spacing tapes evenly
across blind covering
any joins and down
both side seams

Attaching the tapes Wrong sides facing upwards, lay the blind fabric on a large flat surface – the floor is the best place.

With tailor's chalk, mark on the vertical lines for positioning the tape. These must be evenly spaced – about 40cm/16in apart – across the fabric to give good sized swags. If you have joined fabric to make up the complete width, each join must be covered by one of the lengths of tape to disguise the seam. This may mean that you have to adjust the distance between the marked vertical lines slightly – but you must still keep them evenly spaced.

The tape is positioned along these marked lines and also down both outer edges of the blind.

If you are using plain woven tape, cut it into lengths equal to the blind fabric drop plus 1cm/½in. Turn 1cm/½in to wrong side on one end of each tape. Place each length of tape along a marked vertical line (or seamline) with the folded end to the bottom edge of the blind and raw end to the top edge. Place a length of tape down each side of the blind. Tack the tapes in place, then sew down both long edges of the tape.

If you are using Dainty tape or the Austrian blind kit tape, cut each length at exactly the same point on the tape so that when all of the cut lengths are in position the pockets or bars line up across the width. Apply as for the plain tape, ensuring that the pockets or bars face upwards.

Sew heading tape to the top of the blind, as for a curtain, but do not gather up yet.

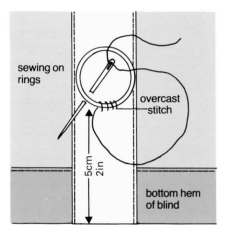

sewing on rings

overcast stitch

5cm 2in

bottom hem of blind

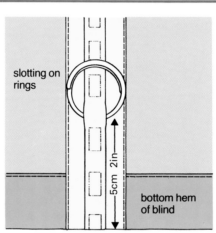

slotting on rings

5cm 2in

bottom hem of blind

Sewn-on rings If you have used plain woven tape on your blind, you will need to sew rings to the tape using overcast stitch. Starting at the bottom left-hand corner, sew the first ring to the tape, placing it 5cm/2in from the bottom edge. Continue up the tape

attaching the rings, spacing them evenly about 20cm/8in apart. Repeat for the other tapes, starting from exactly the same point at the bottom for each one. It's very important to space the rings accurately, because if they do not line up horizontally the blind will not hang evenly.

Slotted-in rings Starting at the bottom left-hand corner, slot a ring through a pocket on the first length of tape, about 5cm/2in from bottom edge. Continue spacing the rings accurately as for the sewn-on rings; you will find them easy to space as you simply count the number of pockets between each ring.

Note: the tape supplied in the Rufflette Austrian blind kit has retaining bars instead of rings. When all the rings are in place, pull up the cords in the heading tape at the top of the blind, gathering up the fabric evenly until it is the correct width for the window.

Cording the blind Lay the blind flat, wrong side upwards. Starting at the bottom left-hand corner, measure the length of the blind, plus the top width plus one metre extra. Cut a piece of cord to this

Hanging the blind

1 Take the batten of wood and fix the curtain track along one of the 5cm/2in sides, close to the top edge. Pull up curtain tape to fit track and insert hooks. Lay the batten on the floor and fit the blind to the curtain track. Turn over so that tape side of blind faces upwards and, with a pencil, mark on the underside of the batten where each tape meets the batten. Remove blind from track.

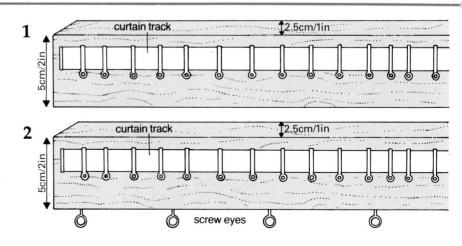

1
curtain track
2.5cm/1in
5cm/2in

2
curtain track
2.5cm/1in
5cm/2in

screw eyes

Adding frills and bows

Frills and bows add extra softness and charm to an Austrian blind, and they are easy to make up and attach.

For the frill Cut and join sufficient 10cm/4in wide strips of fabric to make up double the width of the blind. Turn a double hem (5mm and 5mm/¼in and ¼in) to the wrong side along one long edge and both short edges. On remaining long edge, sew two lines of gathering stitches 1cm/½in and 1.5cm/⅝in from the edge. Draw up gathering threads until the frill exactly fits the bottom of the blind.

With right sides facing, tack and then sew raw edges of frill and blind together, with a 1cm/½in flat seam. Insert piping between frill and blind at this stage if desired. Remove tacking and neaten seam with zigzag or overcasting stitch.

A row of bows are a clever way to conceal the seams in the fabric. For each bow, cut a strip of fabric 70cm×6cm/27½in×2¼in. Fold in half lengthways, wrong sides facing, and cut each end into a point. Trim all edges with bias binding, or bias strips cut from fabric. Tie each fabric strip into a bow. Stitch bows to blind along gathered heading.

Right: Designer touches give a really professional finish to an Austrian blind. Piped seams, a flouncy frill, contrasting binding or a row of bows – choose one or add them all for maximum effect.

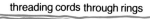

threading cords through rings

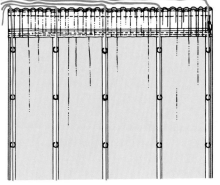

measurement.

Tie this first cord in place to the bottom ring, or bottom bar, of the tape in the bottom left-hand corner and thread it up through the other rings/bars.

Add cords to the other tape lengths in the same way, working across to the right-hand side of the blind.

2 Fix a screw eye in place on each pencil mark along the batten. Screw each end of the batten to the window frame.

Hang the blind on the curtain track.

3 Thread the left-hand cord through the first screw eye and then through all the screw eyes to the right-hand side of the batten.

Repeat for the other cords.

Attach the cleat about half-way down the right-hand side of the window frame.

Above: In a sheer fabric, an Austrian blind lets in softly filtered light.

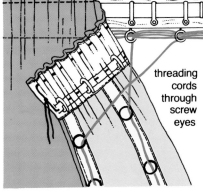

threading cords through screw eyes

To check that the blind pulls up properly, pull the cords evenly together, so that the fabric gathers upwards into soft swags.

Lower the blind, so that it is flat and tie the cords together in a knot, trimming ends to make a neat bunch. Pull the blind up once more, until it is in the desired position and secure the cords around the cleat.

Elegantly ruched festoon blinds

Even more sumptuous than an Austrian blind, a festoon blind remains ruched into soft swags not only when pulled up but also when fully covering the window. Emphasize the pretty scalloped effect of the lower edge with a matching or contrasting frill.

Transform a dull window by making a strikingly decorative ruched festoon blind, highlighting the scallops of the lower edge with a deep gathered frill. Choose a richly printed furnishing fabric, or use a sheer voile for a translucent blind to team with heavier side curtains.

A festoon blind is very similar to an Austrian blind but retains the ruched swags whether raised or lowered and so creates an even more dramatic effect. Read the previous chapter on making Austrian blinds and adapt, as described here, to make a festoon blind. Vertical lines of curtain tape – lightweight Dainty Tape is ideal – gather up the extra length.

A rod or batten encased in matching fabric, stitched to the back of the blind, ensures that the bottom edge hangs well and is easy to raise and lower smoothly. Choose a metal rod about 1cm/½in in diameter or, adding curtain weighting tape to increase the weight if necessary, a wooden batten about 2cm/¾in deep.

Below: Piping and a frill add to the decorative effect of a festoon blind.

You will need

Fabric for the blind, frill and batten casing (see Measuring up)
Rufflette Dainty tape for vertical tapes (see Measuring up)
Blind cord about twice length of tape
Rufflette Standard curtain heading tape to fit width of prepared blind fabric plus turnings
Small split curtain rings
Screw eyes
Metal rod or wooden batten to fit finished blind width
Wooden heading batten, curtain track and hooks to hang blind
Cleat to hold cords
Note: The tape in an Austrian blind kit does not create permanent ruching.

Measuring up

To calculate how much fabric to buy, measure the width and drop of your window (or the area to be covered by the finished blind).
Multiply the width by 1¼ times for a medium-weight fabric or by 1½ times for lightweights and sheers, to find the width of fabric needed. You may need more than one width of fabric to make up this size.
Multiply the drop by 1½-3 times (again, the bulkier the fabric, the less you need; only a fine sheer needs 3 times the drop) to find the required length of blind fabric.
Calculate how much fabric you will need to buy by multiplying the required length by the number of widths needed. You will also need sufficient 20cm/8in-deep strips of fabric to make up a piece 1½ times the width of prepared blind fabric for the frill and a strip of fabric 8cm/3in deep by the width of the finished blind to cover the rod or batten.
Add allowances for pattern matching as necessary.
Calculate the Dainty tape needed as for an Austrian blind, page 70.

Cutting out

Allowing for pattern matching where necessary, cut out lengths of fabric to make up the area of the blind. Also cut 20cm/8in deep strips to make up a frill piece 1½ times the blind fabric width, and a strip for batten casing (see Measuring up).

Making up and hanging the blind

Join widths of fabric if necessary, as for an Austrian blind, page 70. Press a 2cm/¾in turning to the wrong side down each side edge of the blind and tack.
Press a 4cm/1½in turning to the wrong side across the top edge; tack.

Adding the frill

Join the strips of fabric to make up the frill with 1cm/½in flat seams and press seams open. Fold the strip in half along its length, right sides facing, and stitch across both short ends, 1cm/½in in. Fold strip right side out, press and insert two rows of gathering stitches, in easy-to-gather sections, through both thicknesses along the open edge. Pull up the gathering threads until the frill fits the width of the blind, tie the thread ends securely and even out gathers.
Tack the frill across the bottom edge on the right side of the blind, raw edges together, and stitch 1.5cm/⅝in in from the edge. Remove tacking, zigzag stitch or oversew raw edges together; press upwards.

Attaching tapes and rings

Lay the fabric out flat on the floor, wrong side uppermost and, using a tailor's chalk pencil, mark the position of the vertical lines of Dainty tape. Position the two outer tapes 1cm/½in in from the side edges; space the remaining tapes evenly between them 25–40cm/10–16in apart. If possible, arrange the

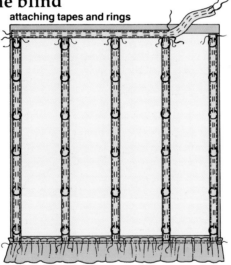

attaching tapes and rings

spacing so that a line of tape will cover any seams joining fabric widths. Cutting 1cm/½in in front of a tape pocket each time, so that they will line up horizontally on the blind, cut the appropriate number of lengths of tape each 5cm/2in longer than blind (excluding frill). Freeing the ends of the gathering cords, turn in 1cm/½in at the lower end of each length of tape, and pin into position from the frill seam to the edge of top turning. Ensure that the edges of the side hems and any seams are covered by tape and that the tape pockets line up. Stitch long edges of each tape.
Freeing the top ends of gathering cords on vertical tapes as shown in diagram, stitch standard heading tape across top of blind covering raw edge and tape ends.
Slot split rings through the tape pockets every 20–25cm/8–10in or so, placing the first ring about 10cm/4in up from the bottom of the tape, with the final ring just below the heading tape.
Gather up each line of tape to the finished length of the blind. Even out the gathering so that the rings line up horizontally across the back of the blind and tie the ends of the cords to secure. Just below each pocket, catch the cords of the gathering tape to the fabric with small invisible handstitches to hold the gathers in place as heavy fabrics may slip when hanging.

Adding a rod or batten

Fold the strip of casing fabric in half lengthwise, right sides facing, and stitch across one short end and down long raw edges with a 1cm/½in seam. Turn right side out.
Slip the rod, or a batten plus weighting tape, into the casing and slipstitch the open end closed.
Lay the blind out flat, wrong side upwards and place the covered rod just below the lowest row of rings as close to the scallops as possible without being visible from the right side. Stitch the top edge of the casing securely in place at the points where it crosses the vertical tapes, making sure the stitches are unnoticeable on the right side.

Cording and hanging

Attach cords and hang the blind in the same way as an Austrian blind.

Roman blinds for a soft pleated effect

Softer than a roller blind and less fussy than an Austrian blind, a Roman blind suits most windows and rooms, and is quick and economical to make. It is also easy to hang and to operate – the pull cords which raise it form attractive layered folds.

A Roman blind is an economical and unusual way of covering a window. When fully lowered it looks similar to a roller blind, but when pulled up, a system of rings and cords on the back concertina the fabric into soft horizontal pleats. There is, therefore, no need to stiffen the fabric, or buy a spring-loaded roller blind kit. A wooden batten running across the blind close to the bottom edge keeps it in shape and hanging straight.

Choosing fabrics

A Roman blind is made from a double thickness of fabric – top blind fabric and lining. The top fabric must not be too sheer or flimsy or it will not fall into crisp pleats. Most smoothly woven furnishing fabrics are suitable – choose one to match your upholstery or the colour scheme of the room. The lining can be ordinary curtain lining, an insulating lining or a complementary fabric that will also look pretty from the outside of the house. Choose closely woven fabrics for both blind and lining and the blind will be light-tight enough even for a bedroom.

The blind is quick and simple to make. After joining fabric and lining, simply stitch vertical lines of tape down its length. Sew rings to the tapes and pass cords through them – when pulled, the cords raise the blind by pleating up the fabric.

Tack the blind to a length of wood for hanging, and fix it to the wall with small angle iron supports, available from most hardwear or DIY suppliers.

Measuring up

The width Measure the width of the window area to be covered by the

Below: An elegant set of Roman blinds.

blind. If the blind is to be hung inside a recess or within a decorative window frame, make sure that the finished width will allow enough clearance for the blind to be raised and lowered without catching on the sides. If the blind is to hang outside a recess, overlap each side by at least 3cm/1¼in. For either style of hanging, add 3cm/1¼in to the finished width measurement for side seams.

It is possible to make a blind for a smallish window from a single piece of fabric. If you do have to join widths of fabric for a larger window, balance the joins evenly – for two widths the join should run down the exact centre of the blind; for three widths, use a complete width for the centre panel with an equal amount of fabric on either side.

For each join required, add 3cm/1¼in to make a 1.5cm/⅝in flat seam.

The length Measure the total drop required and add 3cm/1¼in for top and bottom seams and 1cm/½in for

overlapping the blind fabric on to the wooden heading. If you are hanging the blind outside a recess, add any overlap required at the top or bottom.

The tape Calculate the amount needed in the same way as for an Austrian blind (see page 70).

The finished width of the blind is divided into equal sections by vertical lines of tape spaced at approximately 30cm/12in intervals across the width – with a length of tape on each side edge. To work out the amount of tape required, calculate the number of lengths of tape needed and multiply this by the finished length of the blind plus 2cm/¾in.

You will need
To make the blind
Fabric for the front of the blind (see measuring up)
The same amount of lining fabric
Matching sewing thread
2cm/¾in wide cotton tape (see measuring up)

Non-stretch cord about twice the length of tape
Small plastic or metal curtain rings
Wooden batten about 2cm/¾in wide 1cm/½in shorter than finished width of blind

To hang the blind
A piece of 5cm×2.5cm/2in×1in wood to fit the finished width of blind, for the heading
A metal screw eye for each vertical line of tape
Tacks or staples to attach blind to wooden heading
Angle irons to attach wooden heading to window frame
Cleat to hold cords in place

Cutting out
Cut the fabric to the required length and join widths, if necessary, with 1.5cm/⅝in flat seams. Press seams open. Trim away any excess width taking an even amount from each side. Cut out and make up lining to the same size.

Making up the Roman blind

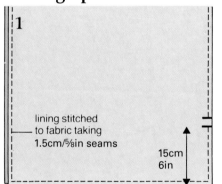

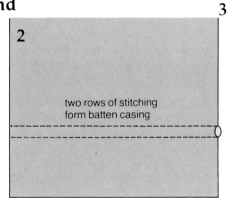

two rows of stitching form batten casing

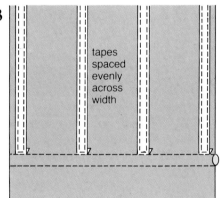

tapes spaced evenly across width

lining stitched to fabric taking 1.5cm/⅝in seams
15cm 6in

Joining fabric and lining Lay the lining fabric wrong side upwards flat on a table or the floor and measure 15cm/6in up from the bottom on one side edge. Mark this point with tailor's chalk.

Measure the wooden batten, add 5mm/¼in to the width and make a second mark on the lining this distance above the first.

1 Lay fabric and lining right sides facing and tack together all round. Sew down both sides and across the bottom edge taking 1.5cm/⅝in seams leaving a gap between the two marks on *one* side of the fabric to insert batten. Turn right side out. Turn 1.5cm/⅝in to the wrong side on both fabric and lining top edges and press. Tack and topstitch the folded edges together close to edge.

2 Lay the fabric out flat with the lining uppermost. With a ruler and tailor's chalk, mark two parallel lines for the batten casing in line with the gap left in the stitching on one side. Sew along these marked lines to form the batten casing.

Attaching tape and rings Mark the position of the vertical tapes on the lining side of the blind by drawing lines with tailor's chalk from the top of the blind to the batten casing. Begin by marking the position of a line of tape 1.5cm/⅝in in from each side edge. Divide the remaining fabric into equal sections with lines for tapes spaced about 30cm/12in apart, adjusting the spacing to suit your blind depth. It is *vital* that the tapes are evenly spaced.

3 Once you have marked the tape lines and checked that the spacing is even, pin and tack the tapes in place, turning 1cm/½in to the wrong side at the top and bottom ends. The tapes should run from the top edge ending at, but not overlapping, the batten casing. Sew the tapes in place, down both long edges and across the bottom edge. Remove tacking.

With tailor's chalk or pins, mark the ring positions about 15cm/6in apart along each line of tape. The first mark should be just above the batten casing and the last approximately 18.5cm/7in down from the top edge of the blind. It is important that the rings are *exactly* aligned horizontally so that the blind pulls up evenly.

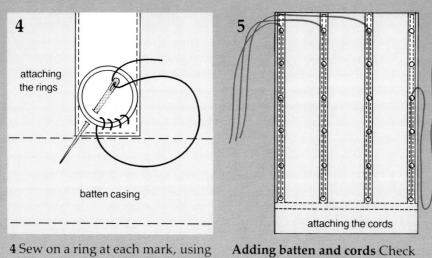

4
attaching the rings

batten casing

5
attaching the cords

4 Sew on a ring at each mark, using overcast stitching worked through the tape and lining but not the top blind fabric.

Adding batten and cords Check that the length of wooden batten is 1cm/½in less than the width of the blind; trim it if necessary. Gently ease it into the stitched casing and neatly hand sew the casing closed.
5 To attach the cords, lay the blind flat on the floor, lining side upwards and tie a length of cord securely to the bottom ring on the left-hand side. Pass the cord through every ring in this first line of tape and across to the left-hand edge of the lining. Allow 1m/1yd or a length that you will be able to reach when the blind is hanging, and then cut the cord.
Repeat for each line of tape, taking the cord up to the top of the blind, across to the left-hand edge and adding approximately 1m/1yd extra before cutting to form the hanging cords which are pulled to operate the blind.

Hanging the Roman blind

Preparing the wooden heading Cut the 5cm×2.5cm/2in×1in piece of wood for the heading to the width of the blind and attach the screw eyes to a wider side, positioning them to correspond with the lines of tape on the blind.
Screw as many angle irons as are necessary to support the blind to the same side of the wood as the screw eyes, placing the bend of the angle iron in line with the edge of the wood.

Below: Use Rufflette Austrian blind tape rather than tape and rings, and thread the cords through the loops.

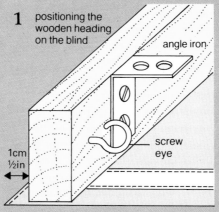

1
positioning the wooden heading on the blind
angle iron
screw eye
1cm ½in

2
cords threaded through the screw eyes

1 With the blind flat on the floor, lining side upwards, lay the narrow edge of the wooden heading (angle irons uppermost), on to the fabric 1cm/½in down from the top edge. Wrap the 1cm/½in strip of blind fabric on the wider side of the wood without screw eyes and tack or staple it securely in place. Make sure that the strip of fabric turned on to the wood is absolutely straight and even or the blind will hang askew.

2 Thread the left-hand vertical cord through the screw eye above it so that it hangs on the left side of the blind. Work across the blind threading each cord through the screw eye directly above and through the other screws along the wood to the left-hand side. When all cords have been inserted loosely knot the dangling ends together. Hold the wood and blind up to the window in the required position and attach the angle irons to the window frame or wall.
Untie the cords and trim to an even length of about 1m/1yd (or as required) then re-tie neatly together.
Pull the bunch of cords downwards and the blind above the batten will pull up in even folds, from the bottom upwards.
Screw a cleat to the window frame in a position within easy reach; wind the cords around this to hold the blind up at the required level.

Trimming a Roman blind

Emphasize the neat, clean lines of a Roman blind with a sharply contrasting trim.
Use a flat tape or straight strips of fabric with raw edges pressed under for the trim. A width of 2.5cm/1in wide gives a bold effect.
Make up the blind as far as attaching the tapes to the lining side. Add the trim before attaching the rings.

Lay the blind out flat, right side upwards, and tack the trim in place down both sides and across the bottom edge, mitring the corners. Set the trim about 1.5cm/⅝in in from the edge so that the blind fabric forms a narrow border.
Machine the trim in place, topstitching down both edges, but do not machine over the batten casing. Remove the

Above: On a border-printed fabric, adjust width by making a tuck and only trim lower edge of the blind.

tacking and back stitch by hand along the trim where it crosses the casing, stitching through the top layer of fabric only, so as not to obstruct it.
Press well, sew on the rings and continue to make up the blind in the normal way.

PART 3

Cushions

Cushions add a decorative and individual touch to a room. Use them to soften the hard lines of some modern furniture, to add a dash of colour and richness to an austere colour scheme or comfort to a window recess, wooden bench or stool. Size and style are almost infinitely variable; use your imagination and the ideas given in the next few chapters to create an eye-catching collection of cushions.

Large floor cushions add supplementary seating for a large number of guests and make for an informal look. Covered foam blocks convert to make an extra bed and sag bags filled with polystyrene granules settle into a cosy supported seat which moulds to your shape.

Smaller cushions add comfort to a sofa or easy chair and can be used as a headrest when sitting up in bed. The basic square, round and rectangular shapes can be left plain or decorated with frills, piping and other trimmings. Add an individual touch using needlecraft skills such as appliqué, needlepoint, embroidery, ribbon weaving – the possibilities are endless – or use these basic techniques to make cushions in more unconventional shapes.

Choosing fabrics for cushions

Almost any fabric can be used, from heavy tapestry weaves to lightweight cottons; the limiting factor is the amount of wear the cushion is likely to get. Avoid very loose weaves and choose fabrics with easy care or washable properties for cushions which will get a lot of use. Remnant counters are a good source of fabrics for the smaller cushions and you can afford to use expensive and luxurious fabrics if only a small amount is required. For a co-ordinated look, save offcuts from your curtains and upholstery.

Ready-made cushion pads are available but if you intend making your own, suitable fabrics are calico, cambric, cotton sheeting and lining material. If the filling is feather or down use a down-proof ticking.

Cushions for comfort

Cushions are just about the most versatile of home furnishings.
They provide a splash of colour, tone or contrast,
and give added comfort to a sofa or chair. Once you have
learned how to make the basic cushion shapes, you
can add frills, piping or fancy borders for a decorative effect.

To make a simple cushion cover all you need is a front, a back, and a method for opening and closing. Before you set to work with the scissors cutting out the fabric, decide on the type of opening you want to use, as this determines the cutting measurements.

A zip, Velcro or overlap opening is the most satisfactory type if you're likely to be laundering the cushion cover frequently, because this makes the cushion pad easy to take out and put back.

A hand sewn opening, although easier to make in the first place, needs to be carefully unpicked and resewn each time the pad is removed.

Choose any furnishing fabric to make up a cushion cover. You can create a bold show mixing style, colour and pattern by buying up fabric remnants or, if you're sewing curtains, loose covers and other furnishings for your home, use left overs from cutting out the fabric to make co-ordinating covers at no extra cost.

The cushion cover itself is sewn to fit over a cushion pad. Never put fillings straight into your cushion cover. All filling has to be enclosed in its own inner cover to give a cushion pad that can be removed from the cushion cover for laundering.

Re-use the pads you've got already if they're still in good condition. If you're buying a new pad, manufactured cushion pads are available in a large number of sizes and shapes, square, rectangular and round, so you should be able to find one with the dimensions to suit your needs.

Right: Cushions in a mixture of shapes and sizes add subtle touches of colour to this cool grey living room.

Making square and rectangular cushion covers

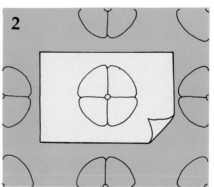

Measuring and cutting

Use a tape measure to size up your cushion pad. It's important to measure right over the pad to take account of its padded out shape. Measure in both directions to find the size of the square or rectangle you will need for the cover and to these measurements add 1.5cm/⅝in seam allowance all round. For a plump-looking cushion, do not add seam allowance so that, after you have sewn the cover together, it fits tightly over the pad.

For each cushion cover, cut a front and a back piece (two sections for the back piece if you've chosen to have a back zip opening, page 85). Lay the fabric on a flat surface and with a ruler and tailor's chalk mark up the sizes of the squares or rectangles.

1 Mark all the squares/rectangles on the straight grain of the fabric with the pattern (if applicable) running in the same direction.

If the fabric has a definite bold pattern, place this centrally on the cushion cover for best effect. To do this, cut a piece of tracing paper to the size of your square/rectangle.

2 Place the tracing paper pattern on the fabric, centring over the main design.

When you're cutting several covers from the same fabric, it helps to estimate the total amount of fabric if you draw up a plan first. On a small piece of paper, mark up the width of your fabric and then draw on, with measurements, the number of fabric pieces needed. Make sure that the combined measurements across the width come close to, but do not exceed, the width of your fabric. To estimate the total length of fabric you will need, simply add up the measurements of the pieces marked down the length.

Hand-sewn side opening This is the simplest of cushion covers to make, its only disadvantage is that you have to resew the opening when the cover is cleaned.
Right sides facing, tack the two pieces of fabric round three sides 1.5cm/⅝in from outer edge with a 90° right angle at each corner. On a rectangular cover, leave a short side untacked. To give rounded corners tack a curve instead of a right angle at each corner. After sewing, trim fabric and notch almost to the seamline.

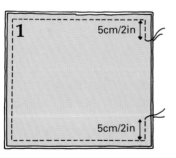

1 On the untacked side, tack 5cm/2in of the seam from both ends, leaving the centre of the seam open. Sew all seams with a 1.5cm/⅝in seam allowance leaving the untacked sections open.

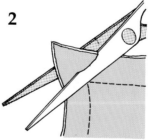

2 On each corner, cut the seam allowance diagonally close to the stitching to reduce bulk. Neaten the raw edges by zigzagging on a sewing machine.

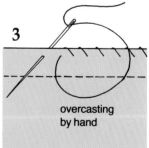

overcasting by hand

3 Alternatively overcast by hand to neaten. Turn to right side and add the cushion pad. Tack the opening closed. Handstitch opening with slip stitches. Remove tacking.

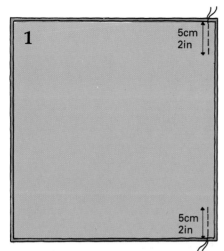

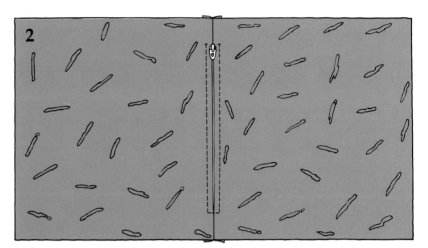

Side zip opening

Lay the two squares/rectangles right sides facing.

1 On one side (short side for a rectangle) tack together for 5cm/2in from each corner along seam allowance. Sew. Remove tacking. Press these short seams flat and press seam allowance to wrong side between the sewn seams. Lay the zip, which should be the same size as the opening, face up on a flat surface and with wrong side of fabric to zip, place open section of seam over the zip teeth. Tack zip in place.

2 On the right side of the fabric, sew down both sides of the zip and across the bottom close to the teeth using the zipper foot on your machine, or as close to the teeth as you can get with the normal sewing foot. Remove tacking. Open the zip and with right sides of the two pieces of fabric facing, tack and sew round the other three sides. Remove tacking. Neaten raw edges. Turn to right side.

Other opening methods In place of a zip you can use a length of press stud tape or Velcro. Make up cover in the same way as for a hand-sewn side opening. Place tape or Velcro on either side of the opening and slip stitch or machine in place.

Making round cushion covers

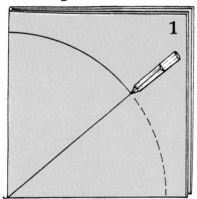

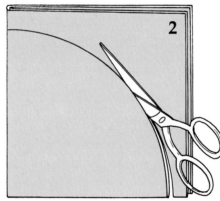

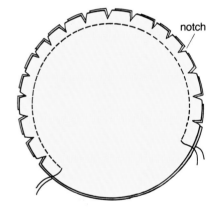

notch

Measuring and cutting

The success of a round cover depends on cutting a perfect circle from the fabric. Measure across the diameter of your cushion pad and add 3cm/1¼in (1.5cm/⅝in seam allowance each side). Cut a square of paper slightly largely than the diameter plus seam allowance.

1 Fold this paper square into four sections. Tie a length of string securely round a pencil and cut this off to half the diameter of the cushion plus 1.5cm/⅝in seam allowance. Again for a plump cushion do not add the seam allowance, and you will get a snug fit. Lay the folded paper on a board and pin the loose end of the string to the point of the folded corner with a drawing pin.

Hold the pencil upright and, at full extent of the string, mark the paper with the pencil in a curve.

2 Take out drawing pin and cut along the curve through all four layers of the paper. Open out the paper and you will have a perfect circle. This circular paper pattern can be made up in tracing paper if you want to see through the pattern to centre it over a fabric design.

Cut two circles of fabric for each cover. A different pattern has to be made for the back of the cover, if you are placing a zip in the back (right).

Hand-sewn side opening

This is the easiest of round cushion covers to make up, as there is no fastening. However, the opening will have to be unpicked and re-sewn each time for washing.

Right sides facing, lay the two circles of fabric together and tack round the circumference with a 1.5cm/⅝in seam allowance, leaving an opening sufficient to squeeze in cushion pad. Sew. Remove tacking. Notch into the seam allowance all round (except the opening) close to stitching line. Turn cover through to right side and add cushion pad. Tack opening closed and slip stitch by hand. Remove tacking.

Creative cushion covers

Once you're familiar with the basic cushion-making skills, you can think more creatively in design terms. Always remember to sew on any motifs or decoration *before* assembling the cushion pieces. As a taster, the ideas (shown right) are simple and effective.

Simple machine patchwork is marvellously quick and uses up odd scraps of fabric.

Ribbons can be sewn on in a plaid design or as a decorative border.

Cotton lace, backed by a piece of taffeta in a contrasting colour, looks pretty for a bedroom.

Appliquéd motifs are fun to make up. As a short cut, you can cut out a motif from left-over curtain material. A fabric with a regular pattern or printed with squares, diamonds or stripes is easy to quilt and makes a soft padded cushion cover.

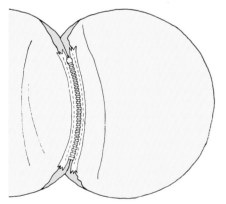

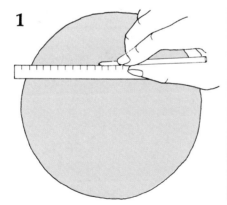

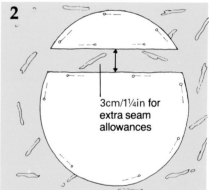

3cm/1¼in for extra seam allowances

Side zip opening

Choose a zip long enough to take the pad. Pin the two circles together right sides facing, leaving an opening in the seam allowance the length of the zip. Tack along the seam allowance for 2.5cm/1in either side of the opening. Sew. Remove tacking and pins. Press short seams flat. Pin the zip into the opening between the stitched seams. This seam is on the curve, so ease the fabric slightly. Tack and sew. Open the zip and place the two fabric circles right sides facing. Tack together round remaining circumference. Sew. Remove tacking. Notch the seam allowance. Turn to right side and insert pad.

Back zip opening

A back zip is easier to sew into a round cushion and looks neater because the zip is sewn between two pieces of flat fabric. Using the circular paper pattern, as before, cut just one piece of fabric (for the front of the cover). Choose a zip length about 10cm/4in shorter than the diameter and using the same circular paper pattern.

1 Mark a straight line across the paper pattern where the zip is to be fitted (you can place this centred or off centre) and cut the paper pattern across this line.

2 Position the two paper patterns on the fabric and mark an extra 1.5cm/⅝in seam allowance along

both straight cut edges. Cut out with the extra seam allowance. Right sides facing, match the two straight edges and tack together. Sew 5cm/2in from either end along the seam allowance. Remove tacking. Sew in zip (as for square cushion cover). Open the zip. Right sides of the front and back circles facing, tack together and sew all round taking 1.5cm/⅝in seams. Remove the tacking. Turn the cover through to right side and add cushion pad.

Single frill with bias edge

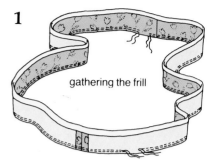

1 gathering the frill

This cushion cover has a frill made from a single thickness of fabric, the outer raw edge of which is finished with bias binding.

Cutting out and making up

Cut out two squares or rectangles of fabric to the cushion pad size with a 1.5cm/⅝in seam allowance all round. The finished width of the frill is a matter of personal choice, but you will find that a frill any wider than 7cm/2¾in finished width is rather floppy. Add 1.5cm/⅝in to finished width of frill for seam allowance. To calculate the length of frill required, measure all round the cushion cover and double this

Add contrast bias for impact.

figure to give an ample frill. For a thick fabric which is more bulky to gather, one-and-a-half times the length is sufficient.

For very fine fabrics only you may need two to three times the measurement.

To the frill length measurement add 3cm/1¼in seam allowance for joining the two short ends and add 3cm/1¼in for any joins that are necessary to make up the length. Cut out the frill and, with 1.5cm/⅝in seams, join the lengths to make a circle.

Neaten the outer raw edge of the

frill with bias binding.

1 Sew two lines of gathering stitches on the inner edge of the frill, 1.5cm/⅝in and 1cm/½in from raw edge. Work gathering stitches along half the length, then cut the stitching threads. Make gathering stitches along the remaining length in the same way.

With right side of frill facing right side of one of the main cushion cover pieces, and raw edges matching, gently ease up the gathering threads along half the frill length, until this exactly fits two sides of the cover fabric. Make slightly more gathers on the corners to allow sufficient fullness.

Pleated frill

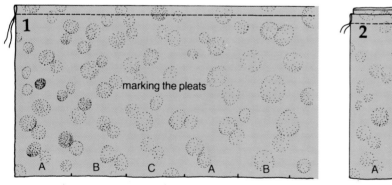

1 marking the pleats

A B C A B

2 making the pleats

A A A A B C

A pleated fabric frill gives a crisp finish to a round or rectangular cushion cover. Piping can also be inserted into the seam for extra decorative effect.

Cutting out and making up

Cut out two squares or rectangles of fabric to the cushion pad size, with a 1.5cm/⅝in seam allowance all round. To calculate the amount of fabric length needed for the frill, measure all round cushion pad and cut fabric to three times this length plus 3cm/1¼in seam allowance for joining the two short ends and add 3cm/1¼in seam allowance for any

joins that are necessary to make up the complete frill length.

To calculate the amount of fabric width needed for the frill, decide on the finished width and add 2.5cm/1in for seams.

Cut out the frill fabric and join the pieces to make one length. On the outer long edge turn a 1cm/½in double hem (5mm/¼in and then 5mm/¼in) to the wrong side and sew.

To pleat up the frill mark the fabric into 3cm/1¼in sections along its length with tailor's chalk. Mark on the right side of the fabric, within the 1.5cm/⅝in seam allowance.

1 Starting at one edge, and using

tailor's chalk, lightly mark each section in a series of consecutive As, Bs and Cs along the length.

2 Make the pleats by folding and pressing the fabric on the right side on the chalk marks so that the mark between A and B is pressed and touches the mark between C and the next A. Continue along the length. From the right side, all the As should be visible and the Bs and Cs folded to the inside. Pin the pleats and tack. Machine 1cm/½in from raw edge. Remove tacking. Tack the pleated frill in place, as for the single frill with bias edge. (To add piping to the seam see under

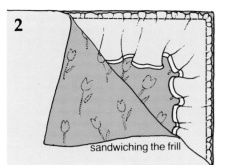
sandwiching the frill

Match and fit the remaining half of frill to the other two sides of the fabric in the same way. Tack the frill in place. Machine 1cm/½in from raw edge. Remove tacking and gathering threads.

At this stage add a side zip, if you want a zip opening.

2 With right sides together, place the second piece of cover fabric on the first, sandwiching the frill inside, and tack all round. Sew all round, allowing a 1.5cm/⅝in seam, and leaving an opening to insert the pad, if a zip has not been added. Remove tacking, turn through to the right side and insert the pad.

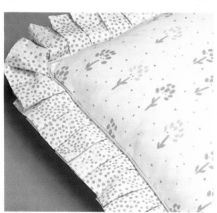

A pleated frill is smart and looks good on round and square cushions.

Professional Touch, right.)

If you want to add a side zip, do so at this stage.

Right sides facing, place the second cushion piece over the first, sandwiching the frill. Sew all round with a 1.5cm/⅝in seam and leave a gap for inserting the cushion pad if a zip has not been added. Remove all tacking. If you have added piping, use a zipper foot to get close up to the piping with the stitching line. Turn through to right side and insert the pad.

Covering piping cord

You can buy piping cord from haberdashery departments. It comes in several thicknesses, and your choice will depend on how prominent you want it to be – the thicker the cord, the more it will stand out from the seam. Piping cord has to be covered with fabric cut on the bias. Either you can make your own bias strips (see page 165) or buy ready-made bias binding. In either case, you will need enough bias fabric to go right round the piping cord and to allow at least 1cm/½in on each edge for seam allowance. So for piping cord that is 12mm/½in in diameter, you will need bias strips at least 3.2cm/1⅜in wide.

1
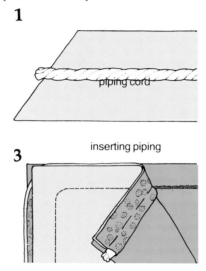
piping cord

inserting piping

2
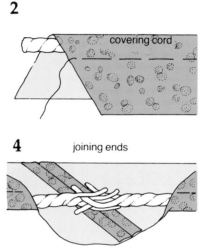
covering cord

joining ends

1 Press the bias strip flat and place the piping cord along the centre, on the wrong side of the fabric.

2 Wrap the fabric round the piping cord and tack the fabric together as close to the cord as possible. Sew, using a zipper foot to get the stitching line close to the cord. Remove tacking.

Adding piping to a seam

Mark seam allowance (1.5cm/⅝in) on the right side of either the front or back of the cushion. cover, using tailor's chalk.

3 Place the piping on the right side of the cover, matching the stitching line of the piping to the marked seam allowance line. The raw edges of the bias piping cord fabric must face outwards to the raw edges of the cushion cover. Tack the piping in place. At each corner, curve the piping round slightly to avoid a sharp angle.

To join the piping first make a

Added to a seam, piping gives a professional and expensive look.

join in the bias strip (see page 165). Join the piping cord by allowing an extra 5cm/2in when you cut the cord to length.

4 Overlap the two ends by 2.5cm/1in and at each end unravel the twisted cords and trim each separate cord to a slightly different length. Intertwine the cords at each end to make a smooth join.

Place front and back of cushion cover together. Tack together, except for the opening and taking a 1.5cm/⅝in seam, stitch as close to the piping cord as possible using the zipper foot on your machine. Sew the piping cord in place along the open edge. Remove tacking.

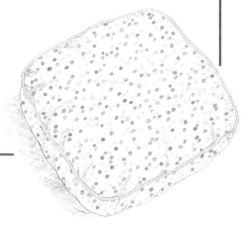

Zigzagged pointed frill

1

2

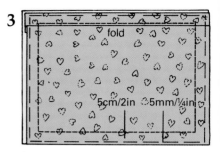
3

This fancy edge is cut to shape with the help of a template and the raw edges neatly finished with a machine zigzag stitch. This type of cover is not suitable for a zip.

Cutting out and making up

Cut out two squares or rectangles of fabric to the cushion pad size plus an extra 8cm/3¼in on both the length and width. Also cut one strip of fabric 8cm/3¼in by the length of the rectangle or square.
1 Place 8cm/3¼in wide fabric strip wrong sides facing on one cushion cover rectangle/square, and with raw edges matching to one of the edges (a long edge if making a rectangular cover). Tack in place.

Take the other rectangle/square and turn 5cm/2in to the wrong side along one edge (long edge if a rectangle). Trim the turn to 3cm/1¼in.
2 Lay the two rectangles/squares together, wrong sides facing, matching raw edges and placing the folded edge of one rectangle/square so that it overlaps the attached strip on the other rectangle/square.
3 Tack all round cover, 5mm/¼in, then 5cm/2in from the raw edges.

Machine along the 5cm/2in tacking line, working from the back, so that the opening is not machined closed. Turn to right side.
To make the pointed frill You will need a cardboard template to cut an evenly pointed edge between the 5cm/2in machined line and the edges of the cushion cover. To make the template, cut a piece of card 30cm× 4.5cm/11¾in×1¾in. Draw a central line through the length. Mark along

making a template

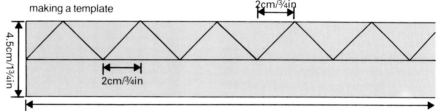

Double gathered frill

This frill is made from a double thickness of fabric. If you are using a fabric with a one-way design, you can create an interesting visual effect by cutting the frill fabric so that the design runs in the opposite direction to that on the cover.

Cutting out and making up

Cut out two circles of fabric to the cushion pad size with a 1.5cm/⅝in seam allowance all round. If you want to insert a back zip, do so at this stage.
To calculate the length of frill needed measure the circumference of your cushion pad with a tape measure. For full gathers cut the frill to double this measurement, adding 3cm/1¼in seam allowance for joining the two short ends and

This frill can be made in either a matching or a contrast fabric.

another 3cm/1¼in for each join necessary to make up the length. Decide on the finished width of the frill, double this measurement and add 3cm/1¼in seam allowance. Join the fabric strips to make up the total length, with 1.5cm/⅝in seams. Join the two short ends.
Fold the frill fabric in half lengthways, wrong sides facing and press. Work two rows of gathering stitches through the layers, 1.5cm/⅝in and 1cm/½in from the raw edges. Work the gathering along half the length, then cut the threads. Resume the gathering along the remaining length.
Fold one of the cushion cover circles

in half, and mark the raw edge at each end of the fold with a tailor's chalk line. Open flat again.
With raw edges matching, and frill length to right side of marked cover piece, place each break in the gathering threads on one of the chalk marks. Gently pull up the gathering threads, evenly around the circumference.
Tack frill in place. If you want to insert a side zip, do so at this stage. Right sides facing, lay the remaining circle of fabric on the first, sandwiching the frill. Tack together and then machine with a 1.5cm/⅝in seam, and leave a gap to insert the pad if a zip has not been added. Remove tacking.
Turn through to right side and insert the pad.

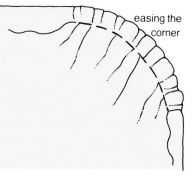
easing the corner

Gathered corners create a plump cushion.

Zigzag points make an unusual edging.

this line every 2cm/¾in and along outer edge of card every 2cm/¾in.
4 Join up the marks with diagonal lines to make a series of points. Cut along the diagonal lines. Lay the template with the straight edge along a section of the stitching and with tailor's chalk mark around the points on to the fabric. Continue in this way all around the cushion cover. At each corner, turn the template at an angle of 45°.
Using a small size, close machine zigzag, stitch along the marked points.
Using small sharp scissors, carefully cut away the fabric close to the zigzag stitching, so that you have a pointed frill. Insert pad.

Gathered corners with piping

This style of cover, suitable for a rectangular or square cushion, has slightly gathered corners.

Cutting out and making up
Cut out two squares or rectangles of fabric to the cushion pad size, with a 1.5cm/⅝in seam allowance all round. Curve each corner by drawing round a saucer or a glass with tailor's chalk. Cut the fabric along the chalked curves.
On both cushion cover pieces work a gathering thread round each corner and gently ease up gathering threads so that each corner is reduced by 3-4cm/1¼-1½in.

Cover the piping cord and stitch to the right side of one cushion cover piece (see Professional Touch on page 87) following the curves on the corners.
If you want to add a side zip, do so at this stage.
Lay both cushion pieces right sides facing and tack together. Sew all round with a zipper foot as close to the ridge of the piping as possible leaving a gap to insert the cushion pad if you have not added a zip.
Turn through to right side and insert pad.

Overlap frill with trimmed edge

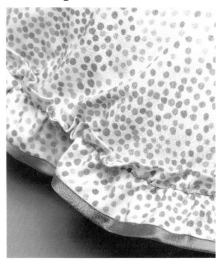

This frill looks best on a round cushion but can be used on a square too.

This is a double fabric frill with the folded edge gathered on to the top edge of the cushion cover. The two raw edges are joined together with satin bias binding.

Cutting out and making up
Cut out two circles of fabric to the pad size with a 1.5cm/⅝in seam

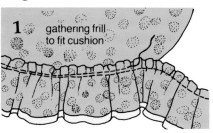
1 *gathering frill to fit cushion*

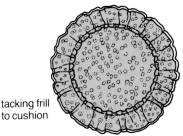
2
tacking frill to cushion

allowance all round.
If you want to insert a back zip, do so at this stage.
Calculate the length and width of frill needed as for the double gathered frill, but do not add a seam allowance to the finished width, as the raw edges are bias bound.
Cut the frill in fabric, join and press in half as for the double gathered frill. Tack the two raw edges together and neaten the raw edges by enclosing them in bias binding (see page 163).
Work gathering stitches in two halves along the folded edge as for the double gathered frill.
1 Gather up the frill to fit the circumference of the cushion, placing folded edge of gathered frill 4cm/1½in in from the raw

edge of the right side of fabric circle, so that the frill overlaps the circle by 4cm/1½in all round. Tack in place.
2 Top stitch frill to the circle of fabric, 2cm/¾in from the folded edge. Remove tacking and gathering threads.
Fold the frill to the centre of the fabric circle.
Insert a zip at this stage, if you are adding a side zip.
Place the remaining circle on first circle, right sides facing, and tack together all round through both layers of fabric – make sure the frill does not get caught in the stitching. Sew with a 1.5cm/⅝in seam and leave a gap to insert the cushion pad if a zip has not been added. Turn through to right side and insert pad.

Gusseted cushions for a perfect fit

Make feather filled cushions luxuriously deep and foam filled cushions neatly tailored, by adding a third dimension – a side gusset – to the cover. Even the plainest of kitchen chairs can be transformed with a bright, comfortable cushion.

Adding a gusset to a cushion cover allows for a deeper, more tailored shape. The gusset, or welt, as it is sometimes known, is a strip of fabric forming the sides between the top and bottom pieces of the cover. The three-dimensional shape produced can be emphasized by piped seams or a decorative or contrasting gusset.

A zip inserted in one side makes it easier to remove the cover for cleaning. If you do not want a zipped opening (or for an inner cover), omit the instructions for a zip. Leave one side unstitched, except for 5cm/2in at the corners, then slipstitch together after inserting cushion pad or stuffing. For soft fillings such as feather, down or foam chips, simply add the zip to one side of the cover and squash the cushion through the opening. For solid fillings such as foam pads, you may have to extend the zip around the adjoining sides – in which case, take this into account when measuring up for the cushion cover fabric.

Before you begin making up these cushions, read the previous chapter for basic instructions.

Right: This antique wooden bench is made more comfortable with a firm, gusseted seat cushion in an attractive print. The round, feather-filled cushions are made in plain, toning fabrics.

Making square and rectangular cushions

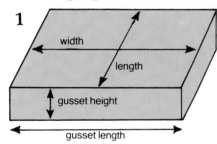

1 For the top and bottom piece of the cushion cover measure the surface of the pad in both directions and add an extra 1.5cm/⅝in seam allowance all round.

For gusset pieces, measure the width and height of each side of the pad and add 1.5cm/⅝in seam allowance all round. The back gusset piece will be cut in half along its length for the zip to be inserted, so add an extra 3cm/1¼in to the height of this piece. For each cushion cover, cut out from fabric one top piece, one bottom piece and the four gusset pieces – one back, one front and two sides.

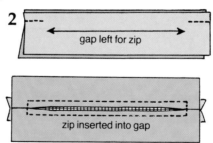

gap left for zip

zip inserted into gap

2 Cut the back gusset piece in half along its length and place the two halves right sides together. Rejoin the cut edge by tacking for approximately 5cm/2in from each corner along the seamline, leaving a central opening to fit the zip. Stitch, press the seam flat and insert the zip.

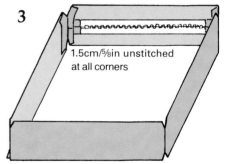

1.5cm/⅝in unstitched at all corners

3 With right sides facing, and taking a 1.5cm/⅝in seam allowance, join the four gusset pieces together to form a square or rectangle. Leave 1.5cm/⅝in at each end of seams unstitched but secure ends of stitching firmly. Press seams open.

4 Matching seams to corners and with right sides facing, pin and tack gusset to one main piece. Machine in place with a 1.5cm/⅝in seam. To ensure a neat square finish at the corners, insert the machine needle right into the fabric at the corner, lift the presser foot, then turn the fabric to correct position for the next row of machining, pivoting it around

Making round cushions

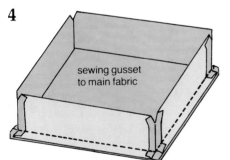

4

sewing gusset to main fabric

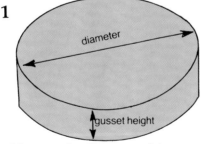

1

diameter

gusset height

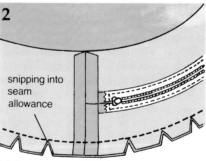

2

snipping into seam allowance

the needle. Replace presser foot and continue stitching.
Snip diagonally across seam allowance at corners, close to stitching, to eliminate bulk. Open the zip, then attach remaining main piece in the same way. Press all seams towards gusset. Turn cover through to right side and insert cushion pad.

1 Measure the diameter of the cushion pad and add 3cm/1¼in to give the diameter of the circles to cut for the top and bottom of the cushion cover.
Measure the circumference and the height of the pad. Cut one gusset piece as a rectangle measuring half the circumference plus 3cm/1¼in by the height plus 3cm/1¼in.
Cut a second rectangle for the zipped half of the gusset but adding a further 3cm/1¼in to the height. Cut this piece in half along its length, place the two halves right sides together, rejoin at each end and insert zip as for square cushion.

Make up gusset as for square one, but forming a circle.
2 With the zip open and right sides together, attach top and bottom circles to the gusset, snipping into the seam allowance all the way round to ease the fabric and give a neat appearance to the seam on the right side. Press all seams towards gusset. Turn cover through to right side and insert pad.
A bolster cushion is simply a variation of a round gusseted cushion, with the gusset height extended to the required length of bolster. Cut the gusset in one piece and insert the zip in the seam.

91

Making shaped cushions

Many chairs have arms or staves that jut out into the seat, so the cushions must fit an irregular shape. If you already have cushion pads to fit the chair, cut the pattern pieces to fit these – adding 1.5cm/⅝in seam allowance all round. If not, make a paper pattern of the seat shape.

1 Measure the width and depth of the chair seat and cut a piece of paper a little larger. Lay the paper on the seat and fold in the edges to the exact outline of the seat. Cut out this shape and check its accuracy by laying it on the seat once more; adjust if necessary. If a back cushion is needed for a sofa or armchair make a paper pattern in the same way, remembering that it will sit on top of the seat cushion, so measure up from the height of this. You can now use these patterns to have pieces of foam cut for the pads. Depending on the amount of padding required, the usual depth for seat pads is 5-10cm/2-4in. Alternatively, you could use your pattern to make up an inner cover in ticking or down-proof cambric, omitting the zip. Stuff with feathers, feather and down or foam chips and sew up opening. Feather cushions look soft and luxurious

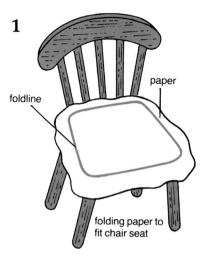

foldline
paper
folding paper to fit chair seat

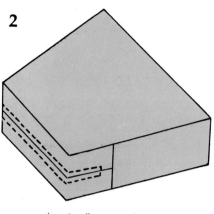

zip extending around corners

but a foam pad retains its shape better and looks neater.

2 After measuring up the shaped pad, calculate the length and position of the zip. On a wedge-shaped cushion, the zip can be inserted into the gusset but it should extend at least 5cm/2in around each adjoining side, so the back gusset piece must be lengthened and the sides correspondingly shortened.

3 For cushions with curved sections cut out to accommodate the arms of the chair, insert the zip into the widest part of the bottom piece of the cushion cover, where it will not show. Cut across your paper pattern where the zip is to go and add 1.5cm/⅝in seam allowance to each edge, before cutting from fabric. The gusset will then consist of side pieces simply joined at the corners, or wherever is most inconspicuous, depending on the irregularity of the shape.

Cut out and make up as for square cushions, placing zip in gusset or main bottom piece as necessary.

Attaching the cushion to the chair

Although the cushions simply lie in place on sofas and easy chairs, when used on wooden upright chairs, stools and rocking chairs they need to be firmly attached. Ties are the simplest solution. They can be made from coloured ribbons or cord, purchased bias binding or tape, or bias strips cut from spare fabric. (Fold raw edges of bias strip to centre, fold strip in half lengthways to enclose them, tuck in short raw ends and slipstitch together). For each tie you need about a 30cm/12in length.

Ties for chairs Place the ties as near to the back corner of the cushion pad as possible, matching up their position to the struts of the chair. Securely stitch centre of tie to cover, then simply tie round chair strut.

Ties for stools Add a tie to each lower corner of the cushion and tie behind stool legs or, for a decorative finish, cross ties behind the legs and tie a bow in front.

Velcro fastenings Use Velcro as an

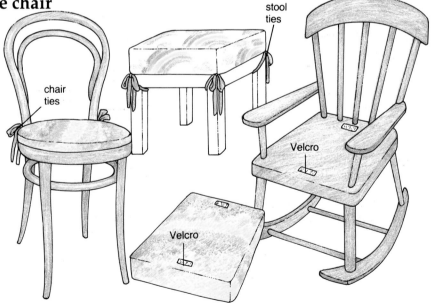

chair ties
stool ties
Velcro
Velcro

alternative to a tie for an invisible fixing – two 5cm/2in lengths are sufficient for one cushion. Stitch one half of each Velcro piece to centre front and centre back of the cushion's underside about 3cm/1¼in

in from the edge. Using a clear household adhesive, stick the backs of remaining Velcro pieces to chair seat to correspond. Allow glue to dry completely before putting cushion in place.

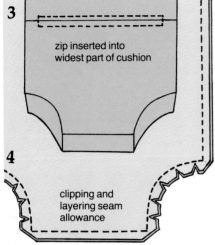

3

zip inserted into widest part of cushion

4

clipping and layering seam allowance

4 To give a perfect finish to the cushion cover, once the stitching is complete, trim away some of the seam allowance to layer the seams and reduce fabric bulk. Snip into the seam allowance on curves, cutting away small V shapes on inner curves, clipping right up to – but not through – stitching line. At the corners, snip off the seam allowance diagonally.

Press all seams towards the gusset. Turn through to right side – all the seams should now lie perfectly flat.

Right: Soften the seat of a rocking chair with a pretty piped cushion.

Finishing touches

To make cushions really special – and individual – add one of the following finishes:

Piped edges These give an elegant tailored finish. Use them to pick out one of the colours on a patterned fabric, or pipe in a toning or contrasting colour to add emphasis to a plain cover. Make up the piping and tack it in position round the edges of both main pieces. Make up covers, sewing the gussets in place using a zipper or piping foot and stitching as close to the piping as possible.

Mix and match fabrics Many fabric ranges now include co-ordinated patterned or plain fabrics, matching borders and positive/negative designs. Use an alternative to the main fabric for the gusset, and perhaps also use the alternative fabric for scatter cushions.

Pleated gussets Join gusset strips to make three times the required length plus seam allowances. Pleat up, tack and then stitch along just inside seamline to hold pleats firmly in position before inserting gusset.

piped gusset

pleated gusset

contrasting gusset

Unusual scatter cushions

These beautifully-styled cushions look so pretty that they would be ideal as an unusual gift, and are surprisingly cheap to make. Learn how to make a shaped cushion pad and start experimenting with these cushion variations to create your own individual look.

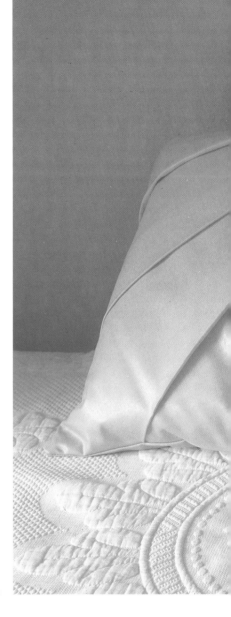

Delightfully pretty and very unusual, these three small scatter cushions will add a decorative touch to any room.

The cushions take surprisingly little material and so can be quite cheap to make – you could, of course, use up suitable remnants.

Because of the unusual shapes though, you'll need to make separate cushion pads from a strong fabric such as curtain lining (now available in many different colours) filled with washable polyester wadding. A fold-over opening in the back of each cushion cover makes it easy to remove the pads for laundering.

The small frilled cushion is decorated with simple machine embroidery. If your machine does not have an embroidery feature, work a few rows of simple hand embroidery or add extra strands of ribbon.

Careful pleating of the fabric produces the dramatic effect of the larger square cushion. The rose in the corner is the only trimming needed.

Little ribbon bows accentuate the shape of the triangular cushion.

Apart from a small central triangle, the front of this cover is made entirely from strips of fabric, folded and stitched to each other in sequence.

You will need
For each cushion:
60cm/24in fabric 120cm/48in wide
Matching thread
Trimmings as follows:
Square cushion
1.60m/1¾yd broderie anglaise
  edging about 5cm/2in wide
75cm/30in satin ribbon 6mm/¼in
  wide
45cm/18in very narrow satin ribbon
Contrasting sewing thread
Triangular cushion
2.40m/2⅝yd broderie anglaise
  edging about 5cm/2in wide
1m/1yd satin ribbon 6mm/¼in wide
Pleated cushion
Small scraps of pink and green
  fabric, wadding and interfacing
To make pads for all three cushions:
60cm/24in curtain lining 120cm/48in
  wide
Matching thread
500gm bag polyester filling

Square embroidered cushion

Make a paper pattern for cushion front from graph on page 96.

Cutting out
From main fabric, cut one front, two back pieces each 22cm×15.5cm/ 9in×6in, and two strips each 20cm×79cm/8in×31in for the frill. Cut two 22cm/9in lengths of very narrow ribbon, and three 25cm/10in lengths of 6mm/¼in ribbon. From curtain lining, cut two 22cm/9in squares for cushion pad.

Making up
Take 1cm/½in seam allowances throughout.
Preparing cushion front Using pattern markings as a guide, pin

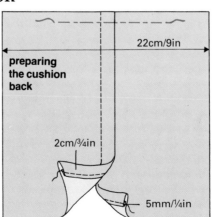

preparing the cushion back

22cm/9in

2cm/¾in

5mm/¼in

ribbons in position on the right side of the cushion front, make a twist in each of the wider ribbons, and tack all in place. Using contrasting

thread, work rows of machine embroidery (or simple hand embroidery if you prefer) parallel to the ribbons. Work further rows in the opposite direction, catching down ribbons, and then remove tacking. Press carefully on the wrong side but do not press over ribbon twists.
Preparing cushion back Press a 5mm/¼in turning to the wrong side down one long edge on both back pieces and stitch close to the folded edge on one piece only. Press a further 2cm/¾in turning to the wrong side on both pieces and, on the unstitched piece only, stitch close to the first folded edge. Overlap the pieces to form a 22cm/

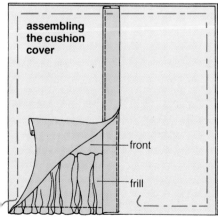

assembling the cushion cover

— front

— frill

9in square, as shown, and tack.

Assembling cushion cover

With 1cm/½in flat seams, join the short edges of frill pieces to form a circle, press seams open and press frill in half, lengthwise, wrong sides together. Join short ends of broderie anglaise edging to form a circle the same size as frill, and tack the two together with raw edges aligned. Run two rows of gathering stitches through all layers close to raw edges and pull up to fit around edge of cushion front. With raw edges together and broderie anglaise side of frill facing right side of cushion front, tack securely together. With right sides facing, tack cushion back to cushion front and stitch all round, sandwiching frill. Clip away excess seam allowances at corners to reduce bulk, zigzag

Above: A colour theme of pink and white links the different styles of cushion.

stitch raw edges together to neaten, then turn right side out through back opening.

Making cushion pad

Place the two pieces right sides facing and stitch all round 1cm/½in in from edge, leaving a 15cm/6in gap along one side. Clip corners, turn right side out and press well. Stuff firmly with polyester filling and close opening by slipstitching edges together.
Slip cushion pad inside cover through back opening to complete cushion.

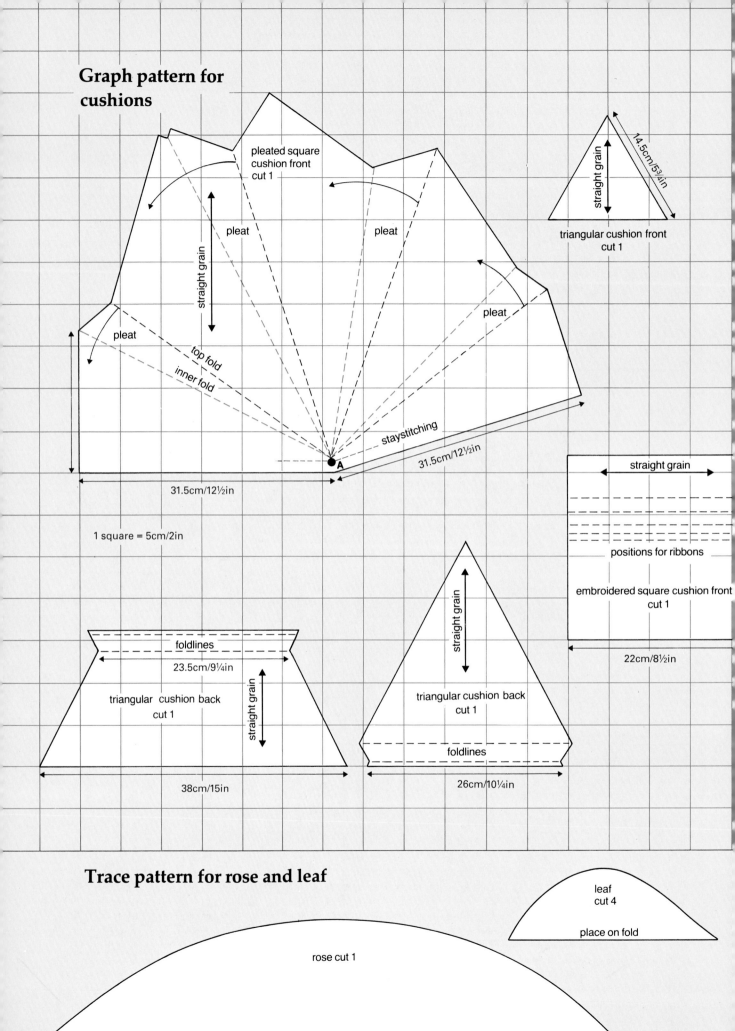

Graph pattern for cushions

pleated square cushion front
cut 1

pleat

pleat

straight grain

pleat

pleat

top fold

inner fold

staystitching

31.5cm/12½in

31.5cm/12½in

A

31.5cm/12½in

1 square = 5cm/2in

14.5cm/5¾in

straight grain

triangular cushion front
cut 1

straight grain

positions for ribbons

embroidered square cushion front
cut 1

22cm/8½in

foldlines

23.5cm/9¼in

triangular cushion back
cut 1

straight grain

38cm/15in

straight grain

triangular cushion back
cut 1

foldlines

26cm/10¼in

Trace pattern for rose and leaf

leaf
cut 4

place on fold

rose cut 1

place on fold

place on fold

Triangular cushion

Make paper patterns for front and both back pieces following the graph.

Cutting out

Using the pattern pieces, cut one front and one of each back piece from main fabric. Cut the remaining fabric into 6cm/2⅜in strips across the width.

For cushion pad pattern, fold in the marked turnings on the paper pattern pieces for back sections, overlap the folded edges, holding them in place with sticky tape, to form a complete triangle and use this as a pattern to cut two triangles from curtain lining.

Making up

Take 5mm/¼in seams unless otherwise stated.

Preparing cushion front With wrong sides facing, fold strips in half lengthwise and press.

1 Place the first strip along one edge on right side of front (small) triangle, raw edges together. Unfold the strip and stitch underneath layer only to edge of triangle. Refold, trim ends level with triangle sides and repeat with second and third strips on other edges of triangle, each time stitching only the underneath layer of working strip to both layers of

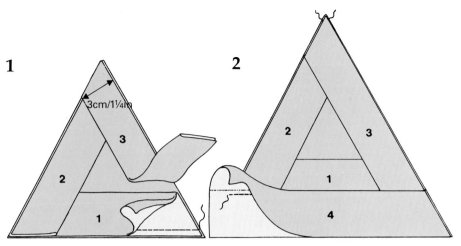

previous strips. Work in a clockwise direction, cutting strips to the correct length as you go.

2 Allowing enough length at each end to extend triangle sides, place folded edge of fourth strip over raw edge of first strip, overlapping it by 1cm/½in. Unfold strip and stitch underneath layer only to previous strip, 5mm/¼in from fold. Refold and trim ends of strip at an angle, so extending sides of triangle. Continue working clockwise round the triangle attaching strips in the same way until there are five strips attached to each edge.

Preparing cushion back On triangular back piece, press a 5mm/¼in turning to wrong side along lower edge and stitch. Press in a further 2cm/¾in turning. On remaining back piece, following pattern markings, press 5mm/¼in

and then 2cm/¾in to wrong side and then stitch. Lap this edge over hemmed edge of triangular back piece and tack together to form a triangle the same size as cushion front.

Assembling cushion cover Join short ends of broderie anglaise edging to form a circle and run two rows of gathering stitches close to raw edge. Gathering up to fit, tack broderie anglaise to right side of cushion front, raw edges together. Place front and back pieces together, right sides facing, and, sandwiching frill, stitch all round edge 1cm/½in in. Clip across corners, turn right side out and press well.

Make three small bows from ribbon and stitch one to each corner.

Make cushion pad as for square cushion to complete.

Pleated square cushion

Make a pattern for the front and, unless adding a ready-made flower, for the leaf and rose.

Cutting out

Cut one front (using pattern from graph) and two back pieces each 33cm×21cm/13in×8¼in from main fabric. Transfer pattern markings onto front piece. Cut one rose piece from pink and four leaf shapes from green fabric.

Cut two 33cm/13in squares of curtain lining for cushion pad.

Making up

Take 1.5cm/⅝in seam allowances except where otherwise stated.

Preparing cushion front Place a 5cm/2in square of interfacing on wrong side of front piece over point A. Staystitch around point A as indicated on pattern, 1.5cm/⅝in

from edge, and clip across seam allowance up to A.

Following the pattern markings, fold pleat lines together to form four tapering pleats, all lying in the same direction; press well and tack.

Prepare cushion back as for embroidered square cushion, but making a 33cm/13in square.

Assembling cushion Place back and front pieces right sides facing and stitch all round edge. Turn right side out and press.

To make flower decoration Back two leaves with interfacing and pair each one with an unbacked leaf, *wrong* sides facing. Zigzag stitch around the edge and through the centre of each leaf.

Fold the rose piece in half lengthwise, wrong sides facing, and sandwich a small piece of wadding in the middle, trimming it to shape.

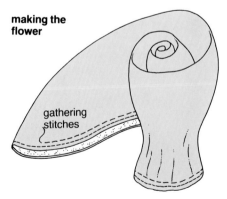

making the flower

gathering stitches

Stitch 5mm/¼in from the edge through all layers.

Work small hand gathering stitches along raw edge. Coil strip into a flower shape and stitch to secure. Pull up gathers tightly to complete. Stitch leaves and rose to the pleated corner of cushion.

Make cushion pad as for other square cushion to complete.

Soft seating: sag bags and floor cushions

*If you're short of space – or of money – for extra seating,
then floor cushions or sag bags provide
the answer. They make comfortable, inexpensive seating units
that can easily be tucked out of the way,
and firm foam cushions will even double as a mattress.*

Use floor cushions or sag bags to replace traditional settees and armchairs for a relaxed informal look that is inexpensive to create and easily varied. They are also ideal as extra seating that can be brought out for visitors then pushed into the background, or into a cupboard, when not required.

Choose a firm furnishing fabric or a tough fabric such as corduroy for the covers. A reasonably dark shade is more practical but all the covers are zipped and easily removed for cleaning.

Sag bags have always been popular with children and teenagers but they are surprisingly comfortable for adults too. Sink into a sag bag and the polystyrene bead filling moulds itself to support your favourite sitting position. This sag bag has a handy

Above: Sag bags are great fun and surprisingly comfortable. For maximum safety, use a fire-retardant polystyrene granule filling.

strap at the top which makes it easy to move around – try one in the garden on a sunny day.

Fabric-covered foam blocks make particularly versatile floor cushions – stack three together against the wall as a simple chair, tie them in line to form a single mattress, use more for a settee, or simply sit on one!

A foam specialist shop will cut the foam to the exact size you require. It is advisable to make a cotton inner cover to protect the foam and help to prevent the corners and edges crumbling with age. This inner cover does not need a zip as it will not need to be removed for cleaning.

Before making up your floor cushion, read pages 90-91 for detailed instructions for cutting out and making up a gusseted cover.

Making a sag bag

Make the sag bag by sewing together six identical pattern pieces, rather like the segments of an orange, and adding a circular zipped base.

Fill the bag with polystyrene granules or beads to about two-thirds of its capacity – the surplus space means you can push the bag into the most comfortable shape for sitting on.

You will need

3.40m/3¾yd of fabric 120cm/48in wide
46cm/18in zip
Matching thread
2.70kg/6lb bag of polystyrene granules

Preparing the pattern pieces

Enlarge the segment pattern piece given below by drawing a grid on which one square equals 5cm/2in and copying the outline on to it square by square. (A 1.5cm/⅝in seam allowance is included.)
Using this as the paper pattern, cut six segment shapes from your fabric. On the wrong side of each segment, draw a chalk line about 5cm/2in down from the pointed end (see graph below).
Cut two strips of fabric each 35cm × 6cm/14in × 2¾in for the handle.
Cut a circle 64cm/25in in diameter for the base. Fold the circle across the diameter and cut in half.

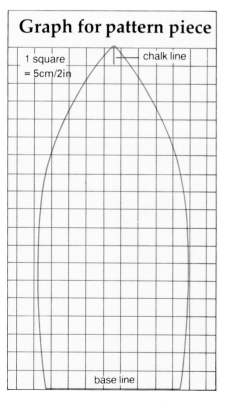

Graph for pattern piece

1 square = 5cm/2in

chalk line

base line

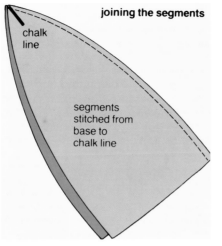

joining the segments

chalk line

segments stitched from base to chalk line

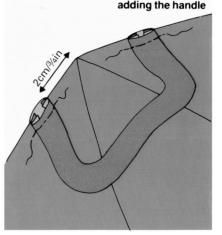

adding the handle

2cm/¾in

Making up

Joining the segments Place two segments right sides together. On one side only, tack and then stitch from the base up to the point where the seamline meets the chalk line. In the same way attach a third segment to the free side of one of the first two, stitching as far as the chalk line.
Repeat this procedure to join the remaining three segments together as a separate half.

Adding the handle Make up the handle by placing the two strips right sides together and sewing down both long edges. Turn right side out, press and tack the ends to the outside edges of one set of three segments 2cm/1in below the top point, raw edges together.
Place the two sets of three segments together, right sides facing, sandwiching the handle ends, and tack and stitch the two remaining outer edges from base to chalk line. Turn right side out and the handle will protrude from the seams. Reinforce the point at which the segments meet with a little hand stitching – this gives added strength to the area most under stress.
Press the seams open, then run a double row of gathering stitches around the base, just within the seam allowance.

Making the base Place the two halves of the circle right sides together and stitch along the straight edge for 9cm/3½in from each end. Press the seam allowances open and insert the zip in the central gap.
With the zip open, and right sides facing, pin the base of three segments around half of the circle,

pulling up the gathers to ease the fitting. Pin the other three segments to the remaining half of the circle; gather, tack and stitch all round. Turn right side out through the open zip.

Filling the sag bag

Fill about two-thirds of the bag with polystyrene granules.
As a precaution against the bag being opened accidentally or by an inquisitive child, hand stitch the pulling tab of the zip to the base of the bag.
Save any left-over granules as they do tend to crush down a bit with time and wear, and the sag bag may need topping up.

Laundering the cover

To empty the bag for laundering, shake the granules to the bottom of the sag bag, hold over a large open plastic sack and open the zip.
Gently shake the granules from the sag bag into the plastic sack – it is easier if you have a helper so that one person can hold the plastic sack while the other tips up.
Turn the sag bag cover inside out, pick out any remaining granules caught in the seams or stuck to the inside of the fabric and wash or dry clean according to the type of fabric.
If your sag bag is likely to be washed frequently, it is worth making an inner cover which can be removed complete with the polystyrene granules while the outer cover is being laundered. Make the inner cover from an inexpensive fabric such as calico, following the sag bag pattern but omitting the handle and zip.

Making foam block cushions

Cover a block of foam with a simple gusseted cover and you have a comfortable floor cushion. Make more than one cushion, inserting ties into the seams, and the potential variations of seating are endless.

The instructions are for a versatile 75cm/30in square cushion, 18cm/7in deep, but alter the measurements to suit your needs, remembering to adjust the fabric requirements accordingly.

You will need

75cm/30in square block of dense, seating quality foam approximately 18cm/7in deep
2.5m/2¾yd of fabric at least 80cm/32in wide for the top cover
The same amount of a firm plain fabric such as pre-shrunk calico for the inner cover, if required
70cm/28in zip
Thread
Strong cotton tape about 15mm/⅝in wide to make the ties

Cutting out

For the top cover cut two pieces of fabric 78cm/31¼in square, three gusset strips each 78cm/31¼in wide and 21cm/8¼in deep, and one strip for the back gusset piece the same width but 24cm/9½in deep.
Cut the inner cover pieces to the same dimensions but make all four gusset strips 21cm/8¼in deep. These dimensions include 1.5cm/⅝in seam allowances.

Making up

Make up the inner cover in the same way as a gusseted cushion cover, insert the foam block and hand stitch the opening together. Make the top cover in the same way as a gusseted cushion cover but cutting the back gusset piece in half, widthways, and inserting the zip between.

Adding ties If you wish to link cushions together, insert ties in the seams while making up.

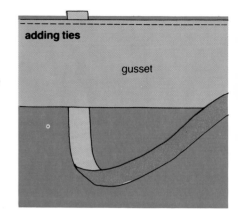

Cut a 30cm/12in length of cotton tape for each tie required. (If you cannot buy the colour of tape to match or contrast with your cushion, dye white tape with a commercial fabric dye.) Eight lengths of tape – two on two opposite sides on both top and bottom – give complete versatility.

Below: Vary the shape and size of cushion to suit your needs – a half-size cushion makes a good back-rest.

Soft floor cushions

These giant floor cushions are quick and easy to make using ready-made cushion pads filled with foam chips or feathers. Simply measure the pad and make up a basic cover as described on pages 82-84, inserting a zip in the side seam for easy removal for cleaning. A combination of large and small floor cushions can make versatile, cheap seating. Use them to replace conventional chairs – an arrangement of low level tables and cushions as shown here gives a feeling of space to a small area and is inexpensive to create. Choose one dominant colour or a combination of toning colours for the best effect. These cushions are made up in a series of black and white checked fabrics, the checks decreasing with the size of the cushions, to give a co-ordinated yet varied look. Alternatively, one or two large

Above: Floor cushions replace the conventional three-piece suite to provide interesting and versatile seating at a fraction of the cost.

cushions are a useful addition to sofa and chairs and a pile of bright covers can add a splash of colour to a dull corner. Bear in mind when choosing fabrics that floor cushions will get a greater amount of wear than a sofa cushion so use a tough furnishing fabric.

PART 4

Bedlinen

A co-ordinated look is easy to achieve in a bedroom. Choose a plain, frilled or pleated look and make up the valance, sheets or duvet cover and pillowcases to match. Add a throwover bedcover or quilted bedspread and a padded cover for the headboard as a final touch.

The sewing techniques are quite simple and are fully explained with step-by-step diagrams and the illustrations give an idea of the wide range of fabrics which are available to suit all styles.

There are also several ideas for the nursery or child's room. You can save money and create a bright cheerful room with cot bedding and bumpers for a baby or a fun sleeping bag for an older child. Transform a bunk bed into a shop, bus or castle or simply add some handy pocketed hangings for toys and books.

Suitable fabrics for bedlinen

Bear in mind that covers which are taken off the bed at night and folded up need to be made from a crease-resistant fabric and that any trimmings added to sheets and pillowcases need to be machine washable.

Polyester cotton sheeting is made in several suitable widths and is widely available with a choice of patterns and colours. It is hardwearing, crease-resistant, machine washable and requires the minimum of ironing. Reversible cotton polyester quilting is ideal for throwover bed covers and ready-quilted fabrics can also be used to cover a headboard. Cot bumpers and sleeping bags need several layers of polyester wadding, hand quilted together.

Bedlinen: flat and fitted sheets

With such a good choice of sheeting fabric now available it is a simple and rewarding task to make bedlinen sets to complement your bedroom decoration scheme. Here are instructions for making flat and fitted sheets, and ideas for pretty trims.

You can save quite a lot of money by making your own bedsheets – you only need to stitch hems on flat sheets or casings on fitted sheets. There are four standard sizes of bed:

Single beds are 90cm wide×190cm
36in wide×75in
and 100cm wide×200cm
40in wide×80in
Double beds are 135cm wide×190cm
54in wide×75in
and 150cm wide×200cm
60in wide×80in

There is also an extra large double-size (king size), not so widely used,
183cm wide×200cm
72in wide×80in

Mattresses are about 18cm/7in deep (though some are slightly deeper). To fit these bed sizes, purchased flat sheets are about 180cm/71in wide×260cm/160in for single, 230cm/90in wide×260cm/106in for double, and 270cm/110in wide×280cm/114in for king size beds.

These sizes allow for approximately 12cm/4¾in tuck-in top and bottom and 20cm/7¾in at the sides.

Fitted sheets are made to fit tightly over the mattress with a turned-under section of about 15cm/6in all round held in place by elasticated corners. Sheeting fabric, which is purchased by the metre, is sold in 228-230cm/89½-90½in widths.

Fabric joins should be avoided as seams in sheeting are uncomfortable. If the width of the sheeting fabric is just over or just under the size you require, you can leave the selvedges at the sides instead of making side hems. Always check when buying fabric to see whether you will need to allow for shrinkage.

Right: Flat sheets are very simple to sew and the top turn-back can be trimmed with a decorative edging for emphasis.

These sheeting samples show the wide choice of styles available.

Flat sheet

Flat sheets are used as top and bottom sheets with blankets, or as a bottom sheet with a duvet. By making your own to measure, you can ensure a good fit.

You will need
Sheeting fabric
Matching sewing thread

Cutting out
Measure the length, width and depth of the mattress.
To the length measurement add twice the mattress depth plus twice the 12cm/4¾in tuck-in allowance plus 10cm/4in for hems. You can increase the tuck-in allowance by up to 30cm/11¾in each end if you wish.
To the width measurement add twice the mattress depth and twice the tuck-in allowance (this can be from 12cm/4¾in to 25cm/9¾in, depending on the width of fabric) and add a further 3cm/1¼in for hems. Cut one piece of fabric to these measurements.

Making up
Make a double hem down each side by folding 5mm/¼in and then 1cm/½in to wrong side of the fabric. Tack and stitch hems in place. (If you are leaving the selvedges, simply omit this stage.)
For the bottom hem, fold 1cm/½in and then 3cm/1¼in to wrong side to make a double hem. Tack and stitch. For the top hem, fold 1cm/½in and then 5cm/2in to wrong side to make a double hem. Tack and stitch. Remove all tacking.

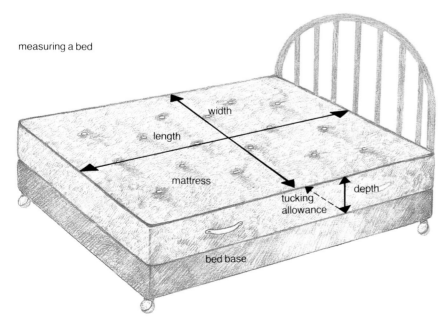

measuring a bed

bed base

width

length

mattress

tucking
allowance

depth

Measuring example

Double bed

135cm wide × 200cm/80in
54in wide × 80in

Mattress length	200cm/80in
Mattress depth × 2	36cm/14in
Tuck-in × 2	24cm/9½in
Hem allowance	10cm/4in
Total length	270cm/106½in

Mattress width	135cm/54in
Mattress depth × 2	36cm/14in
Tuck-in × 2	50cm/19¾in (or less)
Hem allowance	3cm/1¼in
Total width	224cm/88½in

Note: hem allowance need not be added to the width measurement if selvedges are left on fabric.

Fitted sheet

A fitted sheet is a bottom sheet which has elasticated corners to hold it securely in position on the mattress. It can be used either with a flat top sheet and blankets or with a duvet cover to keep the bed looking neat and tidy even when the duvet or blankets are drawn back.

You will need
Sheeting fabric
1m/1yd of 1cm/½in wide elastic
Matching sewing thread

Cutting out
Measure the length and width of the mattress and add 72cm/28¼in to each dimension.
Cut one piece of fabric to these measurements.

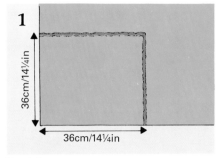

Making up
At each corner, measure 36cm/14¼in from the corner point and mark with tailor's chalk. Measure in from each mark and at right angles draw chalk lines until they meet, forming a 36cm/14¼in square.

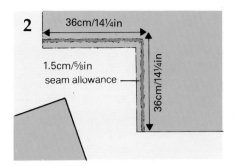

2 Leaving a 1.5cm/⅝in seam allowance outside the marked lines, cut out the resulting square.
3 Making up each corner in the same way, place the two cut edges with the wrong sides together. Tack and stitch 5mm/¼in from edge. Remove tacking. Turn so right sides face and stitch 1cm/½in from edge.

Converting a flat sheet to a fitted sheet

If you have made the change from blankets to a duvet, you may find a fitted bottom sheet more convenient to use than a flat sheet. It will give the bed a neat and tidy look even when the duvet is thrown back. If your existing flat sheet is still in good condition, this can easily be converted into a fitted sheet to save the expense of buying new.

You will need
Flat sheet to fit your bed
1m/1yd of 1cm/½in wide elastic
Matching sewing threads

Cutting out
Measure your mattress and calculate the length/width of fabric needed as for a fitted sheet.
Either cut off or unpick and press out the hems on your flat sheet depending on the dimension of fabric you need.

Making up
Follow the instructions for making up a fitted sheet.

Right: A fitted bottom sheet hugs the mattress neatly by elasticated corners.

PROFESSIONAL TOUCH

To apply corded trim to sheet edge

To imitate the smart finish found on expensive purchased sheets, one or two rows of cording can be added to the top of an upper flat sheet, so that the cording shows when the sheet is folded over the blankets.
Use pearl cotton (a thick embroidery thread) as the cord and the cording foot on your sewing machine or achieve a similar effect by using a twin needle – if your sewing machine will take one.

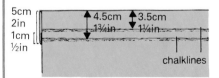

Draw one (or two) tailor's chalk line(s) on right side of top sheet 4.5cm/1¾in (and 3.5cm/1½in) from the folded edge.

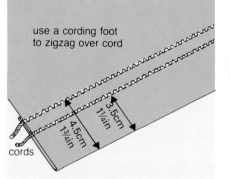

Using the cording foot
attachment on your sewing machine, apply the pearl cotton over the chalk line(s). Choose pearl cotton to match the colour of your sheeting, and stitch with a matching sewing thread. Use either a wide zigzag so that the pearl cotton shows through, or conceal it with a close-up zigzag.

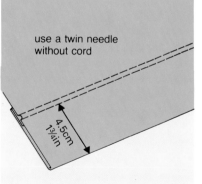

Using a twin needle on your
sewing machine, tighten the tension so that when you sew two rows of stitching you get a raised area between them. (This method needs no cord.)

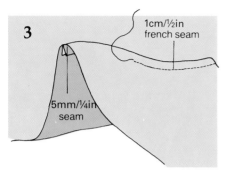

3

1cm/½in french seam

5mm/¼in seam

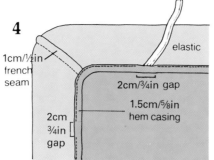

4

1cm/½in french seam

elastic

2cm/¾in gap

2cm ¾in gap

1.5cm/⅝in hem casing

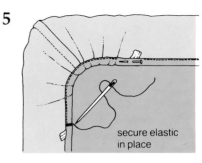

5

secure elastic in place

to form a French seam. Remove tacking.
Turn under a double hem, 1.5cm/⅝in and 1.5cm/⅝in, all round outer edge. Tack, leaving 2cm/¾in gaps 34cm/13½in each side of all four corners. Stitch, close to folded edge – except over 2cm/¾in gaps – to form a hem casing.

4 To gather up each corner in turn, cut a 25cm/10in length of elastic and secure one end on a safety pin. Thread safety pin end of elastic through one of the gaps in the casing and along through the casing until the loose end of the elastic lines up with the gap. Securely pin loose end of elastic in place.

5 Continue pushing elastic along casing until you can draw it out through the second gap (in the process gathering up the fabric on the corner). Remove the safety pin, ease the elastic back into casing and pin, then tack in place. Stitch securely with three rows of stitching. Stitch up casing openings.

Pillowcases to match – plain or fancy

You can give your bedroom scheme a new look simply by changing the pillowcases. Though they are usually made or bought in sets with sheets, you can easily make extra pairs in complementary colours, patterns and styles by following the instructions given here.

Pillowcases can have feminine frills in matching or contrasting fabric, or be left plain for a smart tailored look. Either way they provide an inexpensive way to change the look of your bedding to suit your mood – so why not make several pairs in different styles?

Standard pillows are usually about 74cm × 48cm/29¼in × 19in and pillowcases 75cm × 50cm/29½in × 19¾in. There are variations so measure your pillow in both directions before cutting the fabric. When measuring, remember that the case should fit the pillow loosely and add 3cm/1¼in to each dimension.

There are three basic pillowcase styles: the plain one-piece housewife style, the Oxford (which has a flat border), and the frilled pillowcase. All three have an inner flap to hold the pillow in place and eliminate the need for side fastenings on the case. Sheeting or cotton/man-made fibre mixes are best for pillowcases, but it is not essential to use a wide-width fabric; you can cut out a pillowcase along the fabric length providing that the design/pattern is not one-way only.

Right: A vivid combination of bright, bold colours is eye-catching and practical in a child's bedroom.

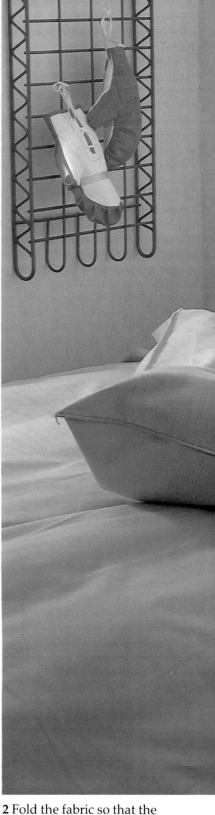

Housewife pillowcase

1

fold

15cm
6in

3.5cm
1⅜in

The plain housewife pillowcase is very easy to make because it can be cut from a single piece of fabric with one end folded in to form the inner flap.

You will need
For each pillowcase:
0.55m/⅝yd of fabric 230cm/90in wide *or* 1.75m/1⅞yd of fabric 90cm/36in *or* 120cm/48in wide (one-way designs in the two narrower widths are not suitable)

Cutting out and making up
From the fabric cut one piece 173cm × 54cm/68in × 21¼in.
1 Turn under a double hem (1.5cm/⅝in and 1.5cm/⅝in) on one short side. Tack and stitch in place.
At the opposite short side, turn under 5mm/¼in, then 3.5cm/1⅜in to make a double hem. Tack and stitch in place.
With wrong sides facing, fold in the short side with narrow hem for 15cm/6in to form the inner flap.

2 Fold the fabric so that the opposite hem meets the fold, enclosing flap.
Tack and stitch both long edges taking 1cm/½in seams. Trim seams to 5mm/¼in. Remove the tacking.
3 Turn through so that right sides face then tack and stitch the long edges again taking 1cm/½in seams (you have now completed French seams). Remove tacking.
Turn pillowcase through to right side. Press.

2

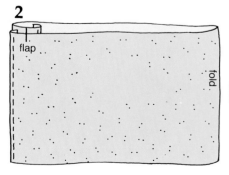

flap

fold

3

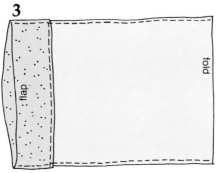

flap

fold

Plain and striped fabrics look effective together.

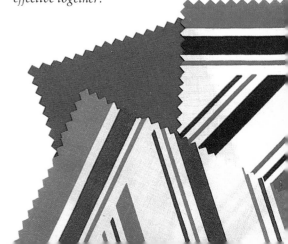

Oxford pillowcase

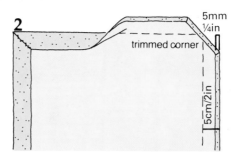

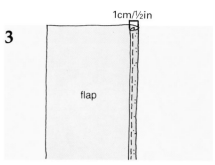

This style has a smart wide border – to give it a decorative, but tailored rather than feminine, finish – and an inner flap to hold the pillow in place.

You will need
For each pillowcase:
0.75m/³⁄₄yd fabric 230cm/90in wide *or*
1.25m/1½yd fabric 120cm/48in wide
or 2.40m/2½yd fabric 90cm/36in wide

Cutting out and making up
From fabric cut the following:
97cm×71cm/38¼in×28in for front
79.5cm×53cm/31¼in×20¾in for back
17cm×53cm/6¾in×20¾in for flap

1 On the back piece, turn under a double hem (1cm/½in and 1cm/½in) along one short edge. Tack and stitch in place.

2 On the front piece, fold 5mm/¼in and then 5cm/2in to the wrong side all round, mitring each corner. Press and slipstitch in place the mitred corners. This mitred hem forms the pillowcase border.
3 On the flap piece, turn under a double hem (1cm/½in and 1cm/½in) along one long edge. Tack and stitch in place.

Frilled pillowcase

This style has a gathered frill all round to give it a soft, feminine look.

You will need
For each pillowcase:
0.90m/1yd fabric 230cm/90in wide *or*
1.70m/1¾yd fabric 120cm/48in wide
or 2.40m/2½yd fabric 90cm/36in wide

Cutting out and making up
From fabric cut the following:
79cm×53cm/31in×20¾in for front
80cm×53cm/31½in×20¾in for back
17cm×53cm/6¾in×20¾in for flap
For frill cut and join (with narrow flat seams), sufficient pieces of fabric 11cm/4¼in wide to make up a 5.30m/5¾yd length

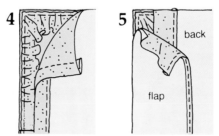

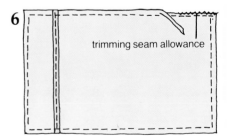

1 Along one long side of flap turn under a double hem (1cm/½in and 1cm/½in). Tack and stitch in place. On one short side of back piece turn under a double hem (5mm/¼in and then 3.5cm/1⅜in). Tack and stitch in place.

2 Stitch together short ends of frill to make a circle, then fold frill in half lengthwise with wrong sides facing. Run two rows of gathering stitches round the frill, 1cm/½in and 1.5cm/⅝in from the raw edges.

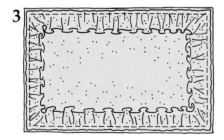

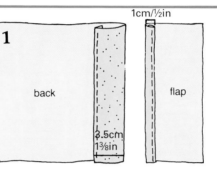

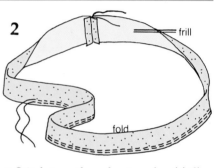

3 Position frill to right side of front, folded edge facing inwards.
Pull up the gathering stitches evenly so that the frill fits the front. Tack frill in place.

4 Place back piece to front piece, right sides facing, sandwiching the frill and matching all edges except the short hemmed edge of the back which must fall 3cm/1¼in short of the length of the front.
5 Place flap with right sides down on to back piece, positioned so that the long raw edge lines up with the protruding front edge.

6 Tack and stitch all round the outer edge of the pillowcase taking 1.5cm/⅝in seams, and being careful not to close up the back hemmed edge in the stitching line.
Trim seam allowance to 1cm/½in and machine zigzag stitch the raw edges together to neaten. Remove tacking. Turn pillowcase to right side, folding flap to inside of front piece. Press.

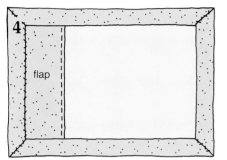
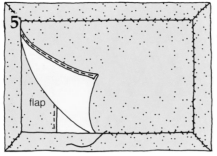
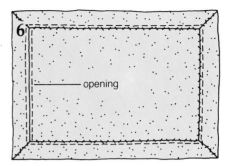

4 With wrong sides facing, place flap to one short side of the front piece, tucking all three raw edges under the mitred hem border by 1cm/½in. Slipstitch mitred hem border to flap along tucked-under long edge.

5 Place back piece to front piece wrong sides facing, with the back piece hem positioned over the flap/mitred hem border join. Tuck the raw edges on the back piece under the mitred hem border by 1cm/½in. Slipstitch mitred hem border in the back piece round three sides, leaving the flap side unstitched.

6 Working from the back side of the pillowcase, machine stitch all round just 3mm/⅛in inside the mitred hem border edge. Be careful not to catch the back piece opening as you stitch.
Remove all tacking. Press.

Above: Frilled pillowcases give a soft and pretty look, while the Oxford-style ones (right) have a chic tailored finish.

Sheets trimmed to perfection

It is the decorative trim applied to flat sheets along the top turn-back, that lifts them out of the ordinary and gives them a designer look. Such sheets are usually expensive, but fortunately it is an easy matter to add a variety of trims yourself.

All of the design ideas suggested here are simple to add to a sheet as you are making it, or they can be applied to a ready-made sheet.

Zigzagged scalloped edge

This pretty scallop shape gives emphasis to the sheet edge, and the machine zigzag stitching around the scallops can be in a contrast colour for extra appeal.

Cut out a paper template for the scallops (see page 178). You will find it easiest to work with a template about 30cm/12in long and use it repeatedly along the edge. Complete the making up of the sheet, but do not sew a hem at the top. On the right side of the sheet, place the template 5mm/¼in from raw top edge.

If you are working on a ready-made sheet, place the template so that it butts up to the finished hem edge. Draw round the scallop outlines with tailor's chalk.

Machine zigzag along the scallop shapes and then, with small sharp scissors, carefully cut away the fabric close to the zigzagging to give the scalloped shape.

Simple border trim

To contrast with or complement a plain coloured sheet, a border of plain or patterned fabric can be sewn along the top edge.

If you are making the sheet, complete the make up with the exception of a top hem.

If you are adding a border to a ready-made sheet, unpick the hem or cut off the corded edge if the length allows this.

Left: A selection of special decorative trims for flat sheets. From top: zigzag scallop edge; a simple border trim and crisp broderie anglaise with a ruffle.

Cut a piece of fabric for the border 23cm/9in by the width of the sheet, plus 3cm/1¼in. Turn 1.5cm/⅝in to the wrong side on each short edge of border piece and tack. Wrong sides facing, fold the border in half along the length and press. Open flat again.

With right sides facing, place one long edge of border to top of sheet and sew with 1.5cm/⅝in seams. Turn border to wrong side of sheet along the foldline and neatly slipstitch along both short ends and the long edge. Press.

Broderie anglais with a ruffle

A ruffle and broderie anglaise trim with two neatened edges, adds a romantic and delicate look.

Whether you are making the sheet or adding a ruffle to a ready-made one, use a minimum-iron fabric for the ruffle. Otherwise, this type of trim can be time-consuming to iron after each laundering.

Complete the make up of the sheet but turn only a single 1cm/½in hem to the right side along the top edge. Cut a piece of fabric for the ruffle 23cm/9in × 1½ times the width of the sheet adding 3cm/1¼in for seams. Turn 1.5cm/⅝in to the wrong side on each short end of ruffle fabric. Wrong sides facing, fold in half along the length and press. Machine stitch across both short ends.

Run two lines of gathering stitches along the length of the ruffle, then gently and evenly pull up the gathering threads until the ruffle fits the width of the sheet.

If you have made the sheet, place the raw edges of the ruffle to the right side of the sheet, 1.5cm/⅝in from the top edge to cover the hem.

If you are adding the ruffle to a ready-made sheet, place the ruffle to the right side of the sheet overlapping the top edge by at least 1.5cm/⅝in. Tack ruffle in place, then lay a length of broderie anglaise trim over the ruffle raw edges and sew in place.

Six pillowcase trimmings

Add a personal touch to pillowcases with simple but effective decorative features. Here are six ideas designed to start you off on the creative track. You will find it easier to stitch embroidery, attach braid or work appliqué before you make up the pillowcases.

You can, however, use all but the piping idea on bought pillowcases, if you take care to stitch through only the front piece of the pillowcase.

Satin stitch embroidery

Initials, bows – or both – are simple shapes to embroider.

First mark the outline with tailor's chalk, then satin stitch by hand or by machine along the outline. Embroidery looks effective on all styles of pillowcase.

Ric rac for emphasis

The bright colours of ric rac braid make a bold colour emphasis as a pillowcase trim, and this is especially jolly for a child's bedroom.

Tack the braid in place, then stitch along the centre. Remove tacking. This type of trim can be added to all styles of pillowcase.

Piping adds style

Piping is a sure way to give a pillowcase style, but it is not suitable for the Oxford pillowcase. You can add piping most successfully to a frilled pillowcase, between the case and frill, or to the

seams on a housewife style (except at the opening). For either style, insert piping between the seams (see page 87) during the making up of the pillowcase.

Points for visual interest

For an unusual pillowcase trim on a frilled or Oxford style, cut the edge into points using a template as your guide (see page 88). Machine zigzag the raw edges with a close stitch and, for a strong visual impact, do this in a contrast colour.

Appliqué accents

Simple motifs cut from fabric can be appliquéd in place down one side, or all round a pillowcase – and this decorative feature can be used on all styles of pillowcase.

Cut out the motifs and tack securely in position. Sew all round with a close machine zigzag stitch.

Lacy looks

Lace is guaranteed to enhance even the most simple of patterns, or to soften the effect of a plain colour. If you are making the pillowcase in the frilled style, you could make the frill from lace as a pretty alternative to fabric.

On a purchased housewife style pillowcase, you can neatly slipstitch a length of lace all round the outer edge. A lace frill is not suitable for an Oxford style pillowcase.

Right and below: Pillowcases acquire a touch of class with a special trimming.

Duvet covers: frilled or reversible

Duvet covers are quick and easy to make using the extra wide sheeting now available. There is a wide range of this easy-care fabric. Choose bold bright colours to make a focal point, a different pattern on each side for versatility or add a frill for a pretty finish.

It is easy to see why more people are changing to duvets – they are light and warm and bed making becomes just a matter of straightening the bottom sheet and shaking the duvet. Duvet covers are best made up in an easy-care cotton and polyester sheeting which, apart from being washable, needs minimal ironing. It can be bought in wide widths so the front and back can each be cut out in one piece, without having to join fabric. Nowadays poly/cotton sheeting is available in a wide variety of plain colours, geometric patterns and floral designs, so there is something to suit any bedroom. It is just as simple to make up the basic cover in two complementary fabrics so that turning the duvet over gives a completely new look.

Duvets should be about 40cm/18in wider than the bed to allow for covering the occupant as well. Duvet covers tend to fall into two sizes: 140cm × 200cm/4ft 6in × 6ft 6in for single beds and 200cm/6ft 6in square for small or standard double beds. King-size duvet covers are 230cm × 205cm/7ft 6in × 6ft 11in and, at the other end of the scale, cot covers are usually 100cm × 120cm/40in × 48in.

Measuring up

If your duvet is not a standard single or double size, measure it and add about 5cm/2in to each dimension for the cover as this should be loose fitting like a pillow case. Alter the fabric requirements accordingly.

Add seam allowances to the finished measurements of the cover: 4cm/1½in to the width and 9.5cm/4in to the length.

This allows for an opening along the bottom edge. If you want a side opening, reverse the seam allowances for width and length and, when making up, apply the instructions given for the bottom edge to one side.

Right: Colour match different patterns, such as the spots and stripes shown here, or use contrasting colourways of the same pattern to make an unusual and reversible duvet cover.

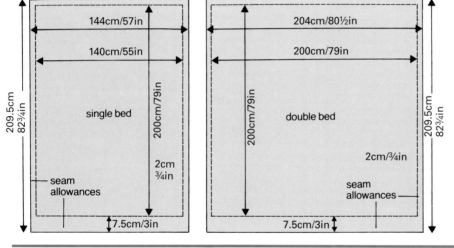

Making the plain duvet cover

A plain duvet cover is simply made by stitching two pieces of fabric together to form a large bag with an opening at one end. The quantities are given below and as sheeting is usually 228cm/90in wide it can be more economical to cut the length of the duvet across the width of the fabric, pattern permitting. Simply double the width of the cover, including seam allowances, to calculate the fabric needed.

You will need
Single: 2.9m/3⅛yd wide sheeting
1m/1⅛yd press fastener tape
Matching thread
Double: 4.1m/4½yd wide sheeting
1.6m/1¾yd press fastener tape
Matching thread

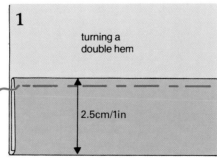

Cutting out and making up
Cut front and back pieces to the required size, including seam allowances, keeping to the straight grain of fabric.
1 On the bottom (opening) edge of each piece, turn a double hem (2.5cm/1in and 2.5cm/1in) to the wrong side. Pin, tack and machine stitch.

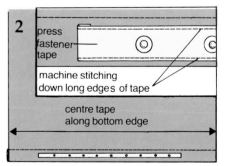

2 Separate the press fasteners and pin one half of the tape to the **right side** of each piece, placing it centrally to the width and next to the stitching. Ensure that the press fasteners correspond on both tapes. Turn raw ends under and use a zipper foot, if you have one, to machine stitch down the long edges of each tape.

3 Place the front and back pieces right sides together, fasten poppers and tack in from each side to just past the tape ends next to the hem edge. Machine stitch from each outer edge along the tacking, then down across the hem and the tape ends.
The other three sides are stitched with French seams.

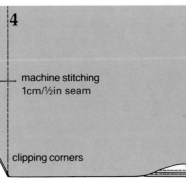

4 With wrong sides together, stitch a 1cm/½in seam down both sides. Trim seam allowance and press. Clip off corners to reduce seam bulk.

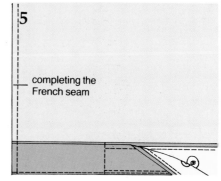

5 Fold cover so that right sides are together and stitch side seams again with 1cm/½in allowance to complete the French seams.
Turn cover right side out and repeat steps 4 and 5 to join top edge with a French seam.
When the cover is complete, turn right side out and press well.

Making a frilled duvet cover

The quantities given below allow for a 12cm/5in deep frill. To calculate the amount of fabric for the frill alone simply subtract the quantities given for the plain duvet from the quantities given for the frilled version. This duvet will not, of course, be reversible, so add any trimmings to the front cover only.

You will need
For a single duvet:
3.5m/3⅞yd wide sheeting
1m/1⅛yd press fastener tape
Matching thread
Trimmings if required
For a double duvet:
4.9m/5⅜yd wide sheeting
1.6m/1¾yd press fastener tape
Matching thread
Trimmings if required

Cutting out and making up
Cut the back and front pieces as for the basic cover.
Cut 15cm/6½in deep strips across the width of the remaining fabric until you have enough to form a strip 1½–2 times the length to be frilled (about 8m/9yd and 10m/11yd for single and double covers, respectively).

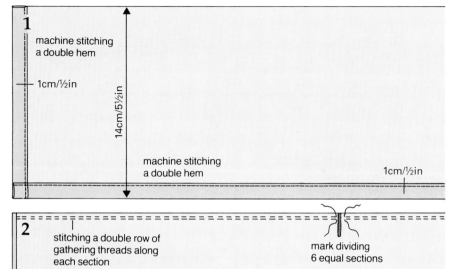

1 machine stitching a double hem
1cm/½in
14cm/5½in
machine stitching a double hem
1cm/½in

2 stitching a double row of gathering threads along each section
mark dividing 6 equal sections

1 Join the frill lengths into one long strip with 5mm/¼in and 1cm/½in French seams. Neaten the short ends by turning a narrow double hem, 5mm/¼in and 1cm/½in, to the wrong side and stitching. Neaten the lower long edge with a double hem (5mm/¼in and 1cm/½in) turned to the wrong side and stitched.
2 Divide the frill strip into six equal lengths and mark. Run two rows of gathering stitches along each section, placing the stitches on either side of the stitching line, which will be 1.5cm/⅝in from the raw edge.
Stitch the hems on the bottom edges of the cover (step 1 of plain duvet cover). Measure down one side, along bottom edge and up the other side on front cover piece and mark this length into six equal divisions.

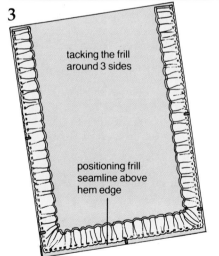

tacking the frill around 3 sides

positioning frill seamline above hem edge

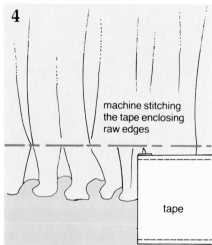

machine stitching the tape enclosing raw edges

tape

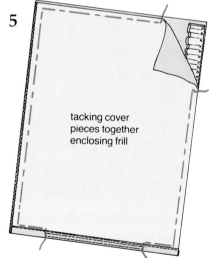

tacking cover pieces together enclosing frill

3 With right sides and raw edges together, pin the frill around the three edges of the front cover, pulling up the gathers evenly so that each section of the frill fits one section of the cover. Allow slightly more fullness at each corner. Start and finish at the top edge seamline and position the frill seamline close to the folded hem edge but not over it. Tack all round.

4 Pin, tack and stitch the press fastener tape into position as for the basic cover but enclosing the raw edge of the frill.
5 Place the cover pieces right sides together and tack a 1.5cm/⅝in seam round the three unfinished sides. Take care not to catch the frill in the top edge seam. Tack in from each side of the bottom edge, next to the hem edge, until just past the tape

ends. Tack across hem and tape. Machine stitch all round the cover following the tacking. Trim down seam allowance on raw edges, then zigzag together to neaten.
Turn cover right side out through opening, spread out frill, and press.

Right: Fold the frill in half widthways to make a reversible cover. Bands of Offray ribbon make an attractive trim.

116

Trimming with lace for luxurious effects

Transform your bedlinen by adding beautiful, delicate lace trimmings. Cobweb-fine lace and fine white cotton give a romantic look while heavier lace has an old-fashioned splendour. Lace trims and inserts can also be added to curtains and tablewear where appropriate.

For centuries, fine lace trimmings have been used to make functional soft furnishings appear as luxurious and decorative additions to the home. Now that machine-made lace is available in an abundance of patterns, designs and textures, an old-fashioned richness of style and character can be added to bedlinen you have made yourself or bought, at relatively little cost.

Use lace as edgings or insertions to soften a patterned fabric, add interest to a plain colour or to highlight an unusual shape. Gather it into frills, or appliqué individual motifs cut from a length of lace, for different effects. Choose a fine, delicate lace for a romantically feminine touch, or a richer, heavier lace to echo a country or Victorian look.

Choosing lace

When picking a lace trimming from the confusing array so often available, it's important to be quite clear as to how it will be applied – whether you will use it as an edging or an insertion, whether it is to be flat or frilled, and whether one, both or neither edges will show. A wide lace trimming with a decorative finish along both edges, for example, would be ideal as a topstitched border or an insertion but unnecessarily bulky – and expensive – when

gathered into a frill or inserted in a seam.

The same design of lace is often available in a variety of widths – choose one to suit the proportions of the item it is to decorate.

For a frilled edging, buy either pre-gathered lace or enough to gather up effectively (at least 1½ times finished length).

Try to match the fibre content of the lace to that of the fabric, choosing a cotton lace for a cotton fabric, nylon for synthetics and so on. This not only gives a better finished look, but also simplifies laundering. A nylon

Below: Mass together lots of lovely lacy items to transform a basic bed – or any dull corner – into a strikingly pretty focal point. Mix old lace and new for a really decorative effect.

lace, for example, could not be washed and ironed at the same high temperatures as a natural fabric.

Avoid putting antique or expensive hand-made lace that should be hand washed or dry cleaned on to furnishings that will require frequent machine washing, unless you are willing to remove them and stitch them on again by hand after each laundering.

Most modern laces are designed to be machine-stitched in place. A straight edge automatically provides a guide-line for stitching; if the lace has a scalloped or shaped edge, machine-stitch either around the shaping or in a straight line just within the shaping. Lace with particularly intricate edges, however, should be attached by hand and so is best avoided if you have a large area of lace to attach, such as down the edges of long curtains.

selection of lace samples

Sewing guidelines

Whether attaching lace by hand or machine, always use a fine sharp needle to avoid snagging and a fine thread in a fibre to match that of the lace.

When machine-stitching lace, it is advisable to practise stitch length and tension on a spare piece of lace and fabric if possible: the tension may have to be loosened slightly to prevent puckering. Tack tissue paper over any lace that will lie on the underside of the fabric while machining, to prevent threads catching in the feeding mechanism. The tissue can be torn away after stitching.

PROFESSIONAL TOUCH

Joining lace trimmings

To join two pieces of lace trimming unobtrusively, or when joining one piece into a circle, overlap the ends – if possible at a point where the pattern matches – and oversew or zigzag stitch the overlapping edge. With small, sharp scissors, trim away the surplus fabric from the underside, close to the stitching.

stitch around motif

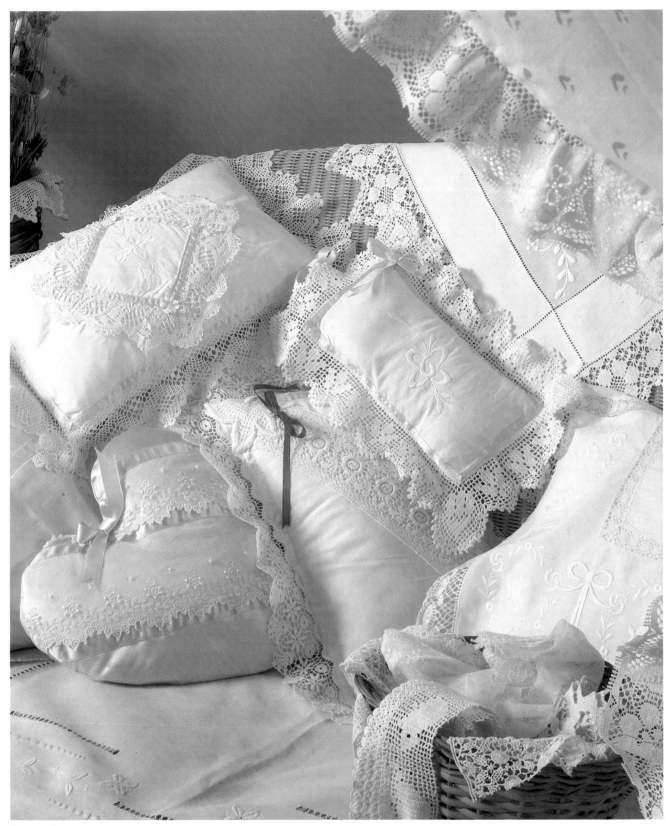

Attaching lace

Where possible, attach lace as part of the making up process as this saves work, enables you to secure raw ends in seams and gives a more professional finish. The exception is when adding precious and very expensive hand-made or antique lace which will need to be sewn on by hand and removed for laundering.

When stitching a lace trimming in place take the smallest possible seam allowance (5mm/¼in or even less on a pre-finished edge) from the lace so as not to lose too much of the pattern, but take the normal seam allowance in the fabric to which it is being attached.

As a seam trimming

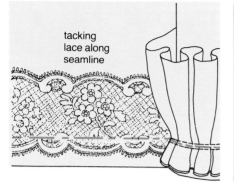

tacking lace along seamline

Insert lace edging into the seams on items such as pillow cases and cushion covers.
With right sides facing, tack the lace along the seamline on one piece of the main fabric so that it will lie sandwiched between the two pieces of fabric while stitching the seam. A fabric frill can be inserted in the seam at the same time.

Left: Lace inserts and frills can also be used on other kinds of soft furnishings such as tablelinen, lampshades, curtains and cushions. White lace complements most colour schemes and always creates a fresh and pretty effect. For a bolder, more dramatic look, dye lace trims in rich or strikingly bright colours, using the appropriate commercial dye.

As an edging

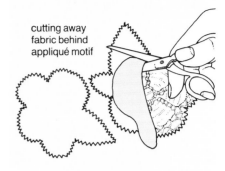

1cm/½in
forming a small inverted pleat at corner
1.5cm/⅝in

Attach a lace edging before making the hem on such items as sheets, tablecloths and napkins where there is only a single thickness of fabric.
Mark the fold of the hem on the right side of the fabric and tack the lace right side down with the plainer edge overlapping the hemline by about 5mm/¼in and facing outwards. Form the lace into a small inverted pleat at all corners so that it will have enough fullness to fan out. Machine stitch along the hemline, then fold under and complete hem as usual, leaving the main part of the lace falling below the fabric edge.

As a border or appliqué

cutting away fabric behind appliqué motif

Simply tack and topstitch lengths of lace in position on the right side of the fabric to form a border. Where possible, let the short raw ends overlap the seamline so they will be caught and hidden in the seams; otherwise turn under the ends to neaten.
Motifs can be cut from lengths of lace and appliquéd on to a fabric background.
To create appliqué with an openwork effect, pin and tack a lace motif to the right side of the fabric and stitch all round the edge with particularly close zigzag stitches, or oversew by hand. Using small sharp scissors and being extremely careful not to cut into the lace, carefully cut away the main fabric from behind the motif.

As an insertion

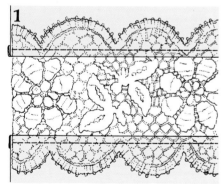

1

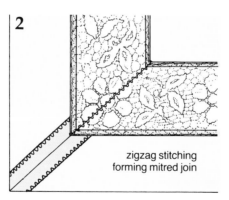

2

zigzag stitching forming mitred join

2 If the lace insertions are to meet at a corner, overlap the two ends at right angles and zigzag stitch across at 45° to form a mitred join. Trim away the surplus fabric on both sides, cutting as close to the stitching as possible.

Lace inserted flat, between two areas of fabric, because it is unbacked, will show up well against the dark wood of furniture underneath, a pretty lining or undercloth, or the light of a window.
1 If the lace has prettily finished edges, tack a very narrow hem along each of the fabric edges. Tack the lace edges on the right side of the fabric over the hems and

topstitch in place, catching down hem turnings at the same time.
If the lace edges are to be hidden, seam one edge of the lace to one piece of fabric, right sides facing and taking only a narrow seam allowance on the lace. Seam the other edge of lace to the second piece of fabric in the same way. Zigzag stitch or oversew turnings together and press away from the lace so as not to show through.

Bed valances in three different styles

A bed looks neater with a valance round the edge concealing the base and legs. The style can be frilled, pleated or plain with pleated corners – they are all quick and easy to make. Co-ordinate the colours and add trimmings to match the bedlinen.

A bed valance fits between the mattress and the base of a bed, hanging down to cover the base, the bed legs and the space under the bed. A valance is particularly necessary for a bed with a duvet and no bedspread to cover the divan base, but it can also be a decorative extra used in conjunction with a bedspread which isn't quite floor length.

The base fabric covers the bed base, fitting under the mattress, and the valance skirt is attached around three sides leaving the head end free. The skirt can be frilled, box pleated or plain with a single inverted pleat at each corner – choose a style to suit the bedroom.

Make it up in an easy-care polyester/cotton sheeting which matches the bedding or complements a throw-over bedspread. Extra wide sheeting requires fewer joins for the skirt and none at all for the base, but to economise use sheeting for the skirt and a cheaper washable fabric, such as an extra wide calico, for the large area hidden under the mattress.

Measuring up

For the valance base, measure the bed base both lengthways and widthways. Add 4.5cm/1¾in to the length and 3cm/1¼in to the width measurements for seam allowances. The base can be cut in one piece from wide sheeting but if you use a narrower fabric, you need to join sections with flat felled seams. For the depth of the valance skirt, measure from the top of the bed base to the floor. The average height is between 30–35cm/12–14in. To this measurement add 6.5cm/2½in for hem and seam allowance.

The finished length of the valance skirt is measured from one head corner, round the base to the other corner (but not across the head end). The actual skirt piece will be cut according to the style of valance.

Right: The deep-coloured valance contrasts with the prettiness of the bedding. If your bedlinen is rather plain, brighten it up with a frilled valance or one in a patterned fabric.

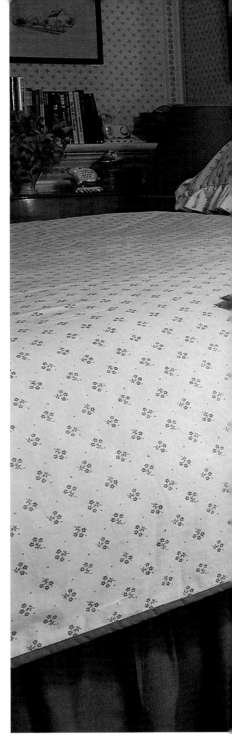

Making a gathered valance

Cutting layout diagram:
- 228cm / 90in (width)
- 260cm / 102½in (height)
- skirt, skirt, skirt, skirt
- **Cutting layout for single bed**
- single valance base

The frilled valance is particularly quick and simple to make.

You will need

For a single bed 90cm/3ft wide:
2.6m/2⅞yd sheeting 228cm/90in wide

For a double bed 135cm/4ft 6in wide:
3.1m/3½yd sheeting 228cm/90in wide

Thread

Trimmings if required

Cutting out and making up

Cut out the valance base with the length across the width of the fabric. Join widths if necessary on narrow fabrics.

The skirt should be 1½–2 times the finished length to allow for gathering. Cut strips across the width of the fabric to make up the length, allowing 3cm/1¼in seam allowances for each join and the two ends.

Fold a double hem (1.5cm/⅝in and 1.5cm/⅝in) along the top edge (head end) of the valance base and machine stitch. Pin, tack and stitch the skirt pieces together into one long strip with French seams.

Fold a double hem (1.5cm/⅝in and 1.5cm/⅝in) at each short edge of skirt strip and machine stitch.

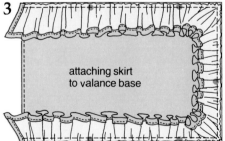

1 dividing 3 sides into 6 equal sections

valance base

1.5cm/⅝in double hem

2 gathering each section

skirt

2.5cm/1in double hem

3 attaching skirt to valance base

1 Measure the three sides – omit the hemmed end – of the base piece and mark into six to eight equal sections. Divide the skirt strip into the same number of sections and mark.
2 Turn a double hem (2.5cm/1in and 2.5cm/1in) along base edge of skirt and machine stitch or hem by hand.

Add any trimmings at this stage. Run two rows of gathering stitches along each skirt section, placing the stitches on either side of the stitching line which will be 1.5cm/⅝in from the raw edge.
3 With right sides together pin the skirt to the base, matching one skirt

section to one base section in turn and drawing up gathering stitches evenly to fit. Allow slightly more gathering round each corner. Tack and stitch skirt in place with 1.5cm/⅝in seams. Trim seam allowance and zigzag stitch together to neaten. Press well to complete.

Making a pleated valance

Box pleats require more fabric than a frill but make a smart valance with a neat finish.

You will need
For a single bed:
3.8m/4¼yd sheeting 228cm/90in wide
For a double bed:
4.2m/4⅝yd sheeting 228cm/90in wide
Thread
Trimmings if required

Cutting out and making up
Measure up for the valance base and skirt depth as before. Cut out the base piece with the length across the width of the fabric. The skirt should be three times its finished length to allow for pleating. Cut strips across the fabric width until you have sufficient length, allowing 3cm/1¼in seam allowances for each join and the two ends.

Decide on the size of pleat you require, finding a figure that will divide evenly into the width of the bed, eg six pleats 15cm/6in wide or nine pleats, 10cm/4in wide, for a 90cm/3ft bed.

Hem the top edge of base piece, join the skirt strips together with French seams and hem the short and lower edges, as for the gathered valance.

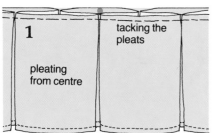

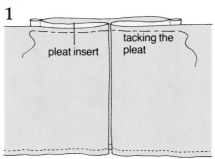

1 Find the centre of the skirt and begin pleating out from this point, folding and pinning the fabric into even box pleats. Try to position the pleats so there will be an inverted pleat formed at each corner.

2 Place the pleated skirt around the three sides of the base with right sides and raw edges together. Adjust the last pleats as necessary to acquire the exact finished length – if they have to be slightly smaller or larger it will not be very noticeable at the head end. Pin, tack and stitch together with a 1.5cm/⅝in seam. Trim seam allowance slightly and zigzag raw edges together to neaten.

Turn right side out and press well to complete.

Making a plain valance with pleated corners

Make the plain valance in a heavier fabric for a more tailored look.

You will need
For a single bed:
2.2m/2½yd sheeting 228cm/90in wide
For a double bed:
2.6m/2⅞yd sheeting 228cm/90in wide
Thread
Trimmings if required

Cutting out and making up
Measure up for the valance base and skirt depth as before. Cut out the base piece with the length across the width of the fabric. The skirt is made from five pieces – two sides, one end and two pleat

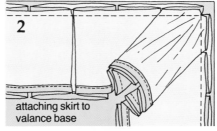

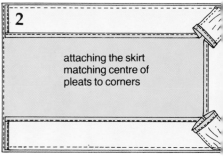

inserts. Each side piece is the bed length plus 10.5cm/4in, the end piece is the bed width plus 18cm/7in and each pleat insert is 18cm/7in. Cut out across the width of the fabric. If a narrower fabric is used, add seam allowances and join widths as necessary. Hem top edge of base as for the gathered valance.

Join the skirt pieces together with French seams (1cm/½in and 1cm/½in seam allowances) to form a continuous strip working in the following order: one side piece, one pleat insert, end piece, second pleat insert and remaining side piece. Hem lower edge and short ends of skirt as for the gathered valance.

Above: Box pleats – simple but smart.

Right: Corner pleat of a plain valance.

1 Mark the finished length of each side piece and of the end piece (working from a central point) on the skirt. Use the excess between to form an inverted pleat; the pleat insert becomes the back of the pleat. Pin and tack the two pleats firmly.
2 Place skirt to base with right sides and raw edges together, matching centre of pleats to corner points of base and clipping into seam allowance on each pleat insert at the corner point. Pin, tack and stitch in place with a 1.5cm/⅝in seam. Trim down seam allowance and zigzag stitch raw edges together to neaten. Press well to complete.

125

Throwover bedcovers – plain or quilted

Create a new look for your bedroom with a stylish throwover bedcover. A striking floor-length version, whether lined or unlined, can be made in an evening; a beautifully quilted coverlet takes a little longer to make but is ideal for chilly winter nights.

As well as adding warmth to the bed, a throwover bedcover introduces a dramatic area of colour or pattern to the room. By making your own, you not only save money, but you have far more scope for choosing a fabric that matches curtains or brightens up the room's colour scheme.

A floor-length bedcover hides boring blankets, an ugly divan base or anything lurking untidily under the bed. Both the lined and unlined versions can be made in an evening.

Use the shorter, quilted coverlet in conjunction with a valance or to show off an interesting, perhaps antique, bedstead. It takes a little more time to make but is not difficult to sew and the finished effect is always luxurious.

Joining widths

As it is unlikely that you will be able to buy fabric wide enough to make a floor-length bedcover from a single piece, you will need to seam together widths of fabric. Think carefully about the position of seams because, as with a curtain or tablecloth, badly placed joins can look conspicuous and unattractive. The centre of the bedcover must be a full width of fabric, with an equal amount of fabric added at each side. Therefore, although two widths of fabric will cover a single bed, don't simply join them with a central seam. Use one width to form a centre panel and cut the other in half along its length to form equal side panels. Join selvedges rather than the cut edges as it is easier to match patterns.

A simple throwover bedcover

This is the easiest of all bedcovers to make, being just a large rectangle of fabric neatened around the edges. As the name implies, you simply throw it over the bed and pillows, and it reaches to the floor on the sides and at the foot of the bed. Make a simple unlined version or add a matching or contrasting lining to add warmth and to look attractive when the bedcover is folded back.

To achieve a more fitted effect without additional sewing, add extra length so that a fold in the cover can be tucked under the pillows before covering them.

Simple trimmings, such as cotton lace, braid or fringing, can be added to match the style of your bedroom furnishings.

Measuring up

Make the bed with the normal amount of pillows and blankets or a duvet.

For the width Measure from the floor on one side of the bed, up and over the width of the bed and down to the floor again on the other side. Add 6cm/2¼in to this measurement for side hems and 3cm/1¼in for each seam joining fabric widths.

Left: Topstitch a plain fabric border around a floor length bedcover to frame a dramatic pattern.

If you want a trimming, such as a fringe, to extend beyond the edge of the cover, subtract twice the depth of the overhanging part of the trimming from the overall width measurement.

For the length Measure from the floor at the foot of the bed, up and along the length of the bed, over the hump of the pillows to the wall or headboard behind. Add 6cm/2¼in to this measurement for hems.

If you want to 'tuck' the bedcover under the pillows, add an extra 40cm/16in to the length.

Remember to allow for pattern matching where necessary.

You will need

Top fabric (See measuring up)
The same amount of lining fabric if required
Matching thread
Trimmings if required

Making up

Unlined bedcover Cut the required lengths of fabric, allowing for pattern matching, and join widths with French seams, taking 5mm/¼in and 1cm/½in seam allowances. Turn a double hem of 1:5cm/⅝in and 1.5cm/⅝in to the wrong side all round the cover, mitring the corners (see page 165). Press and tack. Machine stitch or slipstitch all round to hold hem in place.

If you are adding any trimming, machine or slipstitch it in place around three sides, omitting the headboard end.

Lined bedcover Cut the required lengths of fabric and join the widths, matching patterns with 1.5cm/⅝in flat seams.

Cut out and make up the lining in exactly the same way so that seams lie in the corresponding position to those on main fabric. Press seams.

To join fabric and lining, lay them right sides facing with seams and raw edges lying together.

Tack together all round then machine stitch taking 3cm/1¼in seam allowances and leaving a 60cm/24in gap along one short side. Trim seam allowance to 1cm/½in all round and clip across corners. Turn through to the right side and slipstitch the open edges together.

Adding a trimming, such as a frill or piping, to a lined cover is a very simple matter. When you have the fabric and lining right sides together, simply sandwich the trimming between the two layers and it will be anchored in place as you machine all round the bedcover. When you come to the 60cm/24in gap, machine the trimming to the top fabric only and close gap by hand afterwards.

A quilted throwover coverlet

Make a cosy but smart coverlet by sandwiching a layer of wadding between two layers of fabric and holding with machine-stitched quilting.

Measuring up

Make up the bed with the normal blankets and sheets, or duvet, but do not put the pillows on the bed as they will lie on top of the finished coverlet.

For the width Decide how far you want the coverlet to overhang the sides of the bed, double the overhang depth and add this measurement to the width of the bed. Add 15% to this total width measurement to allow for the 'shrinkage' caused by stitching the quilting. Add 3cm/1¼in for each seam needed to join the fabric widths (see introduction, page 127) but do not add any seam allowance for side hems as the raw edges are neatened with binding.

For the length Measure the length of the bed and add the required depth of overhang for the bottom edge only. This can be either the same depth as on the sides or shorter if it is to tuck inside a decorative footboard. As when calculating the width, add 15% to this measurement but do not add hem allowances.

You will need

Top fabric (See measuring up)
The same amount of fabric for the reverse side
The same area of polyester wadding, either the medium 4oz or the thicker 8oz weight
Enough 5cm/2¾in-wide strips of fabric to bind all round finished coverlet (allow for joins)
Matching sewing threads

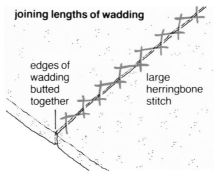

joining lengths of wadding

edges of wadding butted together

large herringbone stitch

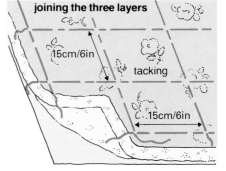

joining the three layers

15cm/6in

tacking

15cm/6in

Making up

Join widths of top fabric, if necessary, with 1.5cm/⅝in flat seams matching patterns. Make up the reverse-side fabric to exactly the same size. Press all seams open flat. Cut wadding to the same size as either fabric piece. Although some specialist shops offer wadding in wide widths so that it can be cut in one piece, you will have to join the more generally available 90cm/36in width.

Joining lengths of wadding Lay the two pieces side by side with edges butting up rather than overlapping and link together with large herringbone stitches.

Lay out the top fabric right side upwards on a solid flat surface such as a tiled floor. Use tailor's chalk to draw on guidelines for the quilting. The quilting lines can be stitched vertically and horizontally to form squares, or as diagonals running in both directions to form a diamond pattern. For either design, the parallel lines must be evenly spaced about 8cm/3in apart. Unless you have a quilting guide bar, chalk in every line as you will find that it is difficult to sew lines by eye.

Joining the three layers Lay the reverse-side fabric out flat, wrong side upwards, and place the

wadding on top. Carefully lay the top fabric over the wadding, right side upwards, and tack all three layers together.

Run the tacking stitches around the edge and then across the width in lines spaced about 15cm/6in apart. Also run lines of tacking down the length of the fabric, again spaced about 15cm/6in apart, so that the three layers are securely held together by the squares of tacking. Quilt the coverlet as described below, re-check coverlet measurements, and trim away any excess so that the quilted fabric is the exact finished size of coverlet. Remove all tacking.

To neaten the edges cut strips of fabric 7cm/2¾in wide, long enough, when joined, to fit all round the outside edge of the coverlet.

Lay the binding right side down on the top side of the coverlet, placing the raw edge of the binding 1.5cm/⅝in in from the edges of the coverlet. Tack in place, mitring the corners of the binding (see page 165). Sew 5mm/⅜in from the raw edge of the binding and then remove all tacking stitches.

Fold the binding over the raw edges of the coverlet to the reverse side. Turn in 5mm/⅜in of the binding to the wrong side and slipstitch.

Quilting large areas

To machine stitch the quilting lines, either place your machine on a table large enough to support the bulk of the coverlet or drape the coverlet over a second table or chair placed next to the machine.

Do not allow the coverlet to hang free as you machine or the weight of the fabric will pull it out of shape as it is stitched and stitch lengths will be uneven.

Try to keep the bulk of the fabric to

the left of the machine, supported by the table, while stitching. As you get into the centre of the quilt roll the fabric tightly to fit under the arm of the sewing machine.

Note On a really large quilt, it may be impossible to fit the bulk of fabric, however tightly rolled, under the arm of the machine. In this case, the widths of fabric and wadding should be quilted together in separate panels and joined as for ready-quilted fabric (see Short Cut).

For 'squared' quilting, stitch all the vertical lines, and then all the horizontal lines. For the 'diamond' quilting, stitch all the diagonal lines running in one direction before stitching those running in the opposite way. This helps to prevent puckering between the quilting lines.

Right: The coverlet is reversible – use two complementary fabrics and simply turn it over for a change.

Using ready-quilted fabric

Quilting very large areas of fabric can be difficult and time consuming so you might prefer to use purchased ready-quilted fabric. Although the selection of fabrics can be quite restricted, try to find a reversible quilting so that your coverlet is different on either side.

Measure up and cut out the fabric as for a machine-quilted coverlet, but without the 15% excess for shrinkage. Joining the widths of pre-quilted fabric requires care, as excess wadding has to be removed from the seams to reduce bulk.

Joining reversible quilting

Carefully unpick the machine quilting lines so that an unstitched strip 3cm/1¼in wide lies along each of the raw edges to be joined.

Lay the two pieces of fabric together right (top) sides facing and tack the two top sides and wadding together, folding back the unstitched strips of reverse side fabric so that it is not caught in the seamline. Machine stitch a flat seam 1.5cm/⅝in wide through the layers of wadding and top fabric, making sure that you do not catch in the reverse fabric. Trim away the wadding from the seam allowances.

Press 1.5cm/⅝in to the wrong side on the two edges of reverse fabric and butt the folded edges together over the seam line of the top fabric. Slipstitch or ladderstitch the butted edges together by hand.

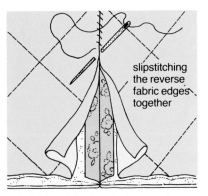

slipstitching the reverse fabric edges together

With hand back stitches and matching thread, restitch the quilting lines that were unpicked, to make continuous lines.

Neatening the edges If you can buy non-quilted fabric to match the ready-quilted fabric, use this to bind the edges as for the quilted coverlet below. If not, use a 25mm/1in wide purchased bias binding.

Beautiful bedspreads made to measure

Frilly and feminine or bold and smart, whatever your bedroom décor, there's a style of fitted bedspread to complement it. Choose a pretty gathered style, one with a stylish box pleated skirt, or a classic design with crisp corner pleats.

It is not always easy to buy a fitted bedspread in a suitable fabric, in the style that suits your room scheme and in a size that will perfectly fit a particular bed. However, making your own bedspreads enables you to achieve a perfect fit in the style and colours of your choice.

All fitted bedcovers consist basically of a top panel that lies over the top surface of the bed and a skirt to fit around the sides. The top panel can be a feature in itself, perhaps made from quilted fabric or a co-ordinating print, but it is the skirt that has the most scope for design variations. A gathered skirt is ideal for a pretty floral print or broderie anglaise and can be trimmed with ribbons or frills. For a stylish look choose box pleats or a plain skirt with corner pleats.

Measuring up

Make up the bed with the normal amount of bedding and, if desired, the pillows. For a tailored fit over high pillows, you will need to include triangular side gussets at the top end when making up the bedspread, although this isn't necessary with a low pillow. However, rather than having a hump of pillows under the bedspread, you may prefer to measure up without them and put the pillows inside pretty daytime covers so that they lie on top of the bedspread during the day as a decorative feature.

The top panel Measure the length and width of the top of your bed and add 3cm/1¼in seam allowances to each dimension to calculate the size of top panel to cut from fabric. If the fabric is not wide enough to cut this in one piece, allow an extra 3cm/1¼in for each seam needed to join widths. Plan the seam positions carefully for the best possible visual effect, having a whole width of fabric down the centre of the panel with an equal amount added on either side rather than one join in the middle of the panel.

The skirt Measure from the top of the bed to within 1cm/½in of the floor for the finished height of the skirt and add 4.5cm/1¾in seam allowance and hem.

Measure down both long sides of the bed and across the foot end as a basis for calculating the width (the longer dimension) of the skirt.

For a gathered skirt, multiply this measurement by 1½ to allow for fullness.

For a skirt with corner pleats, measure each side separately so that seams can be positioned at the corners behind a pleat where possible. Add 40cm/16in to the measurement across the width of the bed and 20cm/8in to the length of each side to allow for pleats and side hems.

For a box pleated skirt, multiply this measurement by 2¼ for spaced pleats or by 3 for continuous pleating.

Optional side gussets Cut a right angled triangle for a paper pattern. Measure the width of the pillows and add 10cm/4in to this measurement for the long base edge of the triangle. Measure the height of the pillows when they are lying fairly flat, rather than puffed up, for the short side of the triangular gusset which lies at right angles to the base. Join these two lines with a curved line that follows the shape of the pillows, then add 1.5cm/⅝in seam allowance all round.

Estimating fabric requirements

Draw out a small scale plan (eg 1cm/½in representing 10cm/4in) of the top panel, side gussets (if any) and skirt.

If your fabric is plain or has a design such as a stripe that can be used sideways to good effect, cut the skirt in one piece along its length to avoid seams. If this would prove uneconomical or if a patterned fabric must be used the right way up, join widths to make up the skirt. You may also have to join widths for the top panel. Subtracting 3cm/1¼in from each fabric width to allow for seams, mark out seam positions to estimate how many widths of fabric are needed for each piece.

Multiply the number of widths by the length to calculate the amount of fabric needed for each piece. Make sufficient allowance for matching patterns when either the top panel or the skirt must be made from more than one width of fabric. After buying your fabric and lining (if you choose to use it), thread is the only other requirement.

Cutting out

Each bedspread consists of a top panel and skirt. Cut out the necessary number of widths to make up each piece to the size calculated by measuring up, allowing for pattern matching.

Right: The simple styling of the straight-skirted bedspread with corner pleats emphasizes the bold stripes of a crisp cotton fabric.

machine stitches as gathering stitches 1cm/³⁄₈in and 1.5cm/⁵⁄₈in down from the top edge. Do not stitch the gathering threads in one continuous length as they would then be impossible to pull up: stitch for lengths of about 60cm/24in and gather up the skirt in sections.

Joining top panel and skirt
With right sides facing, pin the two side edges of the skirt to the top (head) end of the top panel and pin the centre of the skirt to the centre of the bottom edge of the top panel, matching tailor's tacks. Pull up the gathering threads until the skirt fits around the three sides of the top panel, with even gathering all along. Pin, tie off threads securely, tack, and then stitch the skirt in place. Clip into the seam allowance on the curved corners to ease the fabric, if necessary. Remove tacking and press seam.

Completing the bedspread
Turn 5mm/¹⁄₄in and then 1cm/¹⁄₂in to the wrong side to make a hem along the skirt sides and panel top edge and stitch. Turn 1.5cm/⁵⁄₈in and then 1.5cm/⁵⁄₈in to the wrong side to make a double hem along the bottom edge of the skirt and stitch.

To line the top panel press 1.5cm/⁵⁄₈in seam allowance to the wrong side all round the lining, clipping into the seam allowance on the curved corners. Press the top panel/skirt seam towards the top panel and pin the lining and top panel together, wrong sides facing, enclosing all seam allowances. Slipstitch by hand all round the edge of the lining to attach it to the top panel.

Bedspread with gathered skirt

The top panel of the bedspread can be lined for extra weight and warmth. Alternatively use a ready-quilted fabric for the top panel and the matching unquilted version for the skirt.

Making up
Take 1.5cm/⁵⁄₈in seam allowances for flat seams, 5mm/¹⁄₄in then 1cm/³⁄₈in for French seams.

Preparing the top panel Join fabric widths, if necessary, to make up the top panel. Use French seams if the top panel will be unlined, flat seams if it will be lined. Trim the two lower corners of the top panel to a gentle curve, using an object such as a saucer as a guide to ensure that both corners are the same. Mark the centre of the lower edge with a tailor's tack.

If lining is required, cut out, make up and trim to the same size.

If the bedspread is to be unlined, zigzag stitch round the three sides of the panel, omitting the top end, to neaten.

Adding side gussets If including these, zigzag along the two longer sides to neaten, and, with right sides together, stitch a curved edge to each side edge at the top of panel, as in the diagram. Treat the base of the side gusset as the new edge of the top panel. If lining the top panel, join side gussets to lining in the same way.

Preparing the skirt Using French seams, join the skirt pieces together to make one continuous length. Zigzag stitch along the top edge to neaten and mark the centre of the top edge with a tailor's tack. Insert two rows of the largest

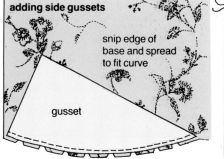

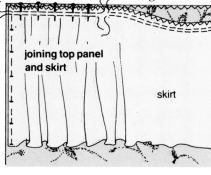

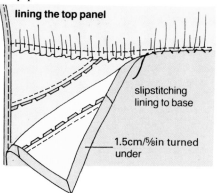

Fitted bedspread with corner pleats

Make this unlined, fully lined or line just the top panel. Use French seams (5mm/¼in and 1cm/⅜in) for joining widths of fabric on any parts that will be unlined to eliminate raw edges. Otherwise, use 1.5cm/⅝in flat seams.

Making up

Prepare the top panel as for the bedspread with a gathered skirt but, before curving the corners, draw a short chalkline at 45° to each of the lower corners. Curve away just the very tip of the corners.

To mark the pleat position measure 1.5cm/⅝in from the curved edge along the diagonal chalkline and mark with a tailor's tack.

Join the side gussets, if needed, to the top panel as before.

Prepare any lining required for the top panel in the same way.

Prepare skirt by joining widths where necessary to make side and end panels (see Measuring up, page 130).

Join a side panel to both short ends of the end panel to make a continuous strip with a side, end, side sequence of panels.

If you are lining the skirt, cut out and join pieces of lining fabric to the same size as the fabric skirt. Place fabric and lining wrong sides facing and tack together along the top edge. From now on, treat the skirt fabric and lining as one.

Mark the exact centre of the top edge of the end panel with a tailor's tack. Also mark the centre of the

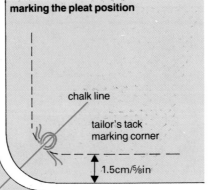

marking the pleat position

chalk line

tailor's tack marking corner

1.5cm/⅝in

lower edge of the top panel with a tailor's tack.

Joining skirt and top panel

With right sides facing and matching the two central tailor's tacks, pin the end panel of the skirt to the lower edge of the top panel as far as the corner tacks.

With the top edge of the top panel and the short side edge of the skirt together, pin the long side edges of panel and skirt together as far as the corner tack, so that the surplus skirt fabric lies on top of the skirt at the lower corners.

To form the corner pleats, fold the surplus fabric at each corner into an inverted pleat, with the centre lying on the corner tack. Clip into the seam allowance on the back part of the pleat so that it will spread around the curved corner. Tack and stitch the skirt in place, catching down the pleats. Neaten the raw edges of this seam unless the top panel is to be lined.

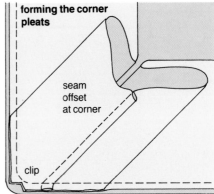

forming the corner pleats

seam offset at corner

clip

Completing the bedspread

Complete an unlined bedspread, or one that has the top panel only lined, in the same way as one with a gathered skirt, adding a lining to the top panel if required.

Complete a fully lined bedspread by pressing a 1.5cm/⅝in turning to the wrong side along the head (top) end of the bedspread (ie skirt sides and top panel). Trim the side edges of the skirt lining so that they lie almost on the fold, tucked under the fabric turning. Turn in the raw edge of the fabric again to make a 1cm/⅜in hem right across head end of bedspread and stitch.

Turn up a double hem (1.5cm/⅝in and 1.5cm/⅝in) around the lower edge of the skirt, trimming and tucking in the lining edge as before, and mitring the corners for neatness. Attach lining to top panel as for the bedspread with gathered skirt.

Bedspread with box pleated skirt

10cm/4in is a good average size for box pleats whether spaced 10cm/4in apart or butted together.

Making up

Cut out and prepare the top panel as for the bedspread with gathered skirt, with side gussets if needed.

Join the skirt pieces into one continuous strip with French seams. Zigzag stitch the top edge to neaten and mark the centre of this edge.

Turn up a double hem (1.5cm/⅝in and 1.5cm/⅝in) along the bottom edge and tack. Rule a vertical chalkline 5cm/2in either side of the central tailor's tack and then every 10cm/4in along the entire length of

the valance. Using these lines as a guide, press in and tack each pleat, spaced or butted.

Joining skirt to top panel. With right sides together and matching centre tailor's tacks, tack the skirt to the top panel, clipping into the seam allowance around curves. If necessary, adjust the pleats or the spaces between at each end of the skirt so that you do not end with part of a pleat, then trim the short ends of the skirt to level them up with the edge of the top panel. Stitch round 1.5cm/⅝in in to join skirt and top panel.

Completing the bedspread

Turn in a double hem (5mm/¼in

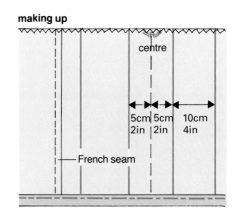

making up

centre

5cm 5cm 10cm
2in 2in 4in

French seam

and 1cm/½in) along the head edge of the bedspread, mitring the corners with the lower hem, and tack. Machine stitch the hem all round the bedspread to complete. Line the top panel, if required.

Practical and decorative fabric bedheads

If you can sew a cushion cover, you can make yourself a striking new bedhead. Simply make up a gusseted cushion incorporating hanging tabs and suspend it from a decorative rail above your bed. Or make a loose quilted cover to put over an existing headboard.

As well as being functional, bedheads can also look very decorative covered in a fabric which co-ordinates with the room or adds a splash of colour.

If the bed already has a fixed headboard, you can make a slip-over cover to give it a new look. If not, you can create a bedhead by simply hanging a cushion from a wooden or brass curtain rail fixed to the wall.

Slip-over bedhead covers

These can be made for most types of fixed headboards, such as the wooden ones normally supplied on a divan bed or padded ones which have become worn or soiled. The bedhead can be any shape, you will have to make a paper pattern of the bedhead before cutting out the fabric for the cover if it is not simply rectangular.

Slip-over covers look best made in quilted fabric as this disguises any indentations in the original bedhead and is more comfortable to lean against. If you buy ready-quilted fabric, making the cover is a very simple matter. However, if you wish to match the cover to curtains or bedding, you can quilt your own fabric.

Hanging bedheads

These are suitable for divans without headboards. To make a hanging bedhead, fix a brass or wooden curtain pole to the wall and hang a cushion – or a pair of cushions – from it.

The pole, measured between end stops, should be at least as wide as the bed. To position it on the wall, sit up in bed and mark the point on the wall where the cushions should be. (You should be able to rest your head in the centre of the cushion.) The pole should be about 6cm/2½in above top edge of cushion to allow for tabs.

You need only one cushion for a single bed. For a double bed, choose either a pair of cushions or one long one. Each cushion will require at least three hanging tabs, an extra-long cushion for a double bed five or more, depending on the width of the bed.

Types of cushion This chapter gives instructions for making two styles of cushion. A solid foam block with a gusseted cover gives a firm long-lasting bedhead with a smartly tailored look; a cushion without a gusset, filled with wadding, feathers or foam chips, is simpler to make and just as decorative, but offers less support.

The width of the cushion should correspond to the pole width and is generally the width of the bed. For a pair of cushions, deduct 5cm/2in from the pole width to allow for the central gap, then divide the measurement in half for the finished width of each cushion.

Cushions can look attractive slightly inset each side of the bed, in which case cut down your measurements accordingly.

Left: To quilt your own headboard cover choose a suitable design such as this floral trellis pattern and quilt along the printed lines and round flower shapes. Below: A slip-on cover made to match a quilted bedspread.

A quilted slip-over bedhead cover

Transform an old-fashioned bedhead with a simple-to-make quilted cover. The instructions given below are for a gusseted cover, but if the wood of your bedhead is thinner than 5mm/³⁄₈in, omit the gusset.

You will need

Enough quilted fabric to cut the front, gusset strip and (optional) the back of the bedhead cover
or fabric and wadding to quilt yourself
Plain fabric for the back of the cover if not using quilted
Matching thread
50cm/½yd strong cotton tape for the ties
Paper to make pattern
Bias binding if required

Making a pattern

Stick together enough large sheets of paper from which to cut the headboard pattern. If the headboard is easily removed from the bed (most simply bolt or screw into place), lay it on the paper and draw round the shape. If you cannot remove the headboard, use very accurate measuring to draw up the pattern. Cut out the paper pattern adding an extra 1.5cm/⅝in seam allowance all round. If your headboard has supporting struts jutting out at the back, make a separate back pattern, drawing round these. Leaving a seam allowance, cut out the strut shapes. Measure the thickness of the bedhead to give the gusset width. Measure up both sides and around or across the top, following any shaping, to give the gusset length. Add seam allowances all round.

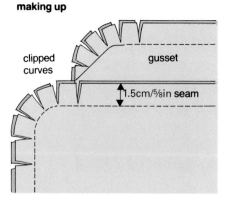

making up

clipped curves

gusset

1.5cm/⅝in seam

Cutting out

Cut the front and the gusset strip from quilted fabric. Cut the back from either plain or quilted fabric.
Note If you are not using ready-quilted fabric, cut a piece of fabric 10cm/4in larger all round than the front pattern piece (quilting tends to 'shrink' the fabric a little). Tack a layer of medium-weight polyester wadding to the wrong side, then machine stitch diagonal parallel lines in both directions to quilt the two layers together. When the quilting is complete, cut out a more accurate pattern piece. There is no need to quilt the back of the bedhead or the gusset strip, although you should back the gusset strip with a strip of wadding to make it look even.

Making up

If you have cut strut shapes from the back piece, neaten the edge with bias binding (see pages 163-165).
With right sides together, tack the gusset strip around the sides and top of the front cover piece. Snip into seam allowance to go round

attaching cover to headboard

tapes securing cover to headboard

curves and corners. Stitch taking 1.5cm/⅝in seam allowance.
Tack and stitch the other side of the gusset strip to the back piece in the same way. (If you are not adding a gusset, simply place back and front pieces right sides together and stitch around sides and top.)
Carefully snip away the wadding from seam allowances to reduce bulk and clip across any corners. Trim away 1.5cm/⅝in of wadding around the open base edge, then turn the unbacked fabric over to the wrong side and turn in the raw edge to make a double hem. Stitch the hem and turn the whole cover to the right side.

Attaching cover to headboard

Cut the cotton tape into four and attach two lengths to the base edge of front piece of cover and two lengths to correspond on the back piece. Position them just inside the supporting struts of the bedhead. Slip the cover over the bedhead an tie back and front tapes together in a double bow. The cover will remain securely in place but is easily removed for laundering.

Solid foam bedhead cushion

Read pages 90-93 first for detailed instructions on cutting out and making a gusseted cushion cover to cover a block of foam.
Foam suppliers will cut foam blocks to the exact size you require; 4cm/1½in is a suitable depth for the foam, but this can be varied according to choice and the distance of the pole from the wall. To prolong the life of the foam, make an inner cover from calico in the same way as a gusseted cushion cover, slipstitching it on to the foam block.

You will need

Foam block 4cm/1½in thick cut to the required size
Enough fabric to cover back, front and side strips of foam and to make tabs
The same amount of calico minus tabs
Thread
Hanging pole and fixings

Cutting out

Using the foam block as a guide, make paper patterns. You will need

a front and a back, four gusset strips to fit top, bottom and side edges, and at least two tab strips for the cushion. Each tab consists of two strips 10cm×20cm/4in×8in plus seam allowances. Add 1.5cm/⅝in seam allowance round all pieces before cutting out.

Making up

Place two tab pieces right sides facing and stitch down the two long edges. Turn right side out and press. Repeat to make all the tabs.

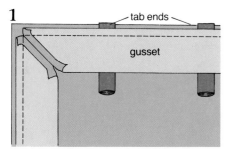

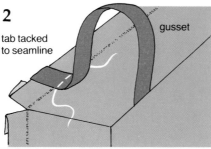

Above: Piped seams add a professional finish to an attractive pair of hanging bedhead cushions. Choose a fabric to match or co-ordinate with your curtains and bedding.

1 Tack one end of each of the tabs into position on the right side of the front piece, raw edges together. Join the short edges of the gusset strips to form a continuous strip,

leaving 1.5cm/⅝in unstitched at each end of each seam. With right sides together, stitch gusset to front piece, enclosing tab ends.

2 Tack the free end of each tab to the

seamline on the opposite edge of the top gusset.
Tack the back piece to the gusset and stitch round except along lower edge, making sure that only the tab ends are caught in the stitching. Clip corners, trim seams and turn right side out. Press well, insert the foam block and slipstitch opening.

Co-ordinated bedding for babies' cots

Make a set of co-ordinated cot bedding as a pretty and practical gift for a baby. Team a quilt or duvet cover, plain or frilled, with a padded bumper and matching sheets, choosing washable fabrics in soft pastels or bold bright colours.

Sewing for a baby is always rewarding and surprisingly little time is needed to make an absolutely stunning set of a cot quilt (or duvet cover) and padded bumper, with sheets trimmed to match.

Use an easy-care fabric such as polyester/cotton sheeting or fast-dyed prints, in a bold and colourful design for the simpler style of quilt, duvet cover or bumper, or a pretty mini-print, broderie anglaise or plain fabric if you choose to make the frilled versions.

The quilt and the bumper are lined with bouncy polyester wadding, which is easy to wash and dry. Press all fabric pieces well before adding the wadding as the finished quilting is best left unpressed.

The sizes given will fit a standard-sized cot of approximately 62cm × 120cm/24in × 48in and a cot duvet of 100cm × 120cm/40in × 48in. Adjust

Reversible bumper and quilt set

Choose colour co-ordinated fabrics with bold pattern lines that can be followed when stitching the quilting. Add an allowance for pattern matching to fabric requirements if necessary.

You will need
1.70m/1⅞yd of fabric 90cm/36in wide
The same amount of fabric for the reverse sides
3.10m/3⅜yd 4oz polyester wadding 90cm/36in wide
1.35m/1½yd contrasting fabric 90cm/36in wide
8×30cm/12in lengths of ribbon
Thread
Tissue paper

Cutting out
For the quilt, cut two pieces of fabric – one from each design – and two pieces of wadding each 90cm×65cm/36in×25½in wide. Also cut 15cm/6in wide strips of contrasting fabric, two 92cm/36¼in long and two 67cm/26½in long, for edging.
For the bumper, cut two pieces of *each* fabric 90cm/36in wide and 40cm/15¾in high, allowing for pattern matching if necessary. Cut two pieces of wadding each 178cm×40cm/71in×15¾in. Also cut 15cm/6in wide strips of contrasting fabric, four 90cm/36in long and two 40cm/15¾in long.

Making up the quilt
Tack a piece of wadding to the wrong side of each main fabric piece

with two diagonal lines of tacking. Tack tissue paper on top of the wadding to prevent it catching in the machine.

Turn the work fabric side up and decide which pattern lines you will follow, or which motifs you will stitch around, to work the quilting. It is not necessary to stitch around every single motif on the fabric but make sure that each quarter of the fabric will be quilted to the wadding at some point. Working from the centre of the fabric outwards, tack just inside any line that is to be a quilting line.

Again working from the centre outwards and with the fabric side upwards, machine or hand stitch along each quilting line. To stitch around shaped motifs, insert the needle at the corner point, lift the presser foot and pivot the fabric around the needle, lower the presser foot, then continue in new direction.

Tear away the tissue paper, place the two pieces of quilted fabric wadding sides meeting, and tack and stitch the layers together all round the edge, 6cm/2¼in in. Remove all tacking.

Binding the edges On both long edges of each edging strip, press 1cm/½in turnings to the wrong side. Fold strip in half lengthways, *right* sides out and press again. Folding in the short ends to fit, pin and tack the shorter strip of edging along the shorter sides of the quilt, enclosing all the raw edges. Topstitch the edging in place,

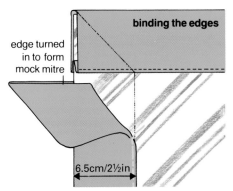

binding the edges

edge turned in to form mock mitre

6.5cm/2½in

stitching through all thicknesses. Pin the remaining strips along the long sides of the quilt, again enclosing raw edges, then trim and turn in the ends to form a mock mitre at each corner. Tack and topstitch edging in place.

Making up the bumper
The two pieces of each fabric are joined to form one side of the bumper. If a seam would be too conspicuous down the centre of the bumper, cut one piece of each fabric design in half and join to either side of the whole pieces, joining selvedges with a 1cm/½in seam. Back each fabric layer with wadding and tissue paper to stitch the quilting. Make up as for the quilt, joining two long edging strips with a narrow flat seam for binding each long edge.

Fold each ribbon in half and, positioning one at each corner and one 30cm/12in either side of the centre points on both long edges, stitch the folded edge to the bumper edge to form ties.

the measurements and fabric requirements for larger cots or cot/beds. Fabric quantities do not allow for pattern matching – you may need to add extra for this or for the positioning of large motifs.

A cot bumper not only protects a baby from draughts but also prevents the child from banging or wedging his or her head against the cot rails. For all-round protection, make two identical bumpers and place one at each end of the cot, to meet at the middle.

To make the set reversible use different but co-ordinated fabrics for back and front, so that turning over either quilt or bumper gives a fresh new look.

The back and front pieces of the bound bumper and quilt are then quilted separately so that the stitching may follow the fabric pattern on each side.

If using a mini-print, broderie anglaise or just a plain fabric for a quilt, sandwich the wadding between the two pieces of fabric and quilt through all layers at once, stitching in simple straight lines, as on the frilled bumper.

The cot sheets can be fitted or flat and trimmed in colours to match other bedding or the nursery décor. With a duvet and cover, of course, only the bottom sheet is needed.

Rather than adding a cot pillow, which is rarely needed and certainly not advised for very young babies, trim a fitted sheet at the corners of the mattress area to give an equally decorative effect without risking safety. As a change from the predictable matinée jacket, a sheet trimmed in this way and paired with a matching flat topsheet makes a delightful gift. Seam allowances are 1.5cm/⅝in throughout unless otherwise stated.

Below: Babies love bright colours so don't be afraid to choose fabrics with eye-catching designs. You can always make one side of the bumper plain and turn this side in to encourage sleep.

Plain duvet cover

Make a baby's duvet cover in the same way as an adult's (see pages 114-116) but following the measurements given. This method is particularly suitable for a cot duvet as French seams enclose all raw edges and ensure that the cover will withstand frequent washing.

Frilled duvet cover

Follow the instructions given on pages 114-116 but adding a doubled frill to make the cover reversible.

You will need

1.80m/2yd of polyester/cotton
  sheeting 230cm/90in wide
or 3.50m/3⅞yd of 120cm/48in wide
  fabric
3.50m/3⅞yd trimming (optional)
70cm/27½in press fastener tape

Left: This delightfully pretty set of frilled duvet cover and matching bumper, is made from practical polyester/cotton sheeting.

Frilled bumper

Choose a firm fabric with a small print that will not be distorted by the quilting lines as they are stitched through both layers at once.

You will need

1.1m/1¼yd sheeting 230cm/90in
  wide
or 2.3m/2½yd fabric 90cm/36in wide
80cm/32in of 8oz wadding 90cm/
  36in wide
Thread
8×30cm/12in lengths of ribbon

Sheet set

Read pages 104-107 first for details of making flat and fitted sheets for beds, adapting the measurements as described for cots and adding individual trimmings.

You will need

1.50m/1⅝yd sheeting 230cm/90in
  wide
or 3.00m/3¼yd winceyette at least
  100cm/40in wide
Thread
80cm/31½in of narrow elastic
Ribbon, lace or fabric off-cuts for
  trimming
Vilene Bondaweb (optional)

Cutting out

Cut the fabric into two pieces each 100cm×150cm/40in×60in, one for each sheet.

Making the flat sheet

Make up the flat sheet as for a bed (see page 104). Stitch a ready-made trimming on to the right side of the top edge to cover the stitching line of the hem. Ribbon, washable braids or lace trims would all be suitable.
Alternatively, cut out pretty motifs from scraps of fabric and arrange them decoratively along the edge of the sheet. Tack in place and zigzag stitch all round the motifs. (Bondaweb may be used to hold the motifs in place, but follow this by zigzagging for durability.)

Making the fitted sheet

Measure the mattress to ensure an accurate fit (most are about 60cm×120cm/24in×48in.) Mark this area with tailor's chalk, tacks or pressed-in fold lines, centrally on the sheet fabric. Leaving a 1.5cm/⅝in seam allowance, cut out the corner squares.
Add trimmings as for the flat sheet

You will need

1.35m/1½yd of polyester/cotton
  sheeting 230cm/90in wide
or 2.70m/2⅞yd of fabric 120cm/48in
  wide – a polyester/cotton mix
  ensures easy laundering
Thread
70cm/27½in press fastener tape

Cutting out and making up

Fold the fabric in half, selvedges
together, and cut two pieces of
fabric each 107cm×132.5cm/
42¼in×51in.
Make up as for an adult's plain
duvet cover, taking the same seam
allowances.

selection of suitable fabrics

Cutting out

Cut two pieces of fabric as for the
plain cover. For the frill cut 15cm/
6in deep strips across the width of
the fabric – three strips of 230cm/
90in wide sheeting or five strips of
narrower fabric.

Making up

Preparing the frill Join the short
sides of the strips together with
narrow seams (1cm/½in) to make
one long strip. Fold in half right
sides facing and stitch across the
two short ends 1cm/½in in.
Turn right sides out and press well.

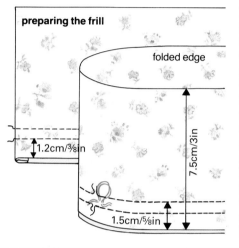

preparing the frill

folded edge

1.2cm/⅜in

1.5cm/⅝in

7.5cm/3in

Fold the strip into four and mark
the quarter sections with tailors'
tacks near the raw edges. Machine
two rows of gathering stitches along
each section, 1.2cm/⅜in and 1.5cm/
⅝in in from the double raw edge,
through both thicknesses. Gather
up to fit three sides of cover.
Continue making up as for an
adult's frilled duvet cover. If adding
an extra trimming such as piping
between the frill and one side of
the cover, tack it round the
seamline on the main cover piece,
raw edges and right sides together,
before adding the frill.

Cutting out

If using wide sheeting, cut two
main pieces of fabric each 178cm/
70in wide and 40cm/16in deep and
two strips across the width of the
fabric each 15cm/6in deep.
If using 90cm/36in wide fabric, cut
four pieces 40cm/16in deep and four
strips 15cm/6in deep, cutting each
across the width of the fabric. Join
these with 1cm/½in flat seams to
make up to the sizes of the sheeting
pieces.

Making up

Prepare the frill as for the frilled
duvet cover. Gathering it up to fit
and with raw edges together, tack
the frill around three sides of one
main piece (omitting the long
bottom edge).
Tack the wadding to the wrong side
of the other main piece and tack
tissue paper over the wadding to
prevent it catching in the machine.
Place the two main pieces together,
right sides facing and making sure

frill is pointing inwards, tack all
round the edge. Machine stitch
leaving a gap of 80cm/30in along the
bottom edge. Trim the wadding
away from the seam allowance,
remove all tacking, turn right side
out and slipstitch over the opening.
Quilt the layers of fabric and
wadding together by machine
stitching around the three frilled
sides, 7cm/3in and 10cm/4in from
the edge.
Add ribbon ties as for other bumper.

but within marked mattress area,
then complete as for fitted bed
sheets, leaving gaps for elastic
20cm/8in from corners.
N.B. If using a stretch fabric such as
stretch towelling, deduct 2.5cm/1in
from the width and length of the
mattress before marking out to give
a snug fit, and machine with a
shallow zigzag stitch.

*Right: A fitted sheet stays in place even
on a slippery, wipe-clean mattress.
Trim the corners with well-secured
ribbons or appliqué, and trim the edge of
a flat top-sheet to match.*

Cat nap with a cosy companion

Sew a super cat-shaped sleeping bag from colourful fabrics, filled with wadding, to create some bedtime fun. Any child would love to snuggle inside this cuddly cat, using its friendly face as a pillow, and it's ideal for afternoon naps or overnight visits.

This colourful cat-shaped sleeping bag makes bedtime really exciting and will persuade the most reluctant sleepy-head to lie down without any fuss. It's ideal for midday naps or to take on holiday, and becomes a reassuring companion on overnight visits to a friend.

The bag is not difficult to make. The cat's arms, legs and collar are made from colourful appliqué motifs easily attached with an iron-on backing. The friendly face is simply zigzag stitched, the head is stuffed to become a soft pillow, and a central zip makes getting in and out very easy. Both top and bottom layers of the sleeping bag are interlined with polyester wadding for warmth and comfort. The tail is optional but great fun, and the sleeping bag is completely washable.

Below: Choose bold primary colours for the cat-shaped sleeping bag, or turn the cat into a tiger or leopard by using all-over stripes or spots.

Choosing fabrics

Make the sleeping bag in a cosy knitted velour, stretch towelling or a brushed fabric. Alternatively, use a less expensive cotton or a polyester and cotton mix: the layer of wadding in both top and bottom sections will provide a reasonable amount of warmth.

You will need

5.1m/5⅝yd fabric 120cm/48in wide
65cm/¾yd contrast fabric 120cm/48in wide for legs and ears
40cm/½yd fabric 120cm/48in wide for arms
30cm/12in fabric 120cm/48in wide for collar
1.8m/2yd medium-weight polyester wadding 150cm/60in wide
2 packets iron-on Vilene Bondaweb
20cm×50cm/8in×20in lightweight iron-on Vilene
65cm/25½in heavy duty zip
Matching and contrasting threads
Small bag of polyester or cotton filling and 50cm/20in fabric 90cm/36in wide for pillow
Dressmaker's carbon paper or pencil

Making the pattern

Enlarge the pattern pieces and the face design from the grid overleaf to make paper pattern pieces. 1.5cm/⅝in seam allowances are included where necessary.

Cutting out

Fold each piece of fabric (except the wadding) in half lengthwise and pin pattern pieces to the double thickness. In this way each leg, arm, etc, will face the opposite way to its pair.

From the main fabric, cut two base pieces (inner and outer), four body pieces (one inner and one top piece facing in each direction), one upper and one lower tail piece and four ear pieces.

From the appropriate contrasting fabrics cut two legs, and two ears, two arms, and two collars.

From wadding, cut one base, two top pieces and two ears.

Cut two pieces for the pillow cover.

Making up the sleeping bag

With either tailor's tacks or chalk, mark all the points shown on the pattern pieces on to the right side of inner base and the two top body pieces.

Stitching the face Use dressmaker's carbon paper to transfer the face design to the head area on the right side of the inner base piece. Iron a piece of Vilene to the wrong side of the head, behind the marked area, to prevent puckering the fabric while stitching. Set your machine to a wide, close zigzag stitch and sew along the marked lines to make the face.

Working the appliqué

Using Bondaweb and following the manufacturer's instructions, back the small ear pieces, the collar edges, and arm and leg edges. Using the marked points as a positioning guide, lay an arm, a leg and a collar piece right side up on the right side of each top body piece. Remove the Bondaweb backing paper and iron into place. Iron each small ear to the right side of a large ear in the same way. Zigzag stitch round each of these appliquéd pieces, except along the outer edges that will lie within a seam, to prevent the fabric fraying. Use either a colour-matched or contrast thread.

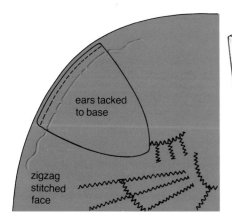

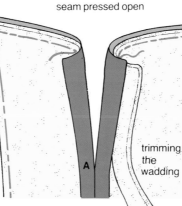

seam pressed open

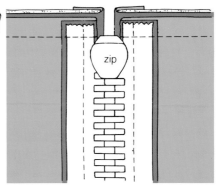

body pieces stitched along top edges

Making the ears

With right sides facing, tack and stitch each appliquéd ear to a plain ear along two long sides. Trim seams, clip into curves and turn right side out. Trim away the seam allowance from all three sides on each of the wadding ear shapes, slip inside the ears and stitch across the base of each ear to hold in place. Tack the ears, appliqué sides down and raw edges together, to the right side of the inner base.

Preparing the body

Tack the wadding pieces securely to the wrong side of inner base and the two inner body pieces.
With right sides facing, tack and stitch the two outer body pieces together from point A to the lower edge. Press the seam open and press in seam allowances from A to top edge. Join the inner body pieces together in the same way and trim wadding away from seam allowance right along the centre edge.

Insert the zip in the outer body piece between A and the top edge. **Place outer and inner body pieces** together, right sides facing, and tack and stitch along the top edges. Turn right side out and press, then slipstitch down the folded edges of the inner body pieces around the zip. Stitch 1.5cm/⅝in around the outer edge to hold both pieces together. **Trim away the wadding**, then insert a row of large gathering stitches from B to B.

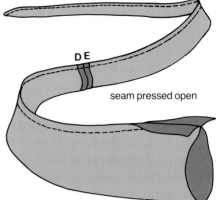

tail stitched along long edge

D E

seam pressed open

Making the tail

With right sides facing, join the tail pieces together along the E-D edge. Press the seam open then fold the tail along its length, right side in, and stitch the long edges together from the top point to the lower edge. Turn right side out, stuff firmly with filling and stitch across the lower edge of the tail to hold.

Left: No more rumpled un-made beds – the cat remains cheerful and decorative even when unoccupied!

Assembling the sleeping bag

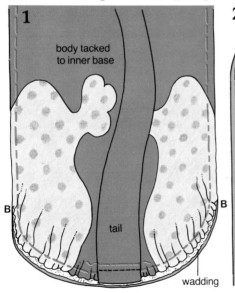

1

body tacked to inner base

B

B

tail

wadding

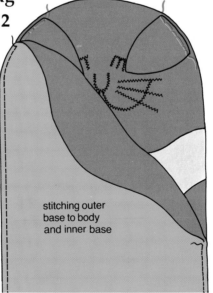

2

stitching outer base to body and inner base

1 Lay the inner side of the body on the right side of the inner base and tack the side edges together from C down to B on each side. Gather up the lower edge of the body to fit the base, matching centre points. Pin and tack securely, then tack tail to the centre of the lower edge, raw edges together.

2 Lay the outer base piece right side down on top of the inner base and body and pin together all round the edge. Tack and stitch together, leaving a gap along one side for turning through.
Remove all tacking, press well and turn right side out.

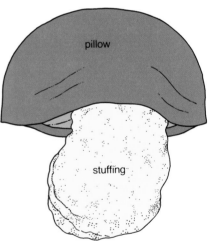

pillow

stuffing

Making the pillow

Place the two pieces of pillow cover fabric together, right sides facing, and stitch together leaving a small gap for turning through. Turn right side out, stuff with the remaining filling, and slipstitch the open edges together.

To complete the sleeping bag, slip the pillow inside the cat's head and, working from the back of the head, catch in place with a few hand stitches made just below the ears. Slipstitch the side opening to close.

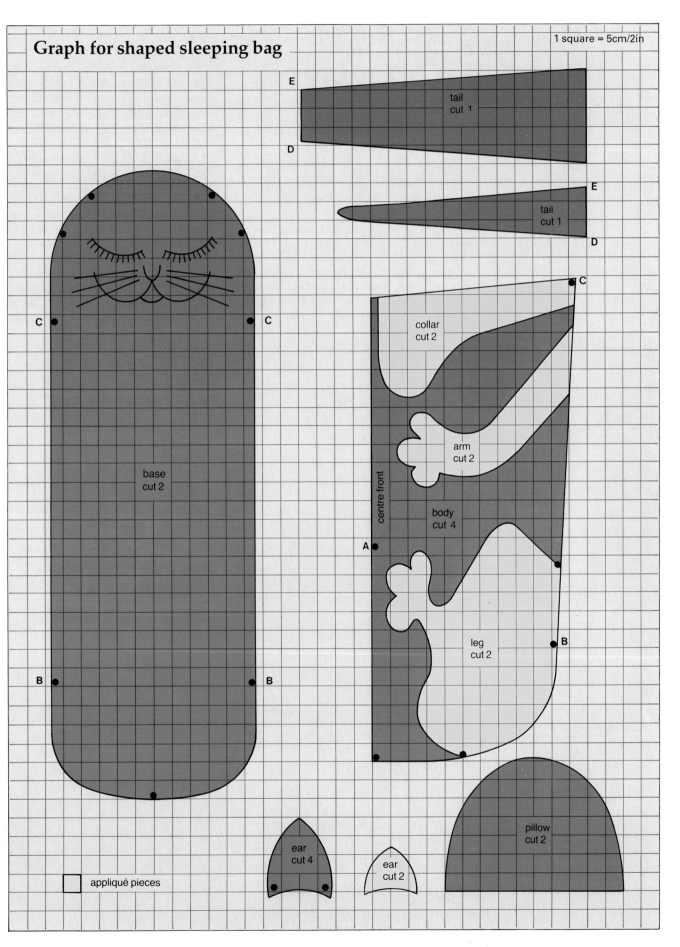

Graph for shaped sleeping bag

1 square = 5cm/2in

E
D
tail
cut 1

E
tail
cut 1
D

C

C C

base
cut 2

B B B B

centre front

A

collar
cut 2

arm
cut 2

body
cut 4

leg
cut 2

C

B

pillow
cut 2

ear
cut 4

ear
cut 2

appliqué pieces

145

Wake up to the fun of bunk bed hangings

Transform bunk beds into a play-shop or café with a simple but effective tie-on hanging. The shop-front has a window for serving through and a blind to let down at closing time! Or adapt the basic idea to create your children's favourite fantasy land.

Children will love the idea of turning their bunk beds into a shop or café, serving customers through the window or snuggling inside with the blind down at closing time! Add even more appeal with the child's own name appliquéd across the top (the sign board panel can easily be replaced if the hanging eventually passes down to younger brothers and sisters). The letters and flowers are appliquéd on to the main panel –

Vilene Bondaweb secures them in place to make stitching round the edge much easier or, with some fabrics, unnecessary. To economise, omit the Bondaweb and tack each piece firmly in place before zigzagging all round.

The dimensions of the finished hanging are 182cm×126cm/72in×49½in: measure your bunk beds and check that this will fit. Tapes or ribbons tie the hanging to the bunk bed frame and allow for some adjustment but, as the design is based on rectangular panels, it's easy to alter the size to fit almost any style of bunk bed.

Any tough cotton fabrics can be used to make the hanging, although they should be 120cm/48in wide to avoid having to adjust panel sizes. Craft cottons or inexpensive lightweight

furnishing fabrics are ideal; Laura Ashley Country Furnishing Cottons are used here. White tape is the most inexpensive for tying on the hanging, but if you have spare ribbons to hand, use these for a prettier effect. Be sure to attach tapes to the sides of the hanging on a level with the lower edge of the window as these provide the tension to keep the window flat. The basic idea of a hanging to turn night-time sleeping space into a daytime play area can be adapted to suit your child's favourite games. Follow the design ideas overleaf, or devise your own, using simple appliqué or fabric paints.

You will need
Cotton fabrics 120cm/48in wide as follows: 2.3m/2½yd floral print, 1.2m/1⅜yd rose pink, 80cm/⅞yd plum, 1.2m/1⅜yd stripe
90cm/1yd pink ribbon 5mm/¼in wide
4.5m/4⅞yd tape or ribbon for ties
20cm/7¾in medium weight iron-on interfacing
Vilene Bondaweb (optional)

Making patterns
Following the graph on page 148, in which one square equals 5cm/2in, make paper patterns for the door and window scallops, flowers and the letters you require.

Cutting out
Following the measurements in the cutting guide, page 148, cut one window panel, one side panel and two door panels from floral printed fabric. Cut a main door piece 48cm×90cm/ 19in×36in, and 28.5cm/11½in deep strips 120cm/48in and 68cm/27in long from rose pink fabric.
From striped fabric, cut a piece for the blind 70cm/27½in deep and 104cm/41in wide, two window scallops and two door scallops.
From plum fabric cut enough 3cm/ 1½in wide bias strips to make up a length of approximately 4.5m/5yd and cut a circle 7cm/3in in diameter for the door knob. Cut one window and one door scallop from interfacing omitting seam allowances.
Back some of the remaining pieces of pink and plum fabric with Bondaweb (if using) and cut two flowers and one flower centre from pink fabric, and one flower, two flower centres and 20cm/8in high letters from plum fabric.

Making up the hanging
Take 1.5cm/⅝in seam allowances (7mm/¼in and 8mm/⅜in for French seams) unless otherwise stated.
To make the door With right sides facing, tack bias strips to right side edges of each floral door panel, placing the edge of the binding 5mm/¼in in from the edge of the fabric. Machine stitch 1cm/½in in from the fabric edge (5mm/¼in in from binding edge). Leaving a 1cm/ ½in binding, fold the bias strip to the wrong side and press without turning in second raw edge.
Position floral panels on pink door piece and machine stitch from right side just inside binding to secure in place, enclosing raw edge of binding underneath panel.
Tack the doorknob in place (first slipping a little wadding underneath if you would like a three-dimensional effect), then zigzag stitch all around edge to attach.
Press a 1.5cm/⅝in turning to the wrong side all around door, then topstitch in place on floral side panel, as indicated on diagram, 7cm/2¾in above lower edge.
To add flower appliqué Removing Bondaweb backing paper, iron a flower centre on to each flower of the opposite colour. Iron flowers

Left: Disguised as a shop or café, bunk beds become an exciting, double-decked play area for 'let's pretend' games.

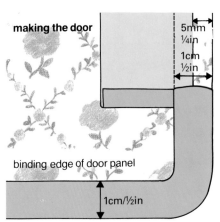

making the door

5mm
¼in

1cm
½in

binding edge of door panel

1cm/½in

into position around bottom left hand corner of hanging as illustrated and zigzag round each one for extra durability. If not using Bondaweb, tack and zigzag stitch each piece.
Place the two main floral panels together, wrong sides facing and top and bottom edges level, and join the short edges above and below window to side panel with French seams.
To hem the lower edge, press a 7cm/2¾in turning to the wrong side, turn in the raw edge by 1cm/½in and machine stitch, except across door – hem this area by hand.
To make window Bind sides and top edge of window opening with bias strips as on door panels but turning raw edge under and slipstitching. Clip diagonally towards the end of the stitching lines at lower corners.

Graph for bunk bed hanging motifs

1 square = 5cm/2in

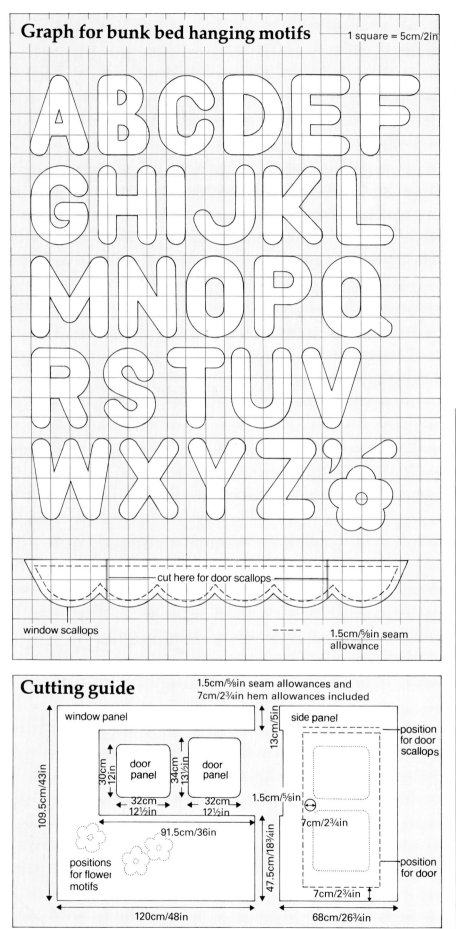

cut here for door scallops

window scallops

- - - - 1.5cm/⅝in seam allowance

Cutting guide

1.5cm/⅝in seam allowances and 7cm/2¾in hem allowances included

window panel

13cm/5in

side panel

position for door scallops

109.5cm/43in

30cm/12in | door panel

34cm/13½in | door panel

32cm/12½in

32cm/12½in

1.5cm/⅝in

7cm/2¾in

91.5cm/36in

positions for flower motifs

47.5cm/18¾in

7cm/2¾in

position for door

120cm/48in

68cm/26¾in

Completing the hanging

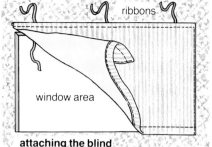

ribbons

window area

attaching the blind

Turn a narrow double hem to the wrong side down each side edge of the blind piece and machine stitch. Machine a deeper double 1.5cm/⅝in hem along lower edge.

Attaching blind With blind lying upside down away from window and right sides facing, pin raw edge of blind 2.5cm/1in above top of window. Cut three 30cm/12in lengths of ribbon and tuck under the blind so that the centre of one ribbon lies at the centre of the blind

More design ideas

Holding the fort . . . playing shops, or taking a ride on an open-topped bus. Or commanding a space-ship, driving a train or fire-engine, running a school – the possible themes for a bunk-bed hanging are endless!

Adapting the instructions for Emily's café, create your own design based on your child's favourite games, extending the hanging around two, three or even four sides of the bunk beds for a really exciting effect. Following the lines of your design, join panels of fabric – perhaps using up all those pieces left over from dressmaking and home sewing projects – to make up the basic rectangular shape. Try to use easily washable, fairly sturdy fabrics to keep the hanging flat. Alternatively use an old (but strong) sheet as the background area. Cover window areas in clear pvc.

Add design details in simple iron-on appliqué, fabric paint or embroidery. Where possible, include personalized extras such as a child's name or a picture of his or her pet.

edge and the others 20cm/8in away on either side. Stitch across blind, 8mm/³⁄₈in from edge. Fold blind downwards, press well, then stitch across top 1cm/½in down to enclose raw edge. Fold up blind, creating a gathered effect, and tie back and front ribbons to hold it.

To make the scallops Place the two door scallop pieces right sides facing and stitch along the shaped edge. Clip into the seam allowance around the curves and at the point between each scallop, turn right side out and press well. Zigzag stitch the raw edges together.

Attaching door scallops Place scallops upside down above doorway with seamline at marked position and stitch across long straight edge. Fold downwards over top of door and slipstitch sides to main panel.

Iron scalloped strip of interfacing

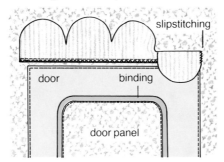

attaching door scallops

slipstitching

door   binding

door panel

to the wrong side of one of the window scallop pieces leaving seam allowance free and then stitch the two pieces together as for the doorway.

Clip and turn right side out. Place the interfaced side to the wrong side on main panel, raw edge level with lower edge of window and stitch edges together. Zigzag to neaten, then fold scallops over to lie on right side of panel and press down.

To make signboard Join short edges of the two pink strips with a French seam to make one long strip. Iron (or tack) required letters in position on right side of strip, leaving at least 2cm/1in clearance all round edge. Zigzag stitch around each letter for extra durability.

Turn a narrow double 1cm/½in hem to the wrong side along top edge and machine stitch. Join lower edge of signboard to top edge of panel with a French seam.

To complete hanging Machine stitch a narrow double hem down each side of the hanging. Cut four 70cm/30in lengths of tape or ribbon, fold in half and sew the folded edge of a tape to each top corner and to each side, level with lower edge of window. If the hanging needs further support, add more tapes as necessary.

DESIGN EXTRA

using the basic design, transform your child's bunk beds into a castle, an open top bus or a shop

Pocketed hangings for nursery or workroom

Organize a place for all sorts of oddments by making a practical wall hanging. The simpler version is hung at the end of a bunk bed so that toys and books are handy at bedtime – a gusseted variation can be adapted for use in kitchen, bathroom or study-bedroom.

A pocketed wall hanging provides an inexpensive storage unit. Make the hanging from a tough fabric chosen to tone with your room décor or to add a splash of colour. With deep gusseted pockets and wooden rods to strengthen top and bottom edges, it holds a surprising number of those annoying items that never seem to have a home.

Use it as a kitchen or bathroom organizer; to create a sewing corner; or to hold an assortment of toys, books

and magazines.

The simpler version is designed to fasten to the end of bunk beds. The bunk bed hanging has large flat pockets that provide a home for all the books and treasured possessions small children must have to hand when they are supposed to be asleep!

Choosing materials

Choose a strong, firm fabric for either of the hanging units. A closely-woven furnishing fabric or a tough

canvas is ideal.

If you are using a fabric narrower than 106cm/42in wide, the pockets must be cut lengthwise and turned to fit across the width of the backing fabric. For this reason choose a plain fabric or one with a pattern which can be turned sideways for the wall hanging.

On a wider fabric, the pockets are cut across the width and there are no pattern limitations.

Neaten the pocket tops and edges

with fold-over braid that is already pressed in half widthways, ready to slip over the raw edge of the fabric. The straps on the bunk bed hanging loop round the bed frame, fastening with large press studs. Button snaps, available from haberdashery shops, give a neater, more professional finish than ordinary press studs. They are quicker to attach – simply clip them to the fabric with the special pliers. These snaps come in a range of colours.

Pocketed bunk bed hanging

Encourage children to keep their room tidy with this fabric storage unit fastened to the end of their beds. Measure the bunk beds before buying any fabric and make size alterations if necessary (see below).

Variations on size

Dimensions given throughout these instructions produce a finished width and length of 73cm/28¾in (excluding straps). Check these measurements against your own bunk beds before buying any fabric. If a slightly greater width or length of hanging would be more appropriate, adjust the measurements and fabric quantities given below.

To simplify this, cut the backing fabric to the larger size but make all the pockets to the size given and centre them on the backing fabric. This gives a wider gap between the pockets and the edges of the hanging, and saves a lot of work when re-calculating fabric requirements.

To make your hanging shorter or narrower, alter the size of the backing fabric as required and reduce pocket sizes to fit.

Twelve straps hold the hanging securely in place by looping round the frame of the bunk bed and fastening with press studs. The length of these will depend on the design of the bed and whether it is made of chunky wood or slim tubular metal. To calculate the length of side straps, measure the width of the bed plus the distance needed to wrap a strap around the upright strut and fasten to itself at each side. Deduct the 73cm/28¾in width of the hanging from this figure and divide the remainder in half to give the finished length of each strap. Add 3cm/1¼in seam allowances.

Measuring vertically, calculate the required length of the top and bottom straps in the same way. Again add 3cm/1¼in seam allowances.

You will need

1.8m/2yd of fabric 90cm/36in wide or 1.3m/1½yd of fabric 120cm/48in wide
3m/3½yd seam binding in matching shade
4m/4½yd fold-over braid in a contrast colour
Matching thread
12 large heavy-duty snap fasteners with tool for attaching

Cutting out

Make pattern following layouts on page 154 or, using tailor's chalk, draw straight on to the wrong side of the fabric. Cut out:
One 76cm/30in square for backing
One rectangle 63cm×30cm/ 24¾in×11¾in for bottom pocket
Two rectangles each 26.5cm×20cm/ 10½in×7¾in for top pockets
Twelve strips each 13cm/5in wide times required length for straps.
Seam allowances are included where necessary.

Making up

Fold in the seam allowance round the edge of the backing fabric when positioning the bound pockets.
Making the pockets Tack fold-over braid all round the edge of each pocket piece, mitring the corners for neatness (see page 164).
Working from the right side, topstitch around the edge of the braid, stitching through all layers.
Tack the bottom pocket to the right side of the backing fabric 5cm/2in from the bottom and side edges.
Tack the two top pockets 10cm/4in

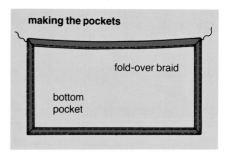

making the pockets

fold-over braid

bottom
pocket

above the bottom pocket, with the outer side edges 5cm/2in in from the backing fabric edges. Topstitch in place.
Making the straps Fold each strap in half lengthwise, right sides facing, and stitch down the length and across one short side, taking 1.5cm/⅝in seam allowance. Trim the seam allowance to 1cm/½in, clip corners and turn through.
Position the straps on the right side of the backing fabric, raw edges together. Place one strap in the centre of each edge and 7.5cm/3in from each corner. Tack and machine stitch the straps in place, sewing 5mm/¾in and 1cm/½in from the raw edges.
With right sides facing, pin the seam binding all round the edge of the backing fabric, 1cm/½in from the edge and enclosing strap ends. Tack and stitch 5mm/¼in from the binding edge. Clip across corners, press the binding and seam allowances on to the wrong side of the backing fabric, and tack. Press straps away from fabric and topstitch on the right side all round close to edge and again 1cm/½in in.
Adding the snap fasteners Wrap the straps of the hanging around the frame of the bunk beds, and pin to hold. Mark the position of the snap fasteners, remove and attach a fastener to each strap, following the manufacturer's instructions.

Design ideas for pockets

Pocketed wallhanging

Lengths of wooden dowelling threaded through the top and bottom hems keep this hanging unit in shape. Trim the pockets with a contrasting fold-over braid, ribbon or straight tape.

You will need

2.4m/2¾yd of fabric 90cm/36in wide *or* 2.1m/2⅜yd of fabric 120cm/48in wide
3.1m/3⅜yd of braid 2.5cm/1in wide when folded in half widthways
Matching thread
170cm/67in of 2cm/¾in dowel
2 small screw eyes
110cm/44in cord or lightweight rope for hanging

Cutting out and preparing fabric

Using a ruler and tailor's chalk and following the diagram overleaf mark out the pattern pieces on the wrong side of the fabric. Cut out one backing piece 90cm×122cm/35½in×48in, two pieces each 106cm×21.5cm/42in×8½in for top

Making up the hanging

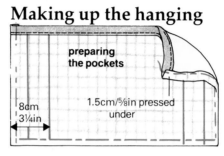

Turn a double hem (1cm/½in and 1.5cm/⅝in) to the wrong side down both long edges of the backing fabric piece and machine stitch.
Preparing the pockets Place a length of fold-over braid over the top (long) edge of each pocket piece and machine stitch in place, catching down both edges of the braid at once.
Work from the right side and leave the braid edges raw at both ends. Press 1.5cm/⅝in to the wrong side round the three remaining edges of each pocket piece and tack down securely. Chalk vertical lines 4cm/1½in and 8cm/3¼in in from the side edges on each pocket piece.

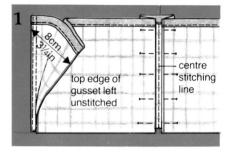

Making the bottom pocket

Fold the prepared piece in half, short ends together, and mark the centre foldline on the right side of the fabric with tailor's chalk.
Open out and place the base edge of the pocket on the *second* chalk line up from the bottom of the backing fabric, matching the centre vertical lines.
Tack and stitch the pocket to the backing fabric along the centre line, then draw a chalk line 8cm/3¼in away on either side of the stitching. Fold the fabric along these two chalk lines, butt the folded edges together along the central stitching line as though forming an inverted

Making the two middle pockets

Fold along the chalk lines at each side to form the gusset pleats and press well.
Draw a chalk line across the width of the backing fabric, 12cm/4¾in above the bottom pockets and place the lower edge of the middle pockets along this line. Position them so that the outer edges are in line with those of the bottom pocket. Tack and stitch the side edges of the pockets and then the lower edge in the same way as for the bottom pocket.

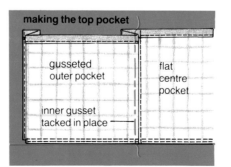

Making the top pocket The pocket piece is divided into three to give a flat centre pocket 15cm/6in wide with a gusseted pocket on each side. Move the vertical stitching lines to adjust the pocket sizes to

suit your requirements.
Draw a chalk line across the width of the backing fabric, 12cm/4½in up from the middle pockets.
Fold the strips of pocket fabric in half, short ends together, and draw a chalk line along the fold on the right side of the fabric. Open the fabric flat and draw a chalk line 7.5cm/3in each side of the centre foldline to mark stitching lines for a central pocket, 15cm/6in wide.
Position the lower edge of the pocket along the chalk line on the backing fabric, matching the centre lines, and tack. Topstitch down the vertical lines to form the central

Right: Patterned pockets add a lively touch to plain fabric.

and bottom pockets, and two pieces each 49cm×26.5cm/19¼in×10½in for middle pockets.
On the right side of the backing fabric piece, draw a chalk line down the exact centre of the fabric from top to bottom. Draw a horizontal line 6cm/2¼in down from the top of the fabric, a second one 6cm/2¼in up from the bottom edge, and one 7cm/2¾in above this.

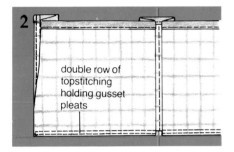

double row of
topstitching
holding gusset
pleats

pleat, and pin in place. The pleats give depth to the pockets.
1 Form gussets on the outer edges of the pockets by folding along the 8cm/3¼in marked lines and then, pleating the fabric back on itself, along the 4cm/1½in lines. Press well and tack the side edges of the pockets to the backing fabric, leaving the top folded edge free. Machine stitch with a double row of top stitching close to the edges.
2 Pin and tack the bottom edge of the pockets to the backing fabric, this time stitching through all layers of gusset pleats. Machine stitch with a double row of topstitching and remove tackings.

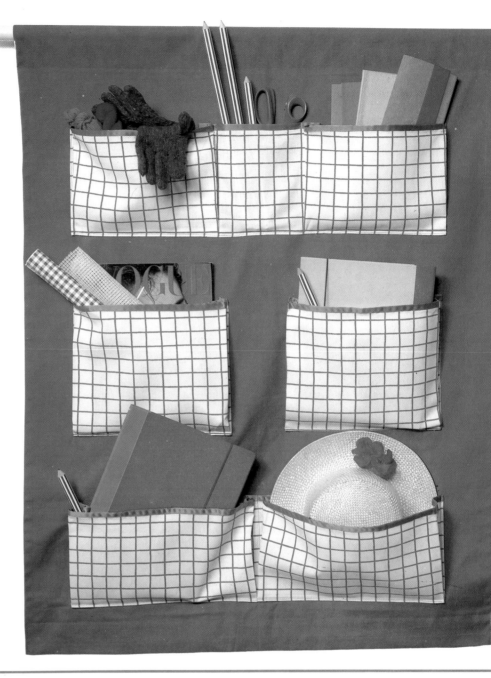

pocket.
Draw a line 8cm/3¼in outside each of the stitched lines. Fold along these and the chalk lines on the outer edge to form the gussets for the two outer pockets; press well and tack the inner gusset pleats in place.
Tack and double topstitch the side edges of the pocket to the backing fabric, keeping the top folded edge free. Sew a double row of topstitching along the lower edge of the pockets through all layers of fabric, as for the bottom pocket.

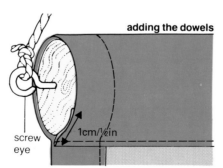

adding the dowels

screw
eye

1cm/½in

Adding the dowel rods
The dowel rods top and bottom give the fabric extra weight and help it to hang straight and flat.
Press 1cm/½in to the wrong side along top and bottom edges of the

hanging. Fold along the top chalk line marked on the backing fabric, turning the area above this to the wrong side. Tack in place and stitch close to the turned in edge to make a casing for the dowel (do not stitch side edges).
Make a casing on the bottom edge in the same way, this time stitching across one end.
Cut two pieces of dowel each 82cm/32¼in long. Insert a screw eye into each end of one piece, gently ease it into the top casing and tie each end of the cord through a screw eye.
Slip the other dowel into the bottom casing and stitch open end together.

Practical pockets

Create a variety of different pock-eted storage units by adapting the instructions for either of the two hangings. Adjust the size of the backing fabric, the arrangement of the pockets and the method of hanging to suit your needs. Use the making up instructions in this chapter as a basic guide to construction.

Choose a fabric that will be appropriate for the purpose of the storage unit – washable, prettily printed, or waterproof – but make sure that it is not too bulky if you wish to have gusseted, rather than flat, pockets.

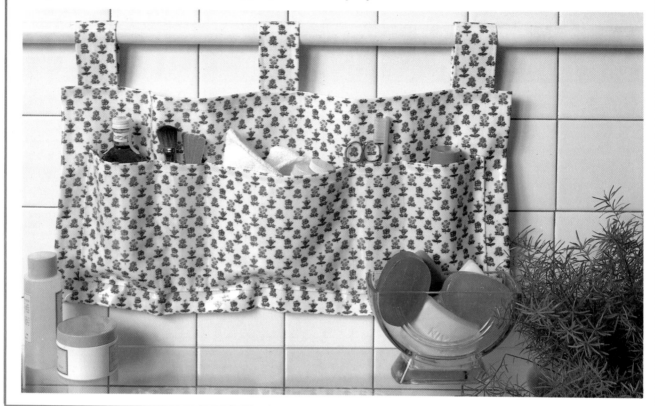

Cutting layouts for pocketed hanging

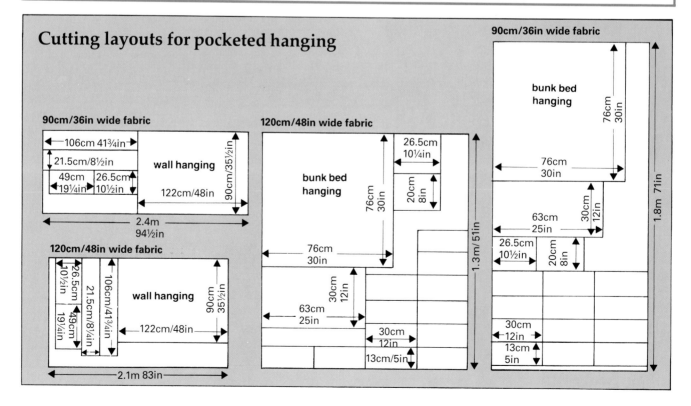

90cm/36in wide fabric

wall hanging
122cm/48in

106cm 41¾in
21.5cm/8½in
49cm 19¼in · 26.5cm 10½in
90cm/35½in
2.4m 94½in

120cm/48in wide fabric

wall hanging
122cm/48in

26.5cm 10½in
21.5cm/8½in
49cm 19¼in
106cm/41¾in
90cm 35½in
2.1m 83in

120cm/48in wide fabric

bunk bed hanging

26.5cm 10¼in
76cm 30in
20cm 8in
76cm 30in
30cm 12in
63cm 25in
30cm 12in
13cm/5in
1.3m/51in

90cm/36in wide fabric

bunk bed hanging

76cm 30in
76cm 30in
63cm 25in
30cm 12in
26.5cm 10½in
20cm 8in
30cm 12in
13cm 5in
1.8m 71in

PART 5

Kitchen and tablewear

Matching sets of tablelinen can be expensive to buy and the colour and pattern you are looking for may not be available. Save money by making your own, tailored to your requirements or make them as a gift for a friend. Several useful sewing techniques are introduced in the following chapters – learn how to add a bound edge trim, a frilled or flounced edge and a shaped appliqué border to cloths, mats or napkins.

A tablecloth which has been designed for a particular table will have the correct amount of drop all round to suit its proportions and the way it is used. Circular tablecloths in particular, whether short or full length, need careful marking out and joining of widths of fabric. Finally, a fitted cloth, made to measure, can transform an old table whatever its shape, and an added topcloth gives a fashionable layered look for a more formal room.

Choosing fabrics for tablelinen

Look in both the dressmaking and furnishing departments for suitable fabrics, checking that they are washable and colourfast. Polyester cotton and seersucker are ideal for tablecloths and napkins as they require minimum ironing. For a more traditional fabric choose fine linen, damask or lace.

Create an original fabric to match your colour scheme with simple machine patchwork, and make use of wadding and ready-quilted fabrics to insulate or to help withstand heat for items such as oven gloves, tea cosies or place mats.

Kitchen companions

Hands burned by the oven, a dress splashed with hot fat, cold tea in the pot – these are easily avoidable mishaps if you have the right protection. Follow these simple instructions and make this inexpensive set of oven gloves, pot holder, apron and tea-cosy.

Ideal as a gift for a friend, or to make for your own home, this kitchen set of apron, oven gloves, pot holder and tea-cosy is very easy to sew, economical on material and, depending on your choice of fabric, can add a splash of colour or a flourish of pattern (or indeed both) to the kitchen. The set looks particularly good when made up to match your kitchen decor.

When you're buying a fabric to make up this set, choose an easily washable (preferably machine-washable) fabric and use insulating material that is washable too because the apron, oven gloves and pot holder, and to a lesser extent the tea-cosy, are items that will come in constant contact with kitchen spills. You can use either furnishing or dress-weight fabric but a cotton or cotton/polyester mix provides an ideal weight of fabric that is easy to launder and quick to iron.

The edges are trimmed with bias binding to give a neat finish. To emphasize this binding you can pick up one of the colours from the fabric or, if you're using a plain fabric, choose a contrasting binding for a really striking two-tone effect.

Bibbed apron

The apron, easy to cut out and make up, has seven pattern pieces and is simply a skirt piece of fabric gathered in to fit a waistband with a bib.

The apron fits most sizes. To adjust the length of the apron skirt, measure from your waist to the required length and compare this measurement with the 60cm/23½in (57cm/22½in when hemmed) length of the skirt pattern piece. If you want to alter the length of the skirt, add extra to the pattern when cutting out, or cut off some of the paper pattern for a shorter skirt.

The neckband on the cutting layout is quite generous so once you have tacked the neckband in place on the bib, you should slip it over your head and hold the bottom of the bib to your waistline. If the band is too long, adjust it to fit, cut off the surplus and re-tack the band in place.

Alternatively, if you prefer to have a neckband which opens at the back, make sure you cut the neckband long enough to allow you to cut it in the middle, neaten the raw edges and add a small piece of Velcro for a quick and easy fastening.

You will need

80cm/⅞yd of 120cm/48in wide fabric
  or 120cm/1¼yd of 90cm/36in fabric
Matching thread
170cm/1⅞yd of 25mm/1in bias binding

Right: The apron with its full skirt and bib protects clothes from household spills and makes a co-ordinating kitchen set with the padded oven gloves, tea-cosy and pot holder.

Cutting out the apron

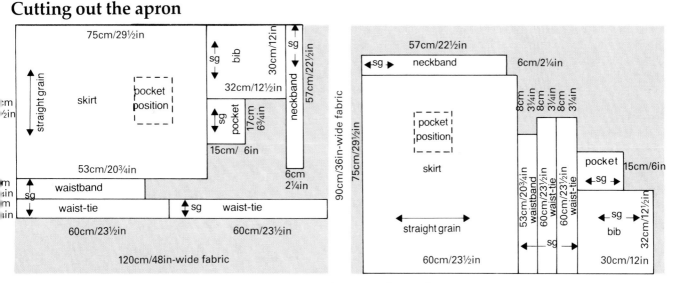

Cut out the pattern pieces in paper following the dimensions given on the cutting layout. Label each pattern piece and mark the straight-grain arrows as shown.
Place the paper pattern pieces on the fabric following the cutting layout for either the 120cm/48in or 90cm/36in fabric. All arrows should lie in the same direction (parallel to selvedges) to ensure that the design of the fabric is the correct way up for each piece.
If you feel confident, miss out the paper pattern stage and draw the pattern pieces directly on to the fabric with tailor's chalk. Cut out the pattern pieces in fabric.

Making up the apron

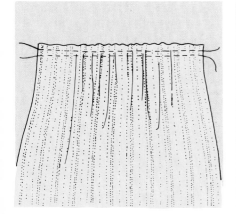

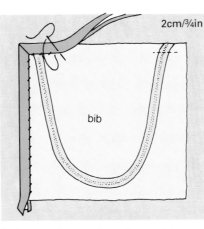

Neaten the edges on the sides and bottom of the skirt piece by sewing a double hem. Turn 5mm/¼in of the fabric to the wrong side, tack in position and turn a further 1cm/½in to wrong side. Tack and stitch hem by machine or slip stitch by hand. Remove tacking.
On each waist-tie, neaten one short edge with a double hem as for the skirt.
Join a waist-tie to each side of the waistband with a 1.5cm/⅝in seam.
1 Stitch two rows of hand gathering stitches or very large machine stitches across the top of the skirt. Pull up the gathering threads until the top of the skirt fits the long edge of the waistband and the gathers are evenly distributed. With right sides

facing, tack together. Sew with a 1.5cm/⅝in seam and remove the tacking and gathering threads. Neaten the long edges of the neckband with a double hem, as for the skirt.
2 With wrong sides facing, position the ends of the neckband on the raw edge of the top of the bib, 2cm/¾in in from the side edges. Tack in place. Neaten the sides and top of the bib raw edges with bias binding (see page 163), taking care to catch only the short ends of the neckband in the binding stitching line.
3 Neatly hand stitch both ends of the neckband to the reverse side of the bias trim to give added strength.

4 With tailor's chalk mark the centre point of the waistband and centre of the bib. With right sides facing, place the raw edge of the bib on the waistband, matching up the centre marks. Tack together and stitch with 1.5cm/⅝in seams. Remove tacking.
Neaten the top raw edges of bib and waistband together by turning in 5mm/¼in then 1cm/½in and topstitching down. Continue neatening along top edge of waist-ties. Neaten skirt and waistband edges together similarly and continue along both edges of ties. Neaten raw edges of pocket with bias binding. Tack pocket in position on skirt, topstitch round sides and bottom and remove tacking.

All-in-one oven gloves

These gloves are made up of a palm piece for each hand joined by a continuous backing piece. They are well padded with insulating material to protect your hands and so make lifting hot and heavy dishes safe.

The fabric you choose for the gloves and the insulating material must be washable and you should check the heat resistance of the insulating material beforehand. Polyester wadding does not give sufficient heat resistance, but one or two layers of blanket (you could cut up an old one) or flannel are suitable.

To test if a fabric is heat resistant, turn the oven up to full and, with the oven glove fabric wrapped round the insulating fabric, use the 'mocked up' glove to lift a dish out of the oven. One word of caution though – lift the dish very carefully and make sure there is somewhere very close to put the dish down, because if your chosen insulating material is not up to scratch, you don't want to find out by dropping the hot dish.

You will need
40cm/½yd of 120cm/48in wide fabric
  or 60cm/⅝yd of 90cm/36in fabric
Matching thread
2.25m/2½yd of 25mm/1in bias binding
1 piece of insulating fabric 72cm × 18cm/28in × 7in and 2 pieces 22cm × 18cm/9in × 7in

Cutting out and making up the oven gloves

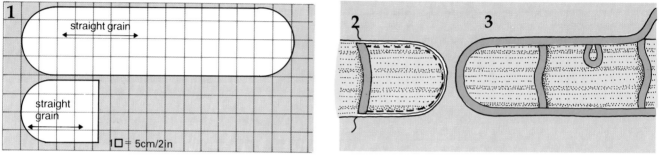

1 Cut out the pattern pieces in paper by enlarging them up from the graph. To enlarge the graph, draw up the same number of squares as the graph, but with each square equal to 5cm/2in, or use dressmaker's graph paper.
Working one square at a time, transfer the design detail from the graph to the larger version.
Mark the straight-grain arrow on each pattern piece.
Cut out two backing pieces and four palm pieces in fabric. All straight-grain pattern arrows should lie in the same direction.
Cut out one backing and two palm pieces in insulating material.
Wrong sides facing, lay the two fabric backing pieces together and slip the matching piece of insulating material between the two layers. Tack all three layers together.
Take two of the fabric palm pieces and place wrong sides facing. Slip a matching piece of insulating material between the two layers and tack all three layers together.
Repeat for the other palm pieces.
Neaten the straight edges of both the palm pieces with bias binding (see page 163) but, after stitching along the first fold of the binding and before turning binding over the raw edge, carefully trim away the excess insulating material from the seam. There is no need to neaten the ends of the binding.
2 Place these palm pieces on the backing, as shown above and tack, except along the bound edges.
3 To make a hanging loop, cut a piece of bias binding 10cm/4in long and fold in half lengthwise, wrong sides facing (raw edges are pre-folded to the wrong side). Top stitch the open edge through all layers. Mark the centre point of the oven gloves with a pin on the raw edge. Place the two raw ends of the binding loop 1cm/½in either side of pin with loop lying inwards. Tack loop ends in place and remove pin. Stitch bias binding all round the outer edge of the oven gloves (see pages 163-164) trimming surplus insulating material from the seam and notching the curve before completing the binding. Remove all tacking.

Pot and kettle holder

Made from just two squares of fabric with insulating material between, this pot holder fits snugly into the palm of the hand and wraps round the pot handle.
The loop allows you to hang it up in the kitchen at a convenient point close to the stove (but not too close because of the obvious fire risks).

You will need
2 pieces of fabric 20cm/8in square
Matching thread
1 piece of insulating material (see oven gloves) 20cm/8in square
110cm/1¼yd of 25mm/1in bias binding

Cutting out the pot holder
Cut out two pieces of fabric 20cm/8in square and one piece of insulating material 20cm/8in square.

Making up the pot holder
Sandwich the piece of insulating material between the wrong sides of the two pieces of fabric and tack.

Make a hanging loop in bias binding as for the oven gloves and tack each end of this loop to one corner, 2cm/¾in out from the corner point in each direction. Sew bias binding all round the outside edges, as for the oven gloves, taking care to catch no more than the loop ends in the stitching. Remove tacking.

Right: The quick and easy pot holder protects against hot pan handles.

Simple padded tea-cosy

Cut from a basic pattern shape, the front and front lining are cut as one piece, and the back and its lining cut to the same size.

Each piece of fabric is folded in half and a piece of wadding slipped between. The folded edges form the base of the cosy, giving it a plump look and allowing it to sit snugly on the table. The two 'sandwiches' are stitched together round the sides and the raw edges are trimmed with bias binding which co-ordinates with the trim on the other kitchen accessories. This method of cutting the main fabric and lining in one piece means that the lining fabric is upside down on the inside of the cosy. If you have chosen a fabric that has a very definite one-way pattern, and do not want this to be upside down inside the cosy, see the Professional Touch below.

The shape and dimensions given for this tea-cosy are for an average sized cosy, but do measure your own teapot before cutting out, and adjust the sizes for height and width if necessary.

You will need
60cm/⅝yd of 90cm/36in wide fabric
30cm/⅜yd of 90cm/36in wide
  polyester wadding (8oz weight)
Matching thread
150cm/1⅝yd of 25mm/1in bias binding

Cutting out and making up the tea-cosy

1 Cut out the pattern piece in paper enlarging it from the graph, as for the oven gloves, so that each square on the pattern measures 5cm/2in. Placing the straight line of the paper pattern on the fold of the fabric, cut out twice in fabric. Open out the fabric and mark the foldline with tailor's chalk.

Cut out the same shape once in wadding. Open out the wadding and cut in half along the fold.

2 Fold one piece of fabric, wrong sides facing, along the foldline and slip a piece of wadding between. Tack together round the outer edges (except the straight folded edge). Repeat for the other half. Lay the two tacked 'sandwiches' on top of each other and tack together round the outer edges (except the straight folded edges).

Neaten the tacked edges by attaching bias binding, as for the oven gloves. Neaten the ends of the binding by turning 5mm/¼in to the wrong side before stitching. Remove tacking.

Right: The tea-cosy, well padded with wadding, sits snugly on the table top.

1 1 square = 5cm/2in

2 fold

Matching the fabric design inside and out

To make a cosy with the pattern the correct way up inside and out, use the same paper pattern but on a single thickness of fabric. Cut four pieces of fabric to the pattern shape, all with the design the same way up, adding 1.5cm/⅝in to each bottom edge.

Right sides facing, sew two pieces together along the straight edge with a 1.5cm/⅝in seam and repeat with the other two pieces. Continue to make up in the same way as the cosy with the folded bottom edge.

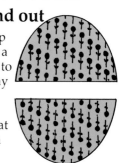

Take notice of pinboards

*Make a bright pinboard or a notice board criss-crossed with
tape to hang in the hall, kitchen,
children's room or study to display all the important dates,
messages, lists and telephone numbers
that are otherwise so easily lost or forgotten.*

Easily made in an evening, a handy notice board can transform hectic family life into a model of streamlined efficiency! Simply cover insulation board in felt and add brightly-coloured drawing pins to make a quick, inexpensive pinboard in whatever size you choose. If you prefer a fabric-covered board – or to avoid pins – add diagonal lines of tape or ribbon, held with map pins, and simply slip items behind them. Either way, you'll always have somewhere safe and constantly visible to put lists of dates to remember, notices of things to do, bills to be paid, children's paintings, favourite pictures or postcards and your New Year Resolutions!

Choosing materials

The fabric Felt is the ideal material for covering a notice board. It lasts far longer than a woven fabric, being able to withstand the sharp points of drawing pins and map pins which soon damage woven threads. It also has the advantage of needing no neatening of edges, as they do not fray, and is available in a wide range of colours and in different widths up to about 180cm/72in. This last is important as joins are best avoided when covering a notice board: because the fabric is pulled taut over the backing board, seams show up rather badly. However, tough loosely-woven fabrics such as hessian may also be used, as pins tend to slip between rather than through the threads. And if you particularly wish to use a furnishing fabric to co-ordinate a notice board with a room scheme (or to economize), use diagonal lines of tape to hold items in place and avoid the damaging effect of pins being constantly moved around.

The board you choose must be soft enough for pushing pins into but not so soft (such as polystyrene) that the surface will soon break up. It should be light enough to hang easily and thick enough to take the full length of a drawing pin or map pin stem (take a pin with you when buying the board to check).

Insulation board has all the necessary qualities and, if your retailer will not cut it to size for you, can be cut to the exact required size with a fine tenon saw or even a sharp craft knife.

Some brand-name boards – often sold specifically for notice boards – have a slightly textured, protective finish to give longer wear. Less expensive, ordinary insulation board will be just as durable if given a quick coat of emulsion paint on back, front and sides, although it can be used as it is.

You will need

Insulation board cut to required size
Felt 5cm/2in larger all round than board *or* fabric 5cm/2in larger all round than board and neatened all round edge
Drawing pins *or* fine metal tacks *or* staple gun and staples
Straight tape to criss-cross board and map pins (optional)
Screw-in hanging ring or 2 rings and picture cord
Picture hook attached to wall

Right: Bright red felt and black and white ribbons create a strong, dramatic colour scheme. Although cotton tape is less expensive, glossy satin ribbons increase the eye-catching effect.

---

a selection of brightly coloured felts and ribbons

Making up the pinboard

Place the felt or fabric right side down on a table or the floor and position the board centrally on top, right side down, with an even border of fabric all round.
Wrap one edge of felt to wrong side of board and secure with a drawing pin or staple in the centre. Pulling fabric taut, secure the centre of the opposite side and then of remaining two sides in the same way.
Working outwards from the centre, on each side in turn, and keeping the fabric perfectly flat, add further pins or staples at about 5cm/2in intervals to within 20cm/8in or so from each corner.

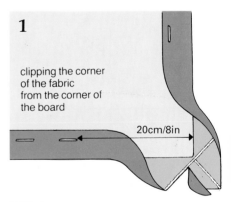

clipping the corner of the fabric from the corner of the board

20cm/8in

Mitring corners

1 On the wrong side of felt or fabric, draw a diagonal line from the corner of the board to the corner of the fabric. Measuring along the line from corner of board mark with a cross the depth of the board plus 5mm/¼in and cut off corner of fabric at this point.

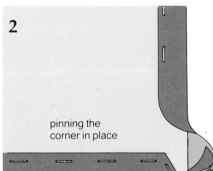

2

pinning the
corner in place

2 Wrap cut edge of fabric over board so that marked cross lies in the corner and hold temporarily with a pin. Fold in the two sides of fabric to meet down the corner of board and secure one side to back of board with as many pins or staples as necessary.

Because of the thickness of the board, you will need to make an extra small tuck in the second side to prevent an 'ear' of fabric protruding beyond the corner. Mitre each corner in turn until all four are neatly finished and the fabric is well secured all round.

Attaching the tapes

Lay the first tape in position running diagonally across the right side of pinboard just below opposite corners (so that tape doesn't have to wrap over point of corner) and, leaving a 5cm/2in extension at each end, cut to fit. Keeping tape taut and flat, wrap ends round to wrong side of board, turn under raw ends by 1cm/½in and pin or staple in place. Attach further tapes running parallel to the first in the same way,

spacing them according to the size of your board – about 15cm/6in apart on an average, medium-sized board. When all tapes running in the one direction are in place, repeat in the opposite direction. Place a drawing pin at each point where the tapes cross one another.

Hanging the board

On smaller boards, screw in a metal picture-hanging ring, slightly below the centre of the top edge, and hang from a picture hook. On larger boards, attach two hanging rings, positioning each one approximately a quarter of the way down and a quarter of the way in from the sides. Tie a length of cord between the two rings.

Tablecloth, mats and matching napkins

To complement both china and furnishings, a tablecloth, placemat and napkin set is quick and easy to sew. To add colour contrast, the edges of the cloth and mats can be trimmed with bias binding, and the napkins made in a plain colour.

Whether you create family meals most of the time or entertain regularly, you'll still be keen to put on a good show with a table setting.

A square or rectangular tablecloth always looks handsome and helps to unify the look of a table and will also cover up a worn table top. If possible, choose a washable fabric that requires a minimum of ironing.

Placemats can be used on their own or can be teamed with a tablecloth and laundered separately if the cloth itself is not soiled.

Napkins should be a generous size to give plenty of cover. Bear in mind that reversible fabrics look better than fabrics only printed on one side.

Colour planning

The fabric chosen for the tablecloth and mats (photographed right) is a good example of the versatility of table-linen in colour co-ordination. It is checked in primary colours on a white background and the edges of the cloth and placemats are finished with bright blue bias binding, picking up one of the primary colours from the checks. The napkins are made in a plain blue to match the blue on the main fabric and to co-ordinate with the bias binding trim.

All corners on the checked tablecloth and placemats are mitred to give a neat accurate 90° square without bulkiness. Alternatively, corners can be rounded and edged with bias binding, or can be finished with a turned-under hem.

As another variation, the placemats can be made up in a ready-quilted fabric to give a softer look. (Polyester wadding used in ready quilted fabrics gives only minimal heat insulation, so use cork mats underneath with hot plates.) Napkins can be made up in plain fabric and trimmed round the edges with bias binding cut from strips of the same fabric used for the cloth, mats or other furnishings.

Remember when using a fabric tablecloth and fabric placemats that the fabric will not protect your table from hot dishes and plates. With tablecloths you need a layer of heat-resistant protective material such as an old blanket or Bulgomme (heat resistant rubberised cotton) between the cloth and table top.

Measuring up

The tablecloth Measure your table top and add an overhang all round. As a rule the cloth should overhang the table to the height of the chair seats.

In many cases, especially if you have a family-sized dining table, standard-width furnishing fabrics are not wide enough to make a cloth without a fabric join. For a centre seam, join two fabric widths together with a flat seam, and cut an equal amount from each width to make up the cloth size so that the seam lies exactly across the centre of the table. Alternatively, to avoid bumps on the table top, join the fabric with a whole width in the centre and a part width either side.

With the bias binding method of finishing raw edges, you need not add any seam allowance to the cloth measurements. For hemmed edges, add 2cm/¾in all round.

Placemats should either be large enough to take a complete place setting or just a dinner plate. (Plates are usually 25cm/10in diameter, but measure your own.) For raw edges finished with bias binding, you need not add any seam allowances, but for hemmed mats, add 2cm/¾in all round to placemat measurements.

Napkins can be any size but 30cm/12in is a good standard size. Add 2cm/¾in all round the napkin for a hem.

The bias binding Measure all round adding 2.5cm/1in for joining.

Right: The tablecloth and placemats have been made up in the same fabric and are trimmed with co-ordinating bias binding. The napkins match the binding.

Below: This placemat, trimmed with bias binding and co-ordinated with a plain-coloured napkin, is large enough to accommodate a dinner plate and cutlery.

Attaching bias binding to straight edges

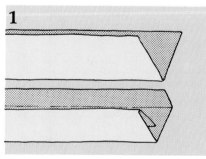

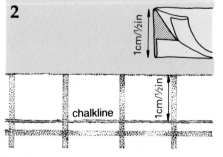

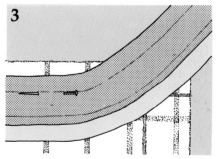

These instructions are for 25mm/
1in-width bias binding which is the
most suitable for trimming
tablecloths and mats.
1 Fold the bias binding in half along
the length, wrong sides facing. On
each long raw edge turn 5mm/¼in to
wrong side. Press. (Most commercial

bias bindings are pre-pressed in this
way, and you only need to complete
this step when you make your own
bias binding strips.)
2 Measure between the centre fold
line and one of the outer fold lines.
Using this figure, measure in from
the raw edge of the mat or cloth and

chalk a line along the right side of the
fabric at this depth.
3 Lay the fabric and bias binding
right sides facing, pinning one outer
edge fold line of the binding to the
chalk-marked line on the fabric.
Pin along one side of the
square/rectangle to the corner.

Mitring square corners with bias binding

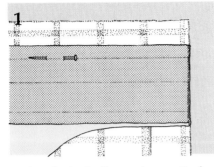

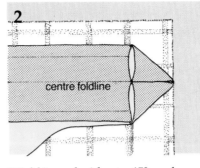

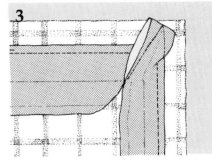

With tailor's chalk, mark a vertical line on the bias binding to correspond with the raw edge of the fabric corner. Unpin a few centimetres of binding.
1 Right sides facing, fold the binding along the line you've marked.

2 Fold in each side at a 45° angle, on to the centre fold line. Press and then open out again.
3 Hand sew along the pressed lines. Pin binding to fabric as far as chalk-marked corner on fabric. Turn corner, making sure none of the

corner binding is trapped. Continue pinning, mitring each corner, then tack. If binding needs joining, tack to within 5cm/2in of join.
4 To join the two ends of the binding, cut one end of binding to a 45° angle. Butt the other end of binding to the

Finishing curved corners with bias binding

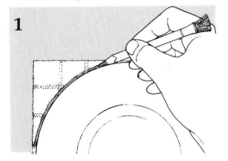

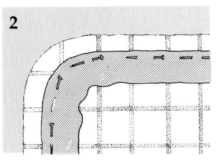

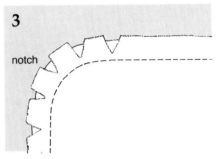

1 To make a rounded corner on a mat experiment by drawing round drinking glasses or saucers to get the curve you want. For a tablecloth, a dinner plate will give a larger curve.
2 Pin the bias to the raw edges of the mat or cloth in the same way as for the square-edged mats but, on the

corners, gently ease the binding to follow the shape of the curve. (Because this binding is cut on the bias (cross) of the fabric, it has a natural stretch which allows it to be eased into shape.) Tack in place, then sew. Remove tacking.

3 If the curve of the fabric is very tight, notch the main fabric almost to the stitching line to give more stretch to the fabric.
Continue to attach the binding in the same way as for the square-edged mats.

Cutting your own binding

Commercially produced bias binding comes in a wide range of plain colours but, if you want a specific colour or pattern to tone with your other furnishings, you can cut bias strips from fabric, and join the strips to make a continuous length of bias binding.
1 To find the bias (cross) of the fabric, lay the piece of fabric flat and fold over one corner at a 45° angle to the selvedge (or lengthwise grain of the fabric). The diagonal fold line is the bias.

Left: The placemat is made in ready-quilted fabric for extra body and the napkins edged with matching bias strips.

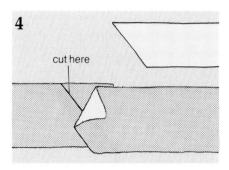

4

cut here

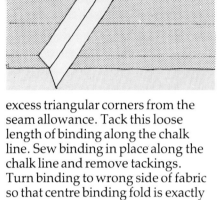

5

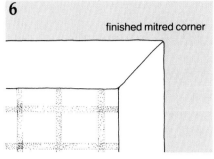

6

finished mitred corner

angled piece, overlapping by 1cm/
½in on the shortest edge. Cut a
complementary angle that overlaps
the first by 1cm/½in.
5 Right sides facing, tack the two
pieces together with 5mm/¼in seams
and hand sew. Press flat. Cut off

excess triangular corners from the
seam allowance. Tack this loose
length of binding along the chalk
line. Sew binding in place along the
chalk line and remove tackings.
Turn binding to wrong side of fabric
so that centre binding fold is exactly

on the raw edge of the fabric. Turn
each corner with care.
6 The corners will be square, with a
diagonal stitching line (the mitred
corner). Tack binding in place on the
reverse side of the fabric, then slip
stitch. Remove all tackings.

Mitring corners

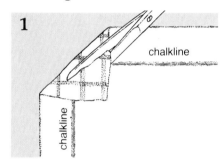

1

chalkline

chalkline

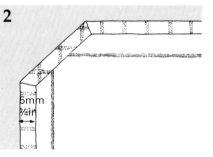

2

5mm
¼in

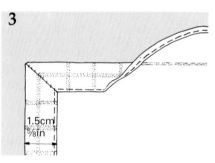

3

1.5cm
⅝in

As an alternative to bias binding, and
for the napkins, fabric edges can be
neatened with a hem and mitred
corners.
When measuring up, allow an extra
2cm/¾in all round. With tailor's
chalk, mark a foldline all round
on the wrong side, 2cm/¾in from

the raw fabric edges.
1 Fold each corner at 45° until the
diagonal touches the point where
the foldlines meet. Cut off the
folded corner leaving 5mm/¼in of
the hem allowance.
2 On the straight edges and corners
turn in 5mm/¼in and tack. Now turn

in remaining 1.5cm/⅝in of the hem
allowance on the sides, along the
foldline.
3 The corners fold to make a diagonal
join (mitre). Tack hem and corners.
Slip stitch diagonal mitre joins and
sew hem by machine, or slip stitch by
hand. Remove tackings.

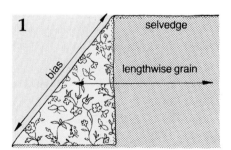

1

selvedge

bias

lengthwise grain

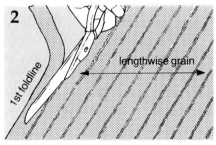

2

1st foldline

lengthwise grain

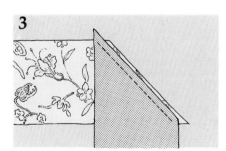

3

2 Mark this foldline with a ruler and
tailor's chalk, then mark a series of
parallel lines. These should be 3.5cm/
1½in apart if you want 2.5cm/1in
finished-width bias binding. For
other widths of binding, take the
finished binding width and add
1cm/½in (5mm/¼in to each edge for

folding to wrong side) and mark your
parallel lines to this width.
3 Join the strips by placing two
lengths at 90°, right sides facing, so
the two diagonals match, leaving an
equal amount of triangular-shaped
fabric each side of the seamline.
Tack. Check the two lengths are level

with each other and, if necessary,
adjust the seam to level the pieces.
Sew with a 5mm/¼in seam. Press
seam open and clip off extending
triangular shapes. Press 5mm/¼in
to wrong side down each long edge,
then fold the binding in half along
the length and press.

165

Circular tablecloths

Pretty circular cloths not only protect a table – they enhance it, providing an effective way of complementing a decoration scheme or livening up one that needs a little extra dash and style. Here are instructions for making long and short versions plus a topcloth for either.

Circular tablecloths are not simply a means to protect a table surface or to conceal a less than perfect one. They also provide a charming way to co-ordinate colours and patterns in decorating schemes.

Don't be deterred by the prospect of cutting a perfect circle of fabric. Simply fold the fabric into four, as shown below, and mark just a quarter of the fabric. Then cut through all layers and you will have a perfect circle.

Measuring up for a short cloth

Measure from the centre point of the table, across the table top and down over the edge to the desired drop. For a short cloth, an average drop is 25-30cm/10-12in from the table top or to just reach a chair seat.

Double this measurement (to give you the diameter) and add 2cm/¾in hem allowance.

Choose the widest possible fabric so that you can cut this cloth in one piece. If joins are unavoidable, make them at the edges of the cloth, not at the centre (see page 168).

Measuring up for a long cloth

Measure from the centre point of the table, across the table top and down to the floor. It is easier if you have help with this stage. If not, weight the tape measure down on the table top and take care not to move it as you measure downwards.

Double this measurement (to give you the diameter) and add 2cm/¾in hem allowance.

Unless you choose a very wide fabric, you will have to join two widths to make up the total diameter. For a really large table, you may need to join three widths.

Right: Strong, plain colours can be both practical and eye-catching.

Cutting out and making up a short cloth

Cut out a square of fabric to the final measurement (diameter plus hem allowance).

1 Fold the fabric in half lengthways, right sides facing, and then in half again widthways, wrong side facing. Lay the folded fabric flat on the floor, or on a table. Pin the edges together, then tack all round to hold the four layers securely together.

Tie a length of string round a short pencil and measure the string to half the diameter plus hem allowance measurement (as above). Tie a single knot in the string to mark the exact length required. Push the drawing pin through the knot and into the folded fabric at the innermost corner (the one with only folded edges). To protect your flooring or table, place a thick piece

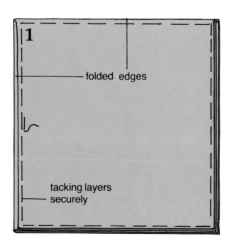

of card or a cork mat under the fabric corner.

If the fabric is particularly fine, use a map pin with a fine point, in preference to a drawing pin.

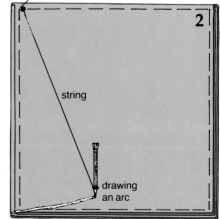

2 Keeping the string taut and the pencil upright, draw a pencil line on the fabric from one corner to another, forming an arc. Remove the drawing pin and string. Tack along the curve just inside the pencil line, through all four thicknesses.

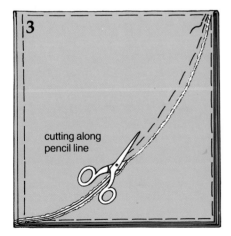

3 Cut out the fabric along the marked pencil line. Remove the tacking, and open out the fabric. To finish the raw hem edge, either make a double hem, or make a single hem with bias binding to give stretch on the curve.

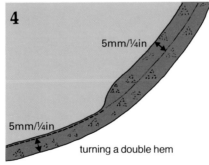

turning a double hem

4 To make a double hem, turn 5mm/¼in and then a further 5mm/¼in to the wrong side and tack in place. Slipstitch by hand, or machine stitch. Do not be tempted to make a deeper hem than 5mm/¼in, as the curve will pucker.
5 To make a hem with bias binding, use 13mm/⅝in width bias binding. Right sides facing, and raw edges matching, sew one long edge of the binding to the hem edge with a

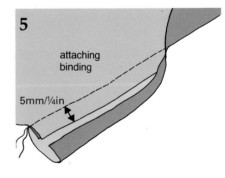

attaching binding

5mm/¼in seam allowance. Press seam towards the binding.
Turn binding to the wrong side of fabric and fold remaining long edge of binding to the wrong side by 5mm/¼in (if not pre-folded when purchased). Tack binding in place. The natural stretch in the bias binding will ease the hem in to place without puckering. Stitch binding in place by machine, or by hand using slipstitch.

Cutting out and making up the long cloth

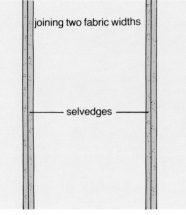

1 joining two fabric widths

selvedges

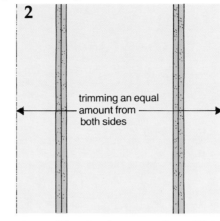

2 trimming an equal amount from both sides

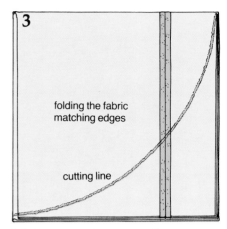

3 folding the fabric matching edges

cutting line

If you have chosen a wide-width fabric, cut a square of fabric to the final measurement (diameter plus hem allowance).
1 If you cannot cut the total square from one piece, cut two (or possibly three for a large table) widths of fabric equivalent to the diameter plus the hem measurement, matching the pattern if necessary. If you have to use two fabric widths, cut one of them in half along its length and tack one to either side of the complete fabric

piece with selvedges together. (This is so that you do not have an unsightly join in the middle of your cloth.) Sew together with 1.5cm/⅝in seams. Press the seams flat, or make fell seams.
If you have to join three pieces of fabric, take 1.5cm/⅝in seams. Press the seams flat, or make fell seams.
2 To adjust the *total* width of the joined fabric to the diameter plus hem allowance measurement required for the cloth, trim an *equal* amount from each side piece of

fabric, remembering to allow 2cm/¾in for a hem. Your fabric will now be a square.
3 Fold the square of joined fabric (or single fabric if you have used a wide width) into four, matching the edges together.
Cut the fabric in a curve to half the diameter plus hem measurement and make up in the same way as for the short circular cloth.

Below: A long cloth looks particularly pretty with a deep, bound ruffle.

A topcloth for emphasis

A square or round topcloth used with a long circular cloth can be made in a contrasting or co-ordinating fabric for extra emphasis.

Cut the topcloth from one piece of fabric to avoid unattractive joins. The raw edges can either be hemmed or given a decorative finish.

Place the long circular cloth on your table and measure the size for the topcloth – this will depend on personal choice – what looks best for the proportions of your table and for the fabric you've used for the cloth. As a general guide, a topcloth should be about 10cm/4in larger than the diameter of the table.

Square or round topcloth Cut a square or circle of fabric to size, allowing 1cm/½in for hems all round. Turn a double hem (5mm and 5mm/¼in and ¼in) all round to wrong side, mitring each corner on a square cloth. Tack, then machine stitch or slipstitch by hand. Remove tacking.

Right: Beautiful tablecloths transform a simple table into a design feature.

DESIGN EXTRA

Decorative hem finishes

These finishes for hems are very effective applied to the edge of a topcloth, but they can also decorate the hem of a short or long circular cloth.

A border, whether in a plain or patterned fabric, accentuates shape and colour. For a square topcloth, you can use a ready-made fabric border or cut your own strips of fabric.

Cut four lengths of border fabric and join them together with mitred corners. Turn the border edges to the wrong side all round and press. Hem the cloth and apply the border to the topside of the cloth, topstitching in place. For a border round the hem of a short or long circular cloth, the border fabric must be cut on the cross (bias) to give the necessary stretch round the curve of the hem.

Motifs, particularly flower shapes, make a very pretty edging on a cloth. Hem the cloth. Then appliqué the motifs on to the edge of the cloth, or sew to the cloth so that they overhang the edge. Cut out the motif shapes, tack in place on the cloth and satin stitch or machine zigzag all round the raw edges.

A bound ruffle is particularly decorative. Hem the cloth. Then cut strips of fabric the required width of ruffle and join to form a strip at least one and a half times the circumference of cloth. Bind both long edges and join short edges to form a circle. Run a double gathering thread along ruffle, draw up to fit cloth edge and topstitch in place along gathering lines.

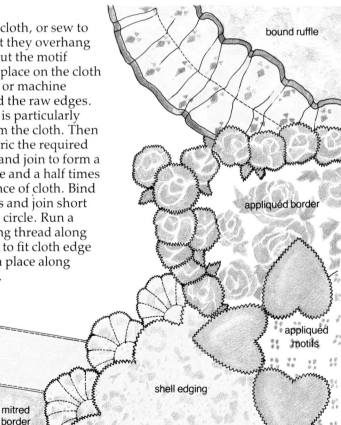

bound ruffle

appliquéd border

appliquéd motifs

shell edging

mitred border

Decorative fitted tablecloths made to measure

Update a dull room by covering a small table in a strikingly pretty, ruffled cloth and using it to display plants, flowers or a collection of favourite items. A fitted, skirted cloth, whether round or square, has endless scope for design variations.

Make a pretty, gathered tablecloth to transform an old table into an attractive piece of furniture, ideal for displaying plants, photographs, lamps or ornaments. If you are unable to find a suitable table lurking in the loft or a junk shop, inexpensive chipboard tables, usually small and circular, are available from many mail order firms.

Making the cloth from two pieces – the shaped top and gathered skirt – enables you to achieve a perfect fit, whatever size and shape your table. It can also be a more economical use of fabric than making a full-length cloth from one complete circle or rectangle, and gives endless scope for design variations.

A deep hem ruffle gives a rich, flounced effect but could be replaced by contrasting bands of fabric, lace insertions or frills, tucks, braid or edge trimmings. To emphasize a

Below: On a ruffled circular cloth, piping and binding in ivory satin trim a subtly patterned, crisp glazed cotton. The overall effect is extremely pretty without being over 'fussy'.

highly patterned fabric, it could, of course, simply be omitted.

The seam between top and skirt also gives scope for adding decorative extras: choose anything from simple piping to a ruched valance or a flamboyant, swagged frill.

Choosing fabrics

The best fabrics to use are those which are washable and easy-care, so a cotton and synthetic mixture, such as polyester/cotton sheeting, is ideal. Seersucker, gingham, lawn, calico, dressweight cottons and lightweight curtain fabrics are equally suitable, but may need more careful ironing! Check whether your material is shrink-resistant, and if not, wash it first, before cutting out. Also ensure that any decorative trimmings are washable, shrink-resistant and colour-fast. Cotton piping cord – as opposed to ready-made piping – should always be pre-shrunk by washing.

Measuring up

Measuring area of table top If the table is circular measure the diameter, add on 4cm/1½in for seams and allow a square of fabric to this size. If the top is square or rectangular, measure length and width and add 4cm/1½in to each dimension.

For the skirt length, measure from the table top to 1cm/½in above the floor and add 2cm/1in for the top seam allowance and a further 2cm/1in lower hem allowance. If adding a frill or ruffle, deduct ¼-⅓ of the skirt length for this before adding seam allowances to both pieces.

Estimate skirt fullness by multiplying by 1½ the circumference of a round tabletop (or the sum of the four sides for a square or rectangular table) and then adding 4cm/2in for seams. The fullness of a frill or ruffle should be 1¼-1½ times this calculated measurement.

To estimate fabric requirements with the least wastage, draw out a rough plan of the cutting layout. With some fabric designs, it may be possible to cut the skirt piece (and frill) down the length of the fabric to avoid seams. If not, and you need to join widths of fabric, allow for extra seams and pattern matching.

Cutting out and making up

Cut out the top piece and required number of skirt and ruffle pieces.
To cut out a circular top piece, fold the square of fabric to a quarter of its size and draw an arc from corner to corner as for a short circular tablecloth (see pages 166-167) before cutting the exact circle. With the fabric still folded in four, cut a small inwards notch in the folded edges of the two outer corners to mark the quarter points of the circle.

Making up

Matching patterns if necessary and with French seams (8mm and 1.2cm/⅜in and ⅝in turnings), join short sides of skirt piece(s) to form a circle. Similarly join ruffle pieces into a circle. Turn up and stitch a double 1cm/½in hem around lower edge of skirt and both long edges of ruffle. (Alternatively, omit seam allowances on ruffle and bind the edges.)

For circular and square cloths, fold the skirt piece into four and mark the quarter points by notching into seam allowance of top edge. Matching these notches to those in the circular top, or to the corners of a square top, will ensure an even amount of fullness on each side. For rectangular cloths, notch the half-way points to correspond with opposite corners, then mark remaining corners according to the ratio between long and short sides. Insert a double row of gathering stitches between each pair of notches 2cm and 1.5cm/¾in and ½in from top edge.

Adding ruffle Insert a double row of gathering stitches, in easy-to-draw-up sections, about 2.5cm/1in from top edge of ruffle and pull up to fit lower edge of skirt. Topstitch ruffle to edge of skirt.

Joining skirt to top

If piping is required, tack it around the seamline (2cm/¾in in) of the top piece, corded edge inwards and raw edges pointing outwards.
Pulling both threads together, draw up each section of gathering to fit the appropriate side (or quarter) of the top and even out gathers. Matching notches of skirt and top and with right sides facing, pin and tack skirt around edge of top. Machine stitch, keeping notches together and pivoting fabric around needle at corners on a square or rectangular cloth.

Remove tacking, trim seam to 1cm/½in and neaten by zigzagging or oversewing raw edges together. Press seam downwards behind skirt so that finished cloth lies smoothly.

Decorative details

For a more elaborate effect, add a ruched or swagged valance to a fitted tablecloth. Simply drape an inserted frill into swags and hold with ribbon bows or use vertical lines of curtain tape to form deep ruching on a valance strip.

DESIGN EXTRA

Above: A pretty but practical tablecloth for everyday use.

Simple patchwork tablecloth

An attractive tablecloth can be made very simply by joining up squares of colourful fabric. The finished size is up to you – make it as large or small as you want, oblong or square to suit your table. Using a sewing machine it should take very little time to make.

Use suitable leftover remnants from your piece bag, provided they are all of similar fabric. For a really well-planned design, buy short lengths of washable drip-dry fabric in co-ordinating prints and plains.

You will also need either bias binding or some plain fabric for a border, and ribbon for trimming is optional. If using easy-care fabric make sure that all trimmings are easy-care as well.

All quantities depend on the finished size of tablecloth.

Preparing the squares

First of all measure your table and decide what size cloth you want. Then choose an appropriate size for the squares (for example 15cm×15cm/ 6in×6in). Work out how many you require, and ensure that you have enough fabric. Then cut out each square accurately, making sure that it is on the straight grain of fabric.

For neatness, you may wish to attach a lining, which should be done when the patchwork is complete. Otherwise neaten all raw edges of each patch, before joining together.

Making up the cloth

Lay out the squares in rows in pleasing colour sequences, each row being the required length of the cloth.

With right sides together, stitch, taking 1cm/½in seams and press seams open. Place strips side by side, tack, and stitch in the same way. Press all seams open.

Finishing outer edges

Finish off the outer edge with bias binding or add a border of plain fabric, choosing one of the colours from the patchwork. Cut strips approximately 10cm/4in deep to fit edges and join them with mitred corners to make a 'frame' for the cloth.

Stitch inner edge of border to cloth, right sides together, and neaten seams. Make a narrow stitched hem around the outer edge. The join can be covered with contrasting ribbon top-stitched in place.

PART 6

Lampshades

Lighting is one of the most important aspects of the decoration of a room and the choice of shade and the fabric it is made up in must be considered with care. The cost of frame, fabric and trimmings is considerably less than buying ready-made shades and, of course, you can make them up to suit yourself. There are many different frame shapes which come in a range of sizes; some are coated with paint or pvc whereas others require taping in order to attach the shade. The techniques for each style are described in detail in the following chapters and a really professional finish is easy to achieve.

Choosing fabrics for lampshades

As a general guide it is advisable to avoid unlined white, red, orange or blue fabrics as these give a most unflattering light. Linings in shades of pink, apricot, yellow or cream give a warm effect. Bear in mind that a heavy furnishing fabric will not allow light to diffuse through it like a lightweight cotton. In this case use a light-coloured lining for maximum light reflection. The choice of fabric is to a great extent governed by the style of shade. For draped handkerchief or pull-on lampshades such as a tiffany shade use cotton, broderie anglaise or lawn. Pleated shades also require soft fabrics such as chiffon, georgette, crêpe or rayon dupions. The more tailored lampshades need fabrics strong enough to stretch over the frame; crêpe-backed satin, shantung, wild silk and some of the lighter furnishing fabrics are all suitable. Finally, drum and other stiffened shades can be made from buckram, parchment or a lighter fabric stiffened using a spray stiffener or backed on to an adhesive base such as Pelmform.

Linings are best made from crêpe, cotton lawn or fine silk. Do not use nylon or any material which is easily flammable.

Straight white cotton tape is used to cover an uncoated frame – use a cold water dye to match the shade fabric if necessary.

Try to choose fabrics and trimmings which are washable whenever possible. To wash a lampshade, immerse it and swirl it about in warm water to which a mild detergent has been added. Rinse and dry as quickly as possible to avoid the frame rusting. A short spell in an airing cupboard or some other warm place will tauten the fabric on the frame.

If the shade is not washable, spray it with a fabric protector such as Scotchguard.

A simple slip-on lampshade

There is no complicated fitting, no special shaping, no taping and sewing to the frame – this is the simplest of lampshades to make. If you attach it to the frame by an elasticated casing at the bottom and a ribboned casing at the top, you can slip it off the frame for cleaning.

Lampshades can be expensive to buy and it is sometimes quite difficult to find exactly what you want to suit your room. The answer is to make your own, combining a frame of your choice with a fabric that co-ordinates with your colour scheme.

Lampshades are surprisingly easy to make and the slip-on style shown here is the simplest of all.

Choosing a frame

To make a simple slip-on lampshade, you will need a frame with a round or oval top and bottom ring. The top ring should be smaller in diameter than the bottom ring and the struts must be straight, or bowed out as in a tiffany. Avoid frames with a shaped or scalloped bottom.

Preparing a frame

Lampshade frames are available in plain metal or coated with white plastic. Plain metal frames must be painted, or they will rust and mark the shade.

Before painting a frame, remove any rust by rubbing down with sandpaper and file off any rough or sharp spots. Paint the struts and rings with white enamel paint, but do not paint the gimbal (the centre ring that attaches to the light bulb holder and pivots for angling the shade).

Is lining necessary?

A lining always makes the shade look neater inside, but whether or not it is necessary depends on the fabric you choose.

With a very thin fabric the light bulb may well be visible through the shade when the light is on, and a lining will solve this problem.

Medium and heavyweight fabrics, particularly in darker colours, should not need lining to conceal the light bulb, but can be lined for a professional finish.

Lining will of course add extra bulk to the shade fabric. If the top ring of the frame is very much smaller than the bottom, as with the large tiffany, this could make it impossible to gather up the fabric tightly enough to fit. In this case, use a lightweight lining such as lawn.

Choosing the lampshade fabric

The thinner and lighter the fabric, the more light will penetrate through the shade. A thick, dark fabric will throw the light from the top and bottom of the shade. If the shade has a narrow top and a wide bottom it will throw a pool of light and be ideal for hanging over a dining table.

You will need

A lampshade frame
Fabric to make the shade
Matching sewing thread
Elastic for the bottom casing
Ribbon for the top casing

Right: A large tiffany shade on a hanging pendant is ideal for lighting a working or eating area. The shade can be made up in a fabric to match furnishings such as curtains or tablelinen.

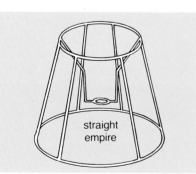

straight empire

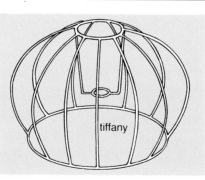

tiffany

tapered drum

Calculating the amount of fabric

For the amount of fabric needed, measure the height of your frame following the curve or slope of the side (A). To this measurement add 4cm/1½in at the top for the casing (B) which will form a gathered frill that stands 1cm/½in above the ring and hides it.

Add an allowance for the elasticated casing at the bottom (C). The depth of the finished bottom casing should be one fifth the height of the frame, (for a 30cm/11¾in high frame you need a 6cm/2¼in casing). So, to calculate casing allowance, double the size of the finished casing and add 5mm/¼in (D). (For a 6cm/2¼in casing add 12.5cm/4⅞in fabric allowance.) Remember that the casing at the bottom of the shade should not prevent heat escaping from the light bulb.

For the width of fabric needed, measure the circumference of your lampshade at the widest point and add 2cm/¾in for seam allowance.

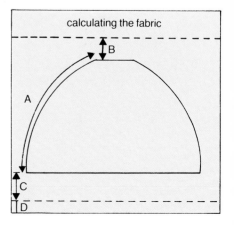

calculating the fabric

Making up the shade

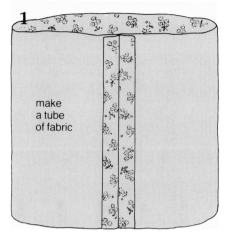

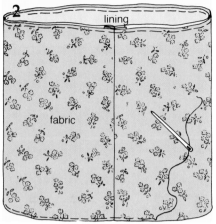

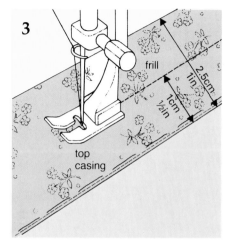

Cut out a piece of fabric to the dimensions required and an identical piece in lining fabric (if applicable).

1 With right sides facing, join the fabric with a 1cm/½in seam to make a tube.

Note: If the circumference is greater than the width of your fabric, join two pieces of fabric. Measure half the circumference on the frame and add 2cm/¾in for seam allowances. Cut two pieces of fabric to these

measurements and, with right sides facing, join with a 1cm/½in seam. Repeat for the lining fabric.

For unlined shades neaten the seam edges with a machine zigzag stitch or oversew by hand. Press flat. If you are lining the lampshade fabric, make up fabric and lining in the same way, but do not neaten the seam edges.

2 Place fabric and lining wrong sides together and tack round all edges. From now on, treat the fabric

and lining as one.

3 Turn 5mm/¼in to wrong side along top edge of fabric and tack. Turn a further 2.5cm/1in to wrong side and tack.

Sew along lower edge of turn and again 1cm/½in higher up to make a casing for the ribbon. Remove tacking.

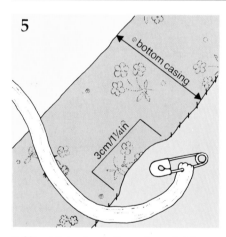

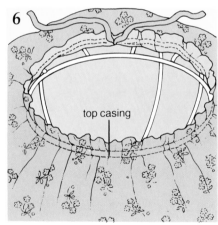

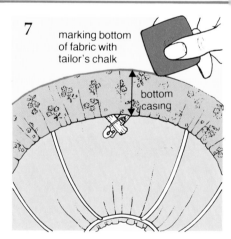

5 Slipstitch along the edge of this casing, leaving a 3cm/1¼in gap. Attach a small safety pin to one end of the elastic and thread it through bottom casing. Pin elastic ends together to secure. Measure top edge, add 20cm/7¾in, and cut a length of 4mm/¼in wide ribbon or tape to this length. Thread ribbon through the top casing as for elastic. Gently pull the fabric over the frame, aligning at least one seam with a metal strut and the top casing with the top ring of the frame.

6 Pull up the ribbon in the top casing until the fabric fits the ring, adjusting so that the gathers are even and a small 1cm/½in high frill stands above it. Knot the two ends of the ribbon around the ring to hold the fabric in place.

7 Unpin the elastic in the bottom casing and pull it up underneath the frame until the fabric is taut. Pin the elastic together.

At this point, if you are adding a frill or trim, mark the bottom point of the lampshade frame all round with a line of tailor's chalk. Untie the top ribbon and remove the fabric from the frame.

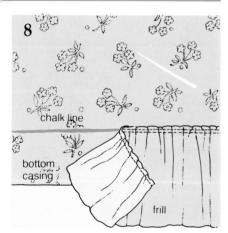

4 With a small pair of pointed scissors, cut a slit on the inside of the casing through only one layer of fabric (and lining if applicable) just large enough to slot the ribbon through. Overcast the edges of this slit to neaten.

Turn 5mm/¼in to wrong side along bottom edge and tack, and then turn fabric again to the wrong side to the depth of the bottom casing (which you have already calculated) and tack.

Finishes for the bottom edge

The bottom of the shade can be left plain, or a sewn-on trim can look attractive. Beads can give an ethnic feel, a frill can make use of a co-ordinating fabric while lace can make your lampshade softly feminine.

To add a frill of fabric or lace, measure round the bottom of the frame and cut a piece of fabric or lace 1½ times this length. Neaten both long raw edges on frill with a double hem and join to make a circle. Gather up evenly to fit the bottom of the frame. Topstitch to the chalk-marked bottom line on the shade, see step 7 below left.

For a beaded bottom edge, calculate how many beaded fringes you need, slot beads on to thread accordingly, then neatly sew ends of threads to chalk-marked line, see step 7 below left.

(*Continued overleaf*)

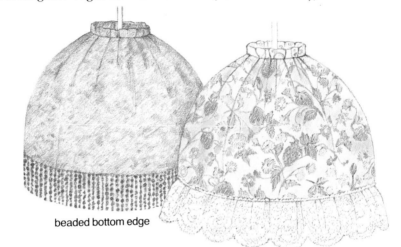

beaded bottom edge

frilled bottom edge

8 Unpin the elastic and attach the frill or trim along the chalk-marked line, taking care not to sew over the 3cm/1¼in gap left in the casing. Add the finish of your choice. Replace fabric on frame, knotting top ribbon in place and pulling bottom casing elastic up to fit. Sew the elastic together securely and cut off any surplus. Close the gap in the casing with slipstitch.

Right: The method used for the tiffany has here been adapted to make a shade for a straight empire frame.

For a scalloped edge make a pattern by cutting a length of paper to the same size as the bottom edge of the frame (plus 2cm/¾in seam allowance to join). Fold the paper in half, then half again and continue folding until you have the paper about half the width of your required finished scallop.

1 Mark the depth of the actual scallop on the folded paper and with a compass or using a coin or bottle top, draw a quarter circle arc to the marked depth.

Cut through all layers of paper along this arc.

2 Open up the paper and you will have a row of even scallops. Use this paper pattern to cut out the scallop edge in fabric. Neaten the raw edges of the scallop fabric and topstitch to the fabric shade.

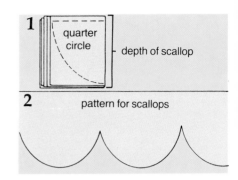

Shade with a lacy finish

This shade is suitable for a frame where the bottom is wider than the top. Make it in broderie anglaise or a similar fabric with one pre-shaped edge to give a ready-made bottom finish to the shade.

Broderie anglaise needs lining because of its fine texture and embroidered holes.

First make the lining in white fabric, or in a matching colour if you have chosen a coloured broderie anglaise. Follow the basic making up instructions for the slip-on lampshade but make a top casing with only the lower line of stitching and thread it with elastic instead of ribbon. This means that the top casing overlaps the ring, rather than making a frill above it.

Fit the lining over the frame.

Now make the shade Cut a piece of fabric to the height of the frame plus top casing allowance and the depth of the drop you want to hang below the frame. For the other dimension, cut to the size of the bottom edge of the frame (plus seam allowance) and hang below the frame.

Make the top casing so that it has an upstanding frill, slotting ribbon through to pull it up to fit. Do not make a casing at the bottom.

Fit broderie anglaise shade over frame and lining and pull up the ribbon to fit at the top. The fabric should overhang the bottom of the shade to give a shaped bottom edge.

Right: Broderie anglaise fabric with a pre-shaped fancy edge has been used to make this delicate shade.

A more formal style of tiffany shade with a panelled cover over a scallop-edged frame. Detailed instructions for making panelled lampshades are given on pages 192-194.

Quick and easy shades

Make a simple but eye-catching lampshade to add the finishing touch to a newly-decorated room or to brighten a dull colour scheme. Choose the pretty handkerchief shade for an informal room, the elegant drum shade for classic styling.

It can become expensive to buy new lampshades every time you re-decorate, but don't let an old shade spoil a

Left: A handkerchief or drum shade (inset) can be made in about two hours.

new room scheme. With a piece of fabric left over from making curtains or cushions, or a pretty remnant, you can make a new shade in less than an evening.

The handkerchief shade is basically

just a square or a circle of fabric draped over a utility ring or a small metal coolie shade. A circle of fabric falls into even folds, whereas a square produces the true 'handkerchief' points. Use a fairly lightweight fabric that drapes easily. and add a lacy trim for extra effect.

The drum-shaped shade is equally simple to make and requires very little fabric. Self-adhesive pelmet stiffening gives the fabric enough body to stand between two single lampshade rings.

Safety note Neither lampshade should be used with a high wattage bulb which might introduce a fire risk.

Stiffened drum lampshade

Use pvc-coated rings, choosing the appropriate fitting for the style of lamp, so that no taping is required.

You will need
Two lampshade rings of same
  diameter, one with lampholder
Piece of 'Pelmform' the height of
  shade by the circumference plus
  2.5cm/1in
Rectangle of main fabric a little
  larger than this
Same size rectangle of lining fabric
Clear fabric adhesive
Braid trim

Making up
Ensure that Pelmform is the exact size required and that all corners are right angles. Press lining and fabric

to remove creases. Place Pelmform on a flat surface and peel away protective paper from one short edge. Anchor edge of wrong side of fabric to this and smooth fabric on to Pelmform, peeling away backing as you go and taking care to keep fabric centred and wrinkle-free. Turn Pelmform over and fix lining in place in the same way. Trim edges of both fabric and lining.

Gluing overlap Place stiffened fabric around rings and hold in place close to top and bottom edges with clothes pegs, adjusting to get a good tight fit. Lightly pencil in overlap line on the inside of shade. Remove fabric from rings and trim overlap to about 1cm/½in. Apply adhesive lightly to the wrong side

of overlap end and position the other end of the shade on to it, making sure it fits true to the line. Place shade, seam down, on a flat surface and weight the seam with a strip of wood or card with a weight on top, for at least half an hour.

Gluing in the rings Position one ring inside the shade about 1cm/½in from the appropriate edge. Run a thin line of adhesive around the inside of the shade about 3mm/⅛in from the edge, push the ring back to this and hold in place with clothes pegs until the adhesive has set. Glue second ring to opposite edge in the same way.

Completing shade Stick or stitch decorative braid around the top and bottom edges of shade to neaten.

Handkerchief style lampshade

To prevent a fire risk, use a low wattage bulb and make sure that the fabric falls well away from it.

You will need
Dropped pendant lampshade ring,
  large utility ring or small coolie
  shade
Enough fabric to cover (see below)
Matching bias binding
Trimming for outer edges (optional)

Measuring up
Measuring correctly is important as the fabric should hang slightly below the bulb on all sides. Attach the ring to the lampholder, insert the bulb and measure from the central flex out to the ring and down

to the base of bulb. Add at least 2.5cm/1in to this measurement and double the final figure to give the minimum size of circle or square needed: increase the size for a deeper shade. A 90cm/36in square of fabric is generally suitable for a 20cm/8in ring.

Cutting out and making up
Fold the fabric into quarters, cut a hole 3cm/1¼in in diameter from the centre as shown and mark outer line for circle, if desired.
Neaten the raw edge around centre hole with bias binding. Neaten outer edges with a narrow double hem, catching in any edge trimming as you go.

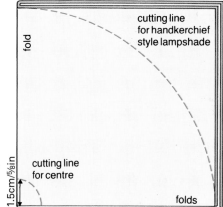

Remove bulb and ring and slip shade over the light flex. Replace ring and bulb and arrange the fabric into evenly-draped folds.

Sun-ray pleated lampshade

One of the simplest of all lampshades to make, but also one of the most stylish, a sun-ray pleated lampshade is ideal for both table lamps and ceiling lights. Make one from a remnant of fabric sprayed with fabric stiffener to brighten a dull room.

There's no excuse for naked light bulbs or dull old shades: a bright and cheerful-looking pleated shade can be made in very little time, for very little money.

Simply spray your fabric with an aerosol stiffener (sold for making roller blinds), press into concertina pleats and attach to a frame. There's no time-consuming taping of the frame, no complicated hand stitching, no neatening or trimming of edges, but the finished shade can look strikingly attractive.

Choosing fabric Any closely-woven lightweight furnishing fabric or heavyweight dress cotton can be used, but avoid sheers or loose-weave fabrics. Use left-over pieces from curtains, cushions or loose covers to create a perfectly co-ordinated look.

Always test fabric spray on the wrong side of a spare piece of fabric before treating the main piece.

Choosing a frame Making sure it has the correct gimbal fitting for the type of light (table lamp, pendant light or standard lamp), choose a straight-sided round frame of your required size. The finished effect depends on the frame shape. Choose one with a silhouette to suit the base. It can be either drum-shaped or one with tapering sides: the method of covering is the same for either.

Alternatively, use a pair of lampshade rings as, except on a very large frame, the stiffened fabric does not need the support of side struts. One ring should have the appropriate gimbal fitting, the other being just a plain circle. The larger the lower ring in proportion to the top ring, the more sloping the sides. Two rings of the same size will produce a drum-shaped pleated shade.

Both rings and frame should be the pvc-coated type which needs no finishing, as they are not taped.

You will need
Pair of lampshade rings of required sizes or a suitable frame, pvc-coated
Medium weight fabric (see below)
Roller blind fabric-stiffening spray
Length of straight rod or dowel
Clothes pegs
Strong thread (button thread)

Right: Making your own lampshade gives you a wide choice of colour and design. The glowing blues and greens of this richly printed glazed cotton ensure a really eye-catching effect.

Measuring up and preparing the fabric

Measure around larger ring and double this measurement, then add on 10cm/4in for shrinkage and turnings. Decide on required height of shade (or length of sloping sides) and add 2.5cm/1in to allow for shrinkage. Cut a rectangle of fabric to these measurements and press to remove creases. If more than one piece of fabric is needed, allow a 2cm/¾in overlap.

Using clothes pegs, attach dowel to one short edge of fabric and suspend dowel from a clothes line (out of doors, if possible, when there's no wind). Spray the wrong side of the fabric evenly all over with fabric stiffener and allow to dry. Remove dowel and press fabric on wrong side. Trim fabric to required depth of lampshade sides by double the circumference of lower ring plus 2cm/¾in, making sure that all corners are true right angles.

Making up the pleated shade

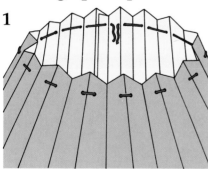

Using a medium-hot iron (and steam if necessary), carefully press the whole piece of fabric into 2cm/¾in wide concertina pleats, parallel to short edges, taking care to keep top and bottom edges level. These pleats form the sun-ray effect when

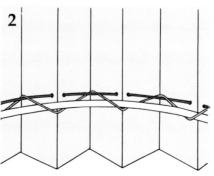

opened out.

1 Thread a large needle with a long length of strong button thread and work along each long side of the shade in turn, picking up a tiny amount of every inner pleat fold 2.5cm/1in from edge as shown.

Arrange the pleated fabric around the large ring, overlapping the join(s) so that the raw edges lie inside pleats, trimming away the end pleat sections if necessary. When pleats fit snugly around ring, tie ends of gathering thread securely together.

2 Attach the pleated fabric to the ring by whipping the gathering thread to the ring with another length of thread as shown, stitching through the shade at the join to anchor the overlap, and tying ends securely together.

Join the top ring to shade in the same way, then carefully distribute the pleats evenly around the shade to complete.

Stylish lampshades – pleated to perfection

Clever lighting can transform a room and these pretty pleated lampshades add the finishing touch. Choose a fabric to emphasize your colour scheme or to match your curtains, cushions or bedspread, for either a smart drum-shaped frame or fashionable coolie shade.

The hand-pleated method of covering lampshades can be used on any frames with sloping or straight sides. A straight drum-shaped shade is quick and easy to cover with even pleating, while a coolie shade, where the top ring is much smaller than the bottom ring, looks particularly effective because the pleats fan out from the top. Frames with bowed sides or with fancy shaping on the top or bottom edges are not suitable.

As these lampshades are unlined, choose a medium-weight fabric with a suitably dense weave. If the fabric is too thin or has an open weave the light bulb and frame will show through. Too dense and thick a fabric will be difficult to form into pleats and won't give enough light. If you do want to use a thin fabric, then you can back it with a soft or medium-weight iron-on Vilene.

The lampshade frames are covered with tape, a technique used in traditional lampshade making.

You will need
Lampshade frame
Strong white cotton tape, 13mm/ ½in wide
Fabric to cover frame
Matching sewing thread
Fabric glue
Bias binding trim for the top/bottom rings (or bias strips cut from the same fabric as the shade)

Preparing the frame
If the frame is not plastic coated, sand down any rough spots and paint the frame, except the gimbal (see page 174).

Right: An oval drum-shaped shade is pleated in the same way as a round one.

Taping the frame

This method of taping is used for any lampshade where the fabric or lining have to be stitched to the frame.

Every strut and the top and bottom rings of the frame must be taped. The tape, which is wound very tightly around the metal, acts as the securing base for the stitches that hold the fabric cover in place. Measure all round the top and bottom rings, and along each strut (but not the gimbal) and multiply this figure by three to give the total length of tape needed.

The tape used should be a strong cotton – not bias binding – and you must be able to tug very hard on the tape without any danger of it breaking.

If you want the tape to match the colour of the inside of your fabric

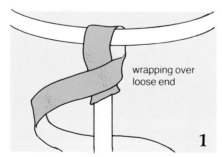

wrapping over loose end

1

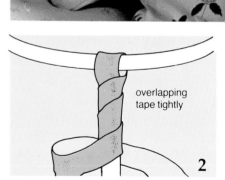

overlapping tape tightly

2

(or the lining, for more complicated shades with linings) dye it with cotton fabric dye:

To start the taping, cut a piece of tape to three times the length of one of the struts.

1 Starting at the top front of one strut, wind the end of the tape over the top ring, round behind, and across to wrap over the loose end.

2 Work down the strut, wrapping the tape diagonally, so that each wrap of the tape slightly overlaps

the previous one. You must pull the tape *very tightly* as you wrap – once the taping is complete it must not be able to move on the strut.

3 When you reach the bottom ring, pass the tape round the bottom ring and back through the last loop to make a knot. Leave the loose end of tape dangling for the time being. Tape each strut except one using this method.

Measure the top ring, the bottom ring and the last untaped strut and

184

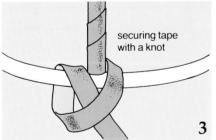
securing tape
with a knot

3

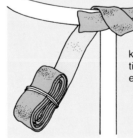
keeping tape
tidy with an
elastic band

4

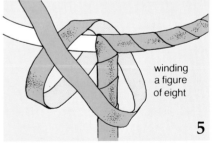
winding
a figure
of eight

5

cut a piece of tape three times this length.

Wind up the tape and secure it with an elastic band, leaving about 20cm/ 8in loose from the bundle. This will keep the tape neat as you work and you won't have to spend a lot of time untwisting it. Once the 20cm/ 8in is used up, free another length.

4 Start taping the top ring at the join with the untaped strut. Hold the end of the tape against the ring at this point, then wind the tape to the inside of the ring and back over the ring again catching the loose end under it. Work right round the top ring as on the struts.

5 When you reach the join between each strut and the top ring, wind the tape round the strut and ring in a figure of eight.

When you have worked all round the top and arrived back at the untaped strut, wind round this in a figure of eight and then tape down its length. When you reach the bottom of the strut, wind round it in a figure of eight and continue to tape the bottom ring in the same way as the top.

As you reach each bottom ring/strut join, trim off the surplus tape from the bottom of the strut leaving a 1cm/½in end. Work the figure of eight over this end to secure it.

To finish off, trim off any surplus tape to leave 5mm/⅜in. Turn this 5mm/⅜in in to the wrong side and handstitch to the bottom ring.

185

Cutting out the fabric

For a drum-shaped shade, measure the circumference of one ring and multiply this figure by three. For a coolie shade, measure the circumference of the larger bottom ring and multiply this figure by 1½. Add 10cm/4in to these measurements to give the total length of fabric needed.

If you have to use more than one width of fabric to make up this length, allow an extra 10cm/4in on each extra piece for joining. (Do not sew the fabric pieces together to join, they simply overlap.)

To calculate the height of fabric needed, measure along one strut and add 5cm/2in.

Cut out a piece of fabric to these measurements.

To stiffen the fabric, cut out both the fabric and iron-on Vilene slightly over size. Iron the Vilene on to the wrong side of the fabric before cutting out accurately.

The side edges of the fabric, unless selvedges, must be machine zigzagged to prevent fraying. The top and bottom edges are left raw as they are neatened with bias binding.

If you are using purchased bias binding, measure the circumference of the top ring and the bottom ring and cut a length of binding to each measurement plus 2.5cm/1in. If you are not using purchased bias binding, cut bias strips (see page 165), 4cm/1½in wide from fabric and join to make up lengths to fit the top and bottom rings plus 5cm/2in to allow for joining.

Right: By making your own lampshades you have a wider choice of colours and shapes. Neaten raw edges with bias strips to match or contrast with main colour.

Attaching fabric to a drum frame

Measure around the top ring between one strut and the next and decide on the size and number of pleats to fit within this to give a pleasing effect and to suit the fabric. *For example* if the measurement between struts is 12cm/4½in, six 2cm/¾in pleats would be suitable. Mark with chalk an overlap allowance of one pleat from the edge of the fabric. Using tailor's chalk, mark out the pleat positions along both edges of fabric, at least for the first section, after which you may be able to pleat up by eye. For each pleat, mark its width, then twice its width for the underlap.

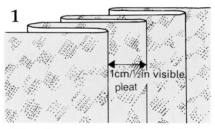

1 Keeping to the straight of grain and leaving the overlap allowance free, fold in the first pleat and pin to the frame so that the chalkline lies on a strut, and the top edge overlaps the frame top by 2.5cm/1in.

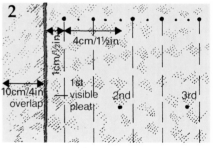

2 Pin the pleats into place around the top of frame between the first two struts, then pin round the lower edge of that section keeping pleats taut, straight and even. If lower ring is larger, adjust pleats.

Attaching fabric to a sharply sloping frame

Because of the size difference between the rings, it is necessary to measure the bottom (larger) ring to calculate the amount of fabric available for each pleat.

Measure around the bottom ring, from one strut to the next and multiply this figure by 1½.

Now measure the distance between two struts on the top ring, and decide on a visually pleasing number of pleats to fit within this. *For example* if the measurement between struts on the top ring is 6cm/2¼in, six pleats would be suitable. If the total amount of fabric available for pleating this section, taken from measuring the bottom ring, is say 30cm/12in (20cm×1½ or 8in×1½) then you have 30cm/12in of fabric in which to form six pleats between struts on the top ring. Six pleats within 30cm/12in of fabric gives you 5cm/2in for each pleat.

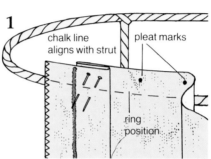

1 The pleats can be overlapped as shown, so (following through the example from above) 1cm/½in forms the visible pleat on the right side of the fabric and the other 4cm/1½in is incorporated into the back of the pleat.

This method may seem to involve a fair amount of mathematics, but it does give a professional look with very even pleating.

2 Using the figures you have calculated mark up the fabric leaving 10cm/4in for the overlap (this is tucked into the last pleat to

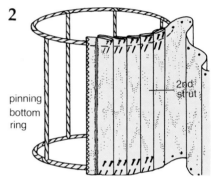

give a neat finish). Use tailor's chalk and mark out the pleat lines on just the first section (the total amount of fabric to be used between two struts).

If you feel skilled enough you can pin the fabric on to the frame by eye without marking the pleats first, but accurate markings, at least on the first section, give a more professional finish.

Fold the first pleat on the top edge, so that the required size of pleat is shown on the right side and the surplus is folded behind.

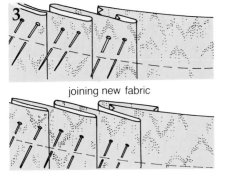

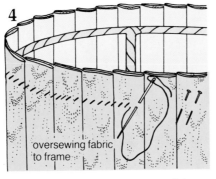

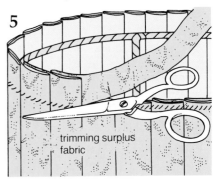

joining new fabric

oversewing fabric to frame

trimming surplus fabric

3 If you have to join the fabric, slip the neatened end (or selvedge) of the new fabric behind or into the last pleat so that no join is visible on the right side of the shade.

4 Oversew all round the top of the frame from the outside, making sure each pleat is firmly stitched on to the taped ring. Repeat round the bottom ring and remove all pins.

5 Trim off the surplus fabric from above the top ring and below the bottom ring, carefully cutting close to the stitching so that the fabric is flush with the frame.

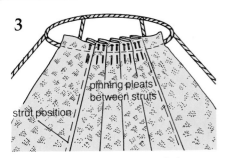

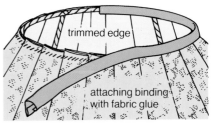

Trimming the shades

strut position

pinning pleats between struts

spacing out pleats around bottom ring

trimmed edge

attaching binding with fabric glue

3 With the overlap fabric left free, pin the pleats to the first section of the top ring as for the drum shade. The last pleat should just reach the next strut.
Check that the spacing of the pleats looks even, then mark the rest of the fabric along the top edge with the same pleating divisions.
4 Now form the same number of pleats in this first section on the bottom ring. Follow the foldline of pleats but pleat up only a tiny amount of fabric so that the pleats are very shallow. Pin them

individually to the bottom ring, making sure that the spacing is even. Pleat each section between struts in this way, pinning the pleats in place to the top and then fanning out on to the bottom ring.
If you have to add another width of fabric, slip the new piece of fabric behind the last pleat (behind several pleats on the top).
To complete the pleating, pin the last pleat over the first overlap. Oversew all round the top and bottom of the frame and trim off the surplus fabric as for the drum shade.

Press 5mm/³⁄₈in to the wrong side on each long edge of the bias binding (this may be pre-pressed on purchased binding) and stick down with fabric glue. Allow glue to dry. Fold the binding in half, wrong sides facing, along its length, press, unfold and glue the wrong side. Stick the binding around the edges of the frame with the centre foldline over the raw edges of the fabric. Join the two ends of the bias by cutting one end at a 45° angle, turning 1cm/½in to the wrong side and lapping it over the other end.

Elegant tailored lampshades with fitted linings

A smartly tailored and lined lampshade adds a distinctive touch and is easy to make. Choose an attractive fabric – a remnant will do – to cover an empire or a drum-shaped frame and line it in a pale colour to help reflect the light or to give a warm glow.

A fitted lampshade cover with a balloon lining gives a professional and elegant effect but is surprisingly simple to make. The lining conceals the struts of the frame and helps to reflect light. It also disguises the outline of the bulb when using fine fabrics. Almost any classic frame with a straight base edge can be used (see below), but spherical or tiffany shades are not suitable for this method.

Choosing fabrics

Soft, easily draped fabric, such as fine cotton, silk, satin and crêpe, are suitable for both the lining and the shade. Crêpe-backed satin is particularly easy to work with. Avoid stiff fabrics with no stretch or those which fray or split easily such as nylon or 100% polyester. If you have to choose a fabric that frays badly, use French seams at the joins.

The shade fabric can be light or dark and should tone with the room furnishings. Choose a pale-coloured lining fabric to increase light reflection. A cream or white gives maximum light while a pale pink or peach sheds a warmer glow, a good choice for a bedroom, for example.

Cutting out

The fabric is usually cut on the cross which makes it easier to mould round the frame and gives a smooth finish. If you are using a patterned fabric where the pattern dictates that the fabric must be cut on the straight, choose a frame which has fairly straight sides.

Preparing the frame

Remove any rough edges from the frame with fine sandpaper before taping, covering and lining as described earlier on pages 174-178 and 184-187.

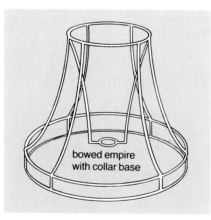

bowed empire with collar base

tall drum

tall bowed oval

suitable lampshade fabrics

Making a lined lampshade

The instructions given here are for a classic shade with the fabric cut on the cross. If you must use your fabric on the straight grain, cut two rectangles and make up in exactly the same way. Keep the vertical grain as straight as possible, especially at the point halfway between the seams.

You will need

A prepared and taped frame
A square of shade fabric which, when folded crosswise, will cover half the frame and allow 4cm/1½in turnings all round.
The same amount of lining fabric
Thread to suit fabric
Enough braid, velvet ribbon or bias strips to trim top and bottom edges
Fine steel glass-headed pins
Tailor's chalk or light pencil

Right: This elegant shade made from furnishing fabric trimmed with ruched velvet would be expensive to buy but is economical to make for yourself.

Preparing the cover and lining

1

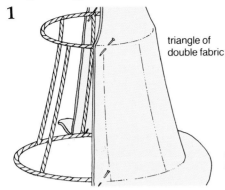

triangle of
double fabric

2

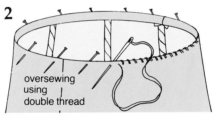

wrinkle-free
fabric pinned
and marked

Fold the square of shade fabric in half diagonally to form a triangle, right sides together.
1 With the folded edge running parallel to the base of the frame, lay the triangle of double fabric over half of the frame. Hold with four pins, one at the top and bottom of two opposite struts.
Place pins halfway down the two

outer struts and in the centre of the top and bottom semi-circle of frame. Pulling the fabric taut, pin outwards from these central pins, working round the frame until the fabric is securely pinned all round and completely smooth and taut. Re-pin wrinkled areas as many times as necessary for a perfect finish.
2 When the fabric is absolutely

wrinkle free, mark with tailor's chalk or light pencil down the two pinned struts on the wrong side of the fabric. Tailor's tack at each end of the lines to mark the position of the top and bottom rings of the frame. Carefully remove the fabric from the frame, keeping the two layers pinned together and cut along the fold.
With the two triangles of fabric still together, right sides facing, stitch along the two pencil lines, extending the seams by about 2cm/1in at each end. Trim down seam allowances to 5mm/¼in and press to one side.
Cut, pin and fit the lining in exactly the same way. As you are working on the *outside* of frame, stitch 3mm/⅛in inside the marked lines to make the lining slightly smaller to fit *inside* the frame.

Fitting the cover to the frame

1

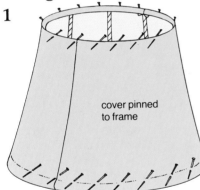

cover pinned
to frame

2

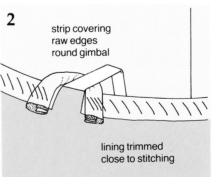

oversewing
using
double thread

1 Slip the cover right side out over the frame. Position the seams along two opposite struts so that they will be less noticeable when the light is switched on. Use the tailor's tacks

as a guide to positioning.
Pin at strut ends and then around top and bottom of the frame, pulling the fabric taut and smooth and re-pinning where necessary until the cover is a perfect fit.
2 Using double thread and small even stitches, oversew the fabric to the tape around the top and bottom rings. Remove pins as you go but keep the fabric taut. Trim off surplus fabric close to stitching.

Fitting the lining to the frame

1

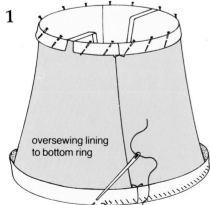

oversewing lining
to bottom ring

2

strip covering
raw edges
round gimbal

lining trimmed
close to stitching

Insert the lining into the shade with the wrong sides of fabric and lining together and matching side seams to those on the outside cover. Pin at strut ends to hold in place. Wrap the surplus fabric over the edge of

the outer cover and, working from the outside of shade, pin around the top and bottom rings, pulling the lining taut as before. Make a slit in the fabric to fit round the gimbal where it joins the top of the frame.

1 Oversew lining in place around the top and bottom rings on the outside of the frame, making sure that the stitches do not show on the lining inside. Trim excess fabric close to the stitching. The stitches and raw edges of fabric will be covered by the trimming.
Cut two short strips 2.5cm/1in wide from the surplus fabric, fold in half lengthwise and press. Press the long raw edges of the fabric in towards the centre fold.
2 Cover the raw edges of the lining around the gimbal with these strips, placing them under the gimbal, over the top ring and pinning the ends (trimmed to fit) to the outside of the cover, close to the top edge of the lampshade.

Trimming the frame

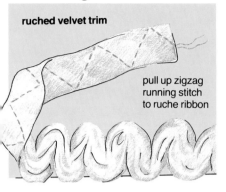

ruched velvet trim

pull up zigzag
running stitch
to ruche ribbon

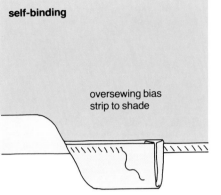

self-binding

oversewing bias
strip to shade

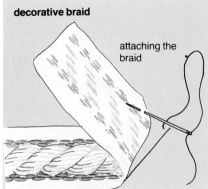

decorative braid

attaching the
braid

Neaten the shade with either a decorative trimming or a subtle self-binding.

Velvet ribbon trimming is one of the quickest and easiest to apply. The texture of the velvet covers the stitching and raw edges without looking lumpy, unlike ordinary ribbon which is not usually heavy enough. Simply stick it into place using a fabric glue such as Copydex, folding in the ends so that they butt together neatly. You must be extremely careful not to get excess glue on the shade.

For a ruched velvet ribbon trim, cut the ribbon twice the required length. Stitch a zigzag line down the centre of the ribbon using small running stitches. Draw up the thread until the ribbon fits the frame, adjusting the gathers for an even scalloped effect. Catchstitch the ribbon to the shade instead of gluing, positioning it so that the scallops slightly overlap the edge.

Self-binding gives a more tailored finish. Cut a bias strip of fabric, double the required width of binding plus 1cm/½in and long enough to go round both the top and bottom edges of the frame. Fold the strip in half, widthways, wrong side in and tuck in the short ends.

Pin the bias strip to the edge of the shade so that the raw edges overlap the shade by 5mm/¼in and the folded edge lies outside the shade. Oversew the strip to the shade, stretching it slightly as you go. Fold the binding over on to the shade

cover – if it has been stretched properly while sewing, it should be flat without needing the top edge slipstitched down.

Decorative braid or fringing can be glued into position but as these trimmings have a tendency to fray easily, the less experienced lampshade maker will find it easier to stitch them on.

Working from behind the braid, take tiny stitches alternately through the top and bottom edges, catching them to the shade fabric. The thread zigzags along behind the braid; do not pull it too tightly or the stitches will leave an imprint on the right side of the braid.

Below: This method of making lampshades is suitable for any size of light fitting.

Panelled lampshades with straight or curved edges

Emphasize the clean lines of a panelled lampshade with a perfectly-fitted cover or follow the same simple method to cover a scallop-edged tiffany frame. Add a professional touch to either shade with a trimming in a matching or contrasting colour.

A panelled cover for a lampshade is cut in sections which are stitched individually to the taped frame. This method is particularly suitable for square, rectangular and hexagonal based frames, half frames for wall-lights and also tiffany and flower-shaped styles with curved edges.

Having separate panels of fabric enables you to repeat a pattern motif on each panel of the lampshade or to use different fabrics for different sides. You could display a piece of appliqué or embroidery on the front panel. Each panel is cut on the straight grain of fabric, making this an economical style of shade to choose. However, if you prefer to work with bias cut fabric or if you are using an unusually bowed frame, cut each panel with the grain running diagonally between opposite corners and adapt the making up instructions accordingly.

Trimmings cover the stitching around each panel and these can either be unobtrusive self-bindings or a decorative feature in a co-ordinating or contrasting colour.

The lining is sewn to the outside of the frame and, as it does not serve to hide the taped frame, is not necessary if your fabric is firm enough to use without a backing.

The same instructions apply both to frames with straight and shaped edges. Simply follow the curve of a shaped edge when stitching lining and fabric to taped frame and when trimming away the excess material.

Making a panelled shade

The same method is used for both angular and tiffany style frames, and for both straight and curved edges.

You will need
Prepared and taped frame
Enough fabric to cut each panel on the straight grain plus a 5cm/2in overlap all round
The same amount of lining fabric
Thread
Enough trimming to cover each strut and top and bottom edges of frame

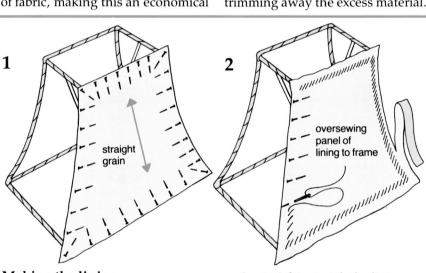

1 straight grain

2 oversewing panel of lining to frame

Making the lining
The lining is cut in panels and sewn to the frame before fitting the top cover.
Measure the height and width of the widest part of each panel of the lampshade frame and add 5cm/2in to each measurement. Cut a rectangle of lining fabric to these dimensions for each panel and mark the centre of each edge.
1 Place the front panel of lining right side down (unless it is to show through a lacy or broderie anglaise fabric) over the frame panel. Making sure that the grain of the fabric is perfectly straight down the centre of the panel and across the middle, pin the centre of each fabric edge to the centre of the corresponding frame strut and at the four corners. Still keeping the

grain straight, stretch the lining fabric outwards over the frame and pin all round the panel. Re-pin and tighten where necessary until the fabric is smooth and absolutely wrinkle-free.
2 Oversew all round the panel, using double thread, to stitch the lining on to the tape of the frame. Trim away excess fabric along the sides of the panel, cutting as close as possible to the stitching, but leave the top and bottom edges untrimmed.
Fit the opposite panel and then the side panels in the same way, again trimming only the side edges.

Right: Cover a simple shade with the main part of a border-printed fabric, cutting strips of the border pattern to make perfectly-matched trimmings.

Choosing materials

Almost any fabric can be used for the top cover although, as with most lampshades, it is better to avoid those that fray easily, such as 100% polyester and similar synthetic fabrics. Silk, particularly one with a slubbed finish, always looks effective; dressmaking and furnishing cottons give a wide choice of colour and pattern; whereas voile, broderie anglaise and lace fabrics appear light and pretty. Lining should be used with all lacy or lightweight fabrics, and dark coloured fabrics, regardless of weight, should be lined with a pale colour or white to reflect the light. It is not necessary to line firm, light coloured fabrics. Choose your lining to suit your top fabric – Jap silk for a silk fabric, crêpe-backed satin for a traditional look or a fine cotton for cotton prints and lacy fabrics.

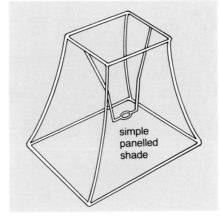

simple panelled shade

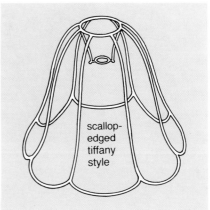

scallop-edged tiffany style

Whatever shape frame you use (see examples above), prepare and tape the frame as described on pages 174 and 184-185. The lining is stitched to the outside of the taped frame before fitting the top cover so the tape will show on the inside. If using a coloured lining, dye white tape to match using a cold water dye and rinsing the dyed tape thoroughly before drying. Alternatively, cut 2.5cm/1in wide bias strips of spare lining fabric, press in a narrow turning along one edge and use this as a binding tape, covering the remaining raw edge as you work.

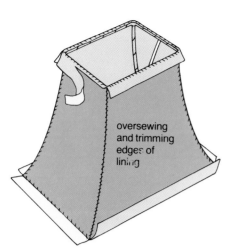

oversewing and trimming edges of lining

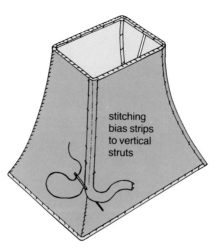

stitching bias strips to vertical struts

Making the top cover

Cut panels of top fabric as for the lining and attach in the same way – this time trimming all four sides of each outer panel close to stitching (take care not to cut into the spare lining fabric). Fold excess lining over top panels to enclose stitching and oversew to frame. Trim closely.

Trimming the shade

Trimming must be added to cover the stitching along each strut and round top and bottom edges of the shade. Apply a narrow trimming to the vertical struts first and cover the raw ends of this with the trimming around the top and bottom edges. Narrow velvet ribbon or decorative braids can be simply glued in place with a suitable fabric adhesive. See page 191 for details of applying these, self-binding and ruched velvet.

Use flexible braid or bias-cut strips of fabric on curved edges.

A narrow bias strip of the lampshade fabric is the most unobtrusive way to neaten the vertical struts and can be combined with a more elaborate bottom-edge trimming. Cut bias strips 2.5cm/1in wide, press 5mm/¼in turnings to the wrong side down both long edges and stitch in place by hand. Work from the top of each strut downwards, passing the needle diagonally behind the bias strip to take a tiny stitch through each edge in turn. Straight-cut strips can be used on straight frame edges. Unusual and more decorative trims are described below.

PROFESSIONAL TOUCH

Unusual trimmings

These elegant trimmings are ideal for the top and bottom edges of panelled lampshades but they can be used just as effectively on other styles.

Double piped trim

Measure round the top and bottom edges of the shade and cut a 4cm/1½in wide bias strip of fabric to this length. Fold right side out over a length of medium piping cord and using a zipper foot and with raw edges together, stitch down the length as close to the piping cord as possible. Place a second length of piping cord inside the bias strip and again stitch down the length, close to the cord. Fold the raw edges to the wrong side, trimming if necessary, and catch down by hand. Hand stitch to the lampshade as for a braid (see page 191).

Two-colour piped trim

Cut the required length of bias fabric 4cm/1½in wide in each of two colours. Insert and stitch one length of piping cord into each bias strip as above. Lay the two corded edges together, wrap all the raw edges to the wrong side, trimming to fit, and catch down by hand. Attach as braid.

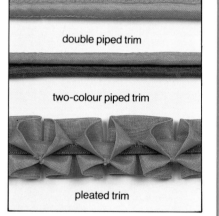

double piped trim

two-colour piped trim

pleated trim

Pleated trim

Cut a 5cm/2in wide strip of fabric on the straight grain, three times the required length. Fold in half lengthwise, right sides together, and stitch down the length 5mm/¼in from the raw edges. Turn right side out and, with seam along centre, press flat, then fold and tack into box pleats 2cm/¾in wide. Machine stitch down the middle to hold the pleats. Lay a length of 7mm/¼in wide ribbon on top of the stitching on the right side and catch in place with a few hand stitches. Join the opposite edges of each pleat in the centre with a few small hand stitches.

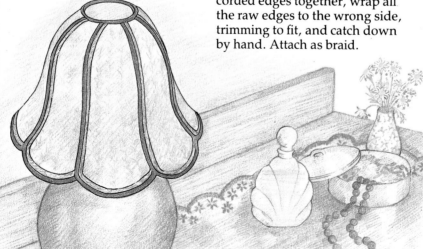

PART 7

Upholstery and loose covers

The following chapters describe the basic techniques for simple upholstery and how to make loose covers for upholstered furniture such as sofas and chairs. There are two kinds of upholstery – the traditional method using horsehair and herringbone or jute webbing and the modern, using foam and rubber webbing. The former should always be used on furniture made before 1940 and if done properly will last for at least fifteen to twenty years. The modern method is cheaper but will only last for about five to seven years before the furniture needs re-upholstering. Instructions are given for re-upholstering and re-covering a simple drop-in seat and a stuffed-over seat as well as the techniques needed for working with foam and rubber.

Choosing fabrics for upholstered seats

Brocade, damask, linen, heavy cotton, twill or wool are all suitable. If you are a needlewoman, a set of needlepoint seat covers can show off your skills to perfection.

Loose covers extend the life of upholstered furniture as well as changing a colour scheme quickly and cheaply. Careful planning and measuring is essential, particularly if the chosen fabric has a large motif or pattern repeat. A sample offcut to hand when planning the cutting layout is useful. Loose covers cannot be used over furniture upholstered in leather or plastic as they will slip out of place, or over velvet as there will be friction between the layers.

Choosing fabrics for loose covers

Fabrics should be tough, firmly woven, colourfast, crease resistant and non-shrink if washable. Buy the best quality you can afford as it is not worth spending time and effort on cheap fabrics which will not last. Do not choose too heavy a fabric as several layers often need to be joined making sewing difficult. Cotton, linen union, twill, cretonne or other lightweight furnishing fabrics are all suitable.

You will probably dryclean loose covers but, if washable, put the covers back on to the furniture while still damp to allow them to stretch to fit, and iron them on the chair. To protect fabric from dirt, spray with a fabric protector such as Scotchguard.

Simple upholstery: re-covering a drop-in seat

If your dining chairs have drop-in seats it is easy to give them a new lease of life by replacing their seat covers. Using basic, very simple upholstery techniques it takes little time to remove shabby old covers and replace them with bright new fabrics

A drop-in seat is a covered wooden frame or base which fits into the recessed top of a chair or stool. It is not fixed and is therefore easily removed for re-upholstery.

Chairs with drop-in seats are mainly used in the dining room and kitchen and the top cover tends to become worn or dirty long before the seat itself needs re-upholstering. Alternatively, you may wish to change the covers to match the decoration of a room or to mount a needlepoint seat cover you have worked.

If you add a calico lining when replacing the top cover this will not only increase the comfort and wear of the top cover but also makes replacing it the next time even easier.

When you have completed covering the seat it is advisable to spray the fabric with an aerosol fabric protector to help resist dirt and stains.

Drop-in seat construction

The traditional drop-in seat consists of a frame with interlaced strips of webbing stretched tightly across to support the stuffing which is usually horsehair or a fibre mixture. Layers of wadding and calico cover the stuffing and hold it in position under the top cover. A black backing fabric on the underside hides the webbing and covers raw edges to complete the seat.

Modern drop-in seats can be constructed on a solid wooden or chipboard base with a foam rubber block for stuffing, although horsehair or fibre are also sometimes used.

The foam block is held in place and squashed into shape by the cover. Although this type of seat is more economical to produce it is not as long lasting or comfortable as a webbed seat.

Right: One advantage of drop-in seat covers is that you can remove them easily for laundering or dry cleaning.

Below: A selection of the materials needed for re-covering a drop-in seat.

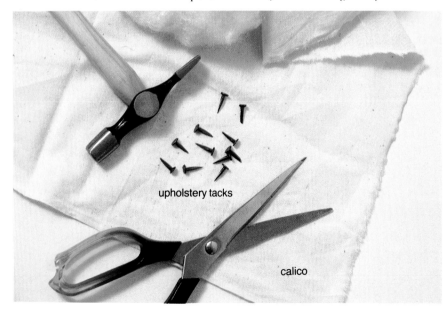

upholstery tacks

calico

Preparing to re-cover

Instructions for re-upholstering a webbed drop-in seat are given on pages 201-203. Re-covering a seat needs no previous experience or special tools and is an ideal introduction to the craft of upholstery.

You will need
Firm, closely woven furnishing fabric 8cm/3in larger all round than seat
The same amount of calico
Black linen or cotton cloth for underside if required
Cotton wadding to cover the seat area
Tack hammer
13mm/½in upholstery tacks

Tack lifter – a screwdriver and
 mallet will do

Removing the old cover
Take the seat out of the chair frame
and remove backing fabric from the
underside if there is any. Lever out
the tacks holding the old seat cover.
To remove an old tack place the
blade of the tack lifter, or
screwdriver, under or beside the
head of the tack. A sharp blow from
the mallet will begin to ease out the
tack. If the head snaps off, leaving a
sharp point, hammer it down into
the frame to prevent it snagging the
new cover.
Keep the old cover in one piece after
removal to use as a pattern guide

when cutting out the new cover.
Unless it is in good condition,
remove the calico lining in the same
way.
If there is any wadding beneath the
lining or top cover it should also be
removed to reveal the stuffing or
the foam block.
With the covers and wadding
removed, you can decide whether
the seat needs re-upholstering
completely or simply re-covering.
The webbing should not sag or be
broken, the stuffing should be firm
and smooth and foam blocks should
not show signs of crumbling edges.
If the seat just has stuffing or a foam
block you could add a layer of
wadding to improve comfort and

durability.
If you are planning to use a heavy
furnishing fabric and a calico lining,
check first that there is sufficient
clearance round the edges of the
frame to enable it to fit into the chair
when covered. If not, you may have
to omit the calico lining.

Cutting out the new fabric
Using the old seat cover as a pattern
guide, cut a piece of calico large
enough to wrap over the seat and
overlap the underside by at least
8cm/3in all round.
Cut your top fabric to the same size.
Cut a piece of wadding to fit the
surface area of the seat without
hanging over the sides.

197

How to re-cover a drop-in seat

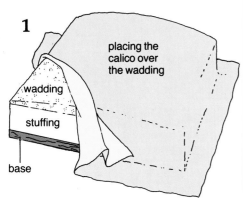

1

placing the calico over the wadding

wadding

stuffing

base

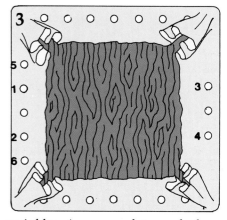

2

2○ 1○

6○ 4○ 2○ 1○ 3○ 5○ 7○

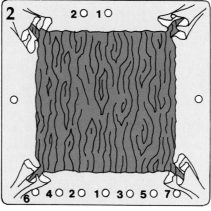

3

5○

1○

○

2○

6○

3○

○

4○

1 Place the wadding on to the seat filling and lay the calico on top. Holding the wadding and calico in place, turn the seat over and wrap the calico over the edges to the underside of the frame or base. The calico is held on to the frame with temporary tacks in the centre of each edge.

Temporary tacking means that a tack is only driven halfway into the frame so that it holds the material in place while you are working, but can easily be repositioned if necessary. A tack hammer with a magnetic tip helps hold the tacks in position while hammering. Make sure that you drive the tack in straight. If it goes crooked, the edge of the head will not lie flat and may

cut into the cover or webbing. Place the first temporary tack in the centre of the back edge, just inside the frame edge. Checking that the grain of the fabric is straight and taut, place a tack in the centre of the front edge, then in each side.

2 Tack along the back edge working outwards from the centre and alternating from one side to the other. Space the tacks about 4cm/ 1½in apart and stop at least 4cm/ 1½in away from the corners. Stretch the calico outwards towards the corners along the back edge as you work.

Pull the fabric from the back to the front and tack along the front edge in the same way. It is essential that the calico is taut and free of

wrinkles. As you work towards the corners, pull the fabric out towards the edge and check that the wadding is not extending over the sides of the frame. Any excess wadding should be trimmed away or tucked back to firm the edge.

3 Still pulling the calico over the seat and diagonally outwards, place a tack either side of the central tacks on one side. Repeat on the opposite side, put in two more on the first side, then on the second side, and so on until both sides are tacked and only the corners are left free. Turn the seat over and check if there are any wrinkles or areas of calico that are not a tight fit. If there are, remove tacks affecting that area, pull fabric taut and replace tacks.

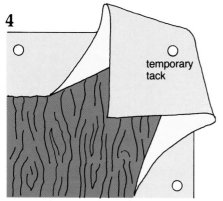

4

○

○

temporary tack

○

○

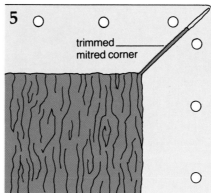

5 ○

○

○

trimmed mitred corner

○

○

○

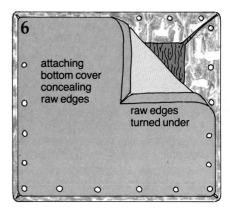

6

attaching bottom cover concealing raw edges

raw edges turned under

4 With the seat cushion side down and working one corner at a time, pull the fabric tightly across the corner and place a temporary tack in the centre. This leaves the surplus fabric on either side of the tack.

5 Tuck the surplus fabric into a mitred fold on each side of the tack. With the fold lines as a guide, trim away excess fabric from the inside of the mitre. Re-fold the mitre and

hold with two tacks. Remove the central temporary tack.

Check that the calico lining is a perfect fit on the right side of seat and make any necessary corrections before moving on to the next corner.

Finally work round the frame hammering all the tacks firmly into place. Trim away any excess fabric. The top cover is added in exactly the same way as the calico lining,

making sure that the second row of tacks does not coincide with first row.

6 A layer of black linen or cotton fabric hides the raw edges of the covers and gives a neat finish. Draw round the seat frame, adding 5mm/ ¼in all round, to make the pattern. Turn 1cm/½in to the wrong side all round the fabric and press. Place the fabric on the underside of the frame, right side out, and tack all round.

DESIGN EXTRA

Needlepoint chair seats

Drop-in seat covers are often worked in needlepoint. First check that there is sufficient room between the seat and the frame for the stitched canvas. Make a pattern for the seat area and allow at least 8cm/3in extra canvas all round. Work the stitching on a frame, to hold the canvas straight and try to keep an even amount of yarn on the back, thus helping it to wear well in use.

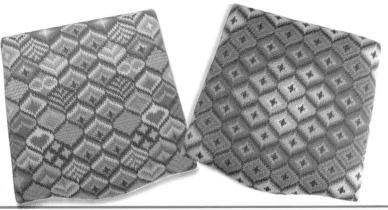

Upholstery techniques for a drop-in chair seat

Upholstery is an exciting and rewarding craft to learn. Follow these instructions for re-upholstering a simple drop-in seat with a webbed base and traditional stuffing, and you will master some of the basic techniques essential to many upholstery projects.

Right: The traditional method of upholstering a drop-in seat is suitable for antique, older-style and modern chairs or stools.

A worn drop-in seat can often be renewed by simple re-covering (see pages 196-198). When removing the old outer covering and calico, however, you may find that the stuffing needs replacing and that the webbing is beginning to sag. This chapter covers the techniques needed for stripping the frame and applying traditional webbing, hessian and stuffing.

Webbing makes a very firm base for a seat yet has a degree of resilience that makes it more comfortable than a solid wooden base. This method of making a webbed seat is suitable for drop-in seats, piano stools, window seats with a base, bench seating and stools. The basic techniques covered, such as applying webbing and making bridle ties, are also used for many other upholstery projects.

Materials and equipment

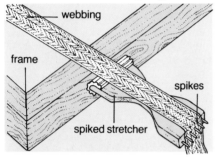

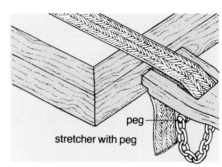

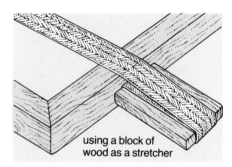

Choose either the traditional black and white herringbone webbing or strong, good quality, brown jute webbing; both are usually 5cm/2in wide. Do not cut the webbing up into lengths beforehand; each piece is cut *after* being tacked in place. The webbing must be pulled taut over the chair frame and this is made easier with a webbing stretcher. There are different types

of stretcher – some have spikes which stick through the webbing to hold it; on others, a loop of webbing slots through the stretcher and is held with a peg. It is worth investing in a proper stretcher if you intend to upholster more than one or two chairs, but if not, use a block of wood about 2cm×10cm×20cm/¾in×4in×8in.

Horsehair is the traditional stuffing used on seats but is expensive and often difficult to obtain. Coconut or other vegetable fibre available from upholstery suppliers is an acceptable alternative. If you can salvage some horsehair from an old seat, use this as the top layer of stuffing, with vegetable fibre underneath.

Preparing the chair

Use a tack lifter or screwdriver in conjunction with a mallet to remove the tacks holding the old covers (see page 197) and keep the old material to use as a pattern guide for new covers. Also remove the stuffing, hessian and webbing. These will be very dusty so spread out a sheet to work on, keep the room well ventilated and have a bin for rubbish and rusty tacks.

The stuffing can often be re-used if you tease it out thoroughly. Horsehair, in particular, is worth re-using, so do not throw it away. Place any you find in a linen bag or old pillowcase and tie up the open end. Wash the whole thing in soapy water, rinse through, hang it out to dry and the horsehair will be as good as new. It will probably be matted together in little bundles, in which case tease out each lump to separate the fibres.

Don't be tempted to keep the original webbing – this would be false economy as just one broken strap can ruin a seat.

If any tack heads snap off while stripping the frame, leaving metal shafts in the wood, knock them right down into the frame using a nail punch if you have one, so that jagged edges do not snag the new materials. Once you have stripped right down to the frame, make sure that the wood is not splitting and the joints are not coming apart. Glue any loose joints before starting to re-upholster. To do this, tap the loose joint a little further apart with a mallet or hammer and place some

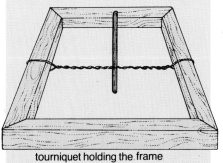

tourniquet holding the frame

wood glue in the space between the two pieces of wood. Tap the joint back together.

Hold the joint with a tourniquet made by tying string round the two frame edges and twisting this round a stick to tighten. Wipe off any excess glue then leave until the glue has thoroughly dried before removing the tourniquet.

Upholstering a drop-in seat

Instructions for completing a drop-in seat are given on page 198.

You will need

Strong jute or black and white herringbone webbing, sufficient for about six straps the width of the seat

Calico and top cover fabric
Tack hammer
Tack lifter or screwdriver
Mallet
Webbing stretcher or block of wood
13mm/½in and 16mm/⅝in upholstery tacks
Sufficient coconut fibre or horsehair

to cover the chair seat and lie 8cm/3in deep before being compressed
Cotton felt wadding or synthetic wadding layered together until approximately 2cm/1in thick to cover seat area
7½oz-10oz hessian 10cm/4in larger all round than the seat
Thin twine and upholstery needle

Applying the webbing

Most chair seats need three strips of webbing evenly spaced in each direction. The central strip must be placed exactly at right angles to the frame – the outer strips can be parallel or slightly angled depending on the shape of the frame.

Particularly large or small seats, however, may need four or two strips, in which case they are spaced evenly across the frame. Estimate their positions before placing the first strip as you won't, of course, start in the centre.

When all the webbing has been correctly attached you will have a very firm base for the stuffing.

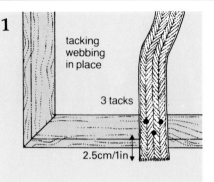

1 Lay one end of the webbing on the centre of the front edge of the frame with an overlap of about 2.5cm/1in and tack it in place with three 16mm/⅝in tacks positioned as in the diagram. Hammer your tacks in very straight – the edge of a bent or

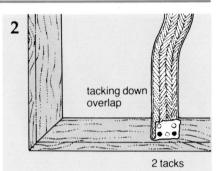

angled tack head could cut into and weaken the webbing.
2 Fold the overlap back over the three tacks and hammer in a further two tacks positioned close to, but not overlapping, the first three, as in the diagram.

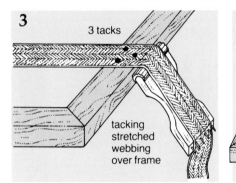

3 Pull the webbing across to the opposite side of the frame, attach it to a webbing stretcher or wrap it around a block of wood, and hold the webbing under light tension with the stretcher or wood wedged against the chair frame. Ensure that the webbing is lying straight across the seat frame.

Press the end of the stretcher furthest from the chair frame downwards, gradually drawing the webbing tighter.

Continue pushing downwards until the webbing is so taut that you feel some bounce when you drop a hammer or screwdriver on to it. Alternatively, tap it with your

fingers – it should sound hollow like a drum and have no 'give' at all. With the webbing held taut – a vice or second person holding the frame down may make this easier – hammer in three tacks as before to hold it in place.
4 Release the stretcher and cut the webbing off leaving a 2.5cm/1in overlap. Fold this back over the three tacks and hammer in the final two tacks.

Complete all the webbing running in the same direction in the same way, spacing the strips about 5cm/2in apart. Three strips are generally all that is needed on a small drop-in seat. If the front of the frame is

wider than the back, splay out the strips.
5 Attach the webbing running in the opposite direction in the same way but weave each strip in and out of the opposite strips *before* tacking down the first end. If the first strip goes over, under, over, the adjacent strips will go under, over, under – and so on.

Upholsterer's knot

Begin with an upholsterer's knot when stitching bridle ties as this holds the end of the twine securely in place. Make a stitch through the hessian leaving a short end of twine lying parallel to the main piece. Tie as in the diagrams; pull up to complete.

1 stitch through hessian · short end · long end

2 hessian · pull to complete knot

Stuffing the seat

adding hessian

hessian

making bridle ties

adding stuffing

Adding hessian

Cut a piece of hessian large enough to overlap the seat frame by about 2.5cm/1in all round and place it directly on top of the webbing. Insert a temporary tack (see page 198) at the centre of each side to hold it. Adjust tacks if necessary to straighten the grain, then drive the four tacks fully in. Fold back the excess material to lie on top of the hessian and tack all round. Work outwards from the centre to the corners pulling the hessian taut as you go. Position the tacks at intervals of approximately 5cm/2in, 1cm/½in from the edge, and mitre the corners.

Making bridle ties

Bridle ties prevent the stuffing slipping around or bunching underneath the cover. They are simply loops of strong thread sewn on to the hessian and the stuffing is tucked under them.

Using twine and an upholstery needle, take giant back stitches starting at the centre of the hessian and spiralling out towards the edge. Push the needle straight up and down through both hessian and webbing, leaving a top loop large enough to fit loosely over your hand. Take care that in pulling through the thread of one stitch you do not decrease the loop of the previous one.

Adding stuffing

Again starting from the centre, pack generous amounts of stuffing under each bridle tie or loop until you have reached the final loop in the outer edge and covered the entire seat. Aim for an even depth of 6-8cm/2-3in.

Gently pat the stuffing all over the surface to feel if there are any gaps or low spots and fill them by tucking in more stuffing, until you have a firm, even surface.

The stuffing should not overlap the frame edge on a drop-in seat or it will no longer fit into the chair.

Completing the seat

Cut a piece of wadding to approximately the same shape as the frame and lay it on top of the stuffing. It, too, should have very little overlap. The seat is then ready to be covered with a fitted calico cover which will pull the seat into its final shape, as described on page 198. If the stuffing still appears lumpy or uneven during this stage, push the end of a long, strong, upholstery needle or a regulator through the calico and manoeuvre it to eliminate any lumps or dips.

Complete the seat with a top cover and black cloth on the underside.

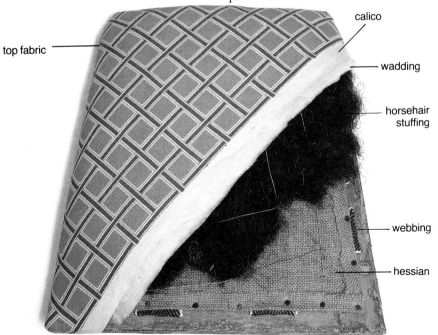

top fabric · calico · wadding · horsehair stuffing · webbing · hessian

Left: Fill in any gaps or low spots to complete a firm, even layer of stuffing before adding the wadding.

Upholstering a simple stuffed chair seat

*A stuffed-over chair seat – one in which the seat is worked
directly on to the chair frame – involves
the more advanced upholstery techniques. However, much the
same effect can be achieved by the less
experienced upholsterer by firming the seat with an edge-roll.*

*Above: Restoring the upholstery on
Victorian or Edwardian chairs often
requires making a stuffed-over seat.
The simplest way to achieve the firm
edges which ensure a long-lasting seat is
to make an edge-roll.*

On many chairs, the seat is upholstered directly on to the wooden frame as an integral part of the chair, rather than being made as a separate drop-in seat. This type of seat is called a stuffed-over seat and can be built up in several different ways. The simple method explained here uses an edge-roll (sometimes called a tack-roll) to form firm, rounded edges which contain the central stuffing. It is suitable for dining-type chairs such as the one illustrated above, which do not require a particularly deep sprung seat.

Many of the traditional upholstery techniques used to make a drop-in seat are also used on this type of simple seat. Read pages 196-198 and 200-203 for details of equipment, attaching webbing, hessian, bridle ties and stuffing, and completing the underside.

New techniques introduced in this chapter include making an edge-roll, fitting the calico around back-struts and corners, and finishing with gimp or decorative nails.

The only additional piece of equipment you need is a curved upholstery needle. Stitching areas such as corners, where the fabric is backed by solid upholstery or the chair frame, is much easier to do with a curved needle.

A stuffed-over seat with an edge-roll

Webbing and a hessian base support the edge-roll and the seat stuffing, which are then covered by calico and a top-cover.

Preparing the frame

Cover a table with a blanket and place the chair on this so that you can work on the chair standing up with a straight back. Remove the old upholstery as described on page 201, putting everything except any re-usable stuffing and the old top cover (if it is to be used as a size-guide) in the dustbin. It is worth spending time on the frame at this stage – a neglected, wobbling frame is often the downfall of a good chair with years of life left in the upholstery. Clear the frame of old tacks, smooth away any splinters or sharp edges and renew glue in joints if necessary. Clean down the show wood – any polished wood that will be visible on the finished chair – while there is no chance of spoiling upholstery in the process.

You will need

Strong jute or herringbone webbing
Webbing stretcher
Tack lifter or screwdriver
Mallet and tack hammer
13mm/½in and 16mm/⅝in upholstery tacks
A piece of 7½–10oz hessian 12cm/5in larger all round than the seat
Coconut fibre or horsehair for seat stuffing
Cotton felt/wadding or synthetic wadding to overlap stuffing
Calico and top fabric 10cm/4in larger all round than the seat
Twine, heavy duty thread, needle
Curved needle
Gimp or decorative nails
Black cloth for underside

Upholstering the seat

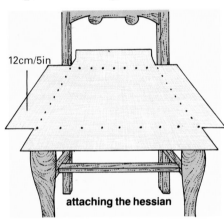

attaching the hessian

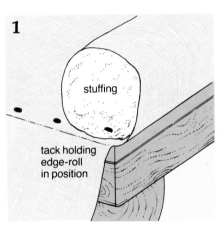

stuffing

tack holding edge-roll in position

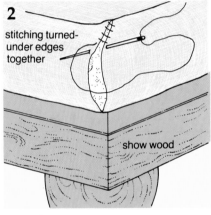

stitching turned-under edges together

show wood

Attach the webbing to the seat area of the chair frame with 16mm/⅝in tacks, as for a drop-in seat. Remember to wedge the stretcher against unfinished wood to avoid marking any show wood.

Attaching the hessian

Lay the hessian over the chair frame so that it overlaps the seat by 12cm/5in all round. Tack in place as for a drop-in seat but working on only the single thickness of material.
When the hessian is taut and firmly tacked all round, cut away a square of fabric from each corner as in the diagram. The remaining overlap of hessian is used to make the edge-roll.

Making the edge-roll

1 For each side in turn, form a firm sausage of waste filling (stuffing fibre, cotton wadding, shredded materials, or a mixture of the three) the length of the side. Lay the sausage of filling along the overlap of hessian and roll the hessian tightly around it, rolling in towards the row of tacks on the frame. Alter the thickness of the edge-roll by adjusting the amount of filling, re-rolling tightly, until the height of the roll is the required height (no more than 5cm/2in) of the finished seat edge.
When you are satisfied with the size and firmness of the roll, insert a tack under the stuffing at each end, attaching the base of the hessian roll to the frame. The edge-roll should protrude over the edge of the frame by about 1.5cm/½in.
2 After making all four rolls, butt the ends together at the seat corners – in effect making a rough mitre – and stitch through the hessian to hold. This ensures firm corners and encloses the filling. The completed edge-roll forms a firm, continuous surround to the seat area, ensuring that it retains a good shape and remains comfortable to sit on.

Stuffing the seat

Stitch bridle ties to the hessian and tuck fibre or horsehair under these to fill the area enclosed by the edge-roll. The stuffing should be deep enough to protrude over the edge-roll and form a crown at the centre of the seat.
When the stuffing is firm and even, lay the wadding on top and trim so that it covers the edge-roll round to the wooden frame. Check again for any low or flat spots in the seat filling and add more stuffing underneath or patches of extra wadding or felt on top.

Fitting the calico cover

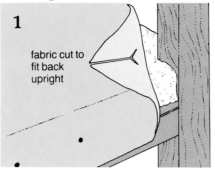

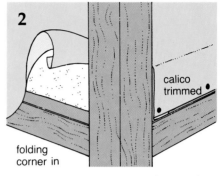

The calico wraps round to the underside of the frame on some styles of chair, but on chairs with polished show wood around the base of the seat, tack it to the strip of unfinished wood just above this. Lay the calico over the seat and hold with three 13mm/½in temporary tacks in the centre of each edge.
The back corners have to be fitted around the chair back uprights.
1 Fold back a triangle of fabric at each corner and cut diagonally through the triangle point towards the corner of the wooden upright, then make two very small cuts to form a Y shape. Do not make the initial cuts too deep – try fitting the calico around the uprights and if it creases, cut a little further.
2 Once the calico can be stretched tautly across the stuffing, fold in the cut edge at each of the back corners and temporary tack. Use a regulator or screwdriver to tuck in the small tongue of fabric. Complete tacking all around the frame, except around the front corners.

Right: Adapt the techniques of fitting a calico cover around back and front corners of a chair to work around arms, or other obstructions. Avoid back-ache by working with the chair on a table.

Completing the front corners and top cover

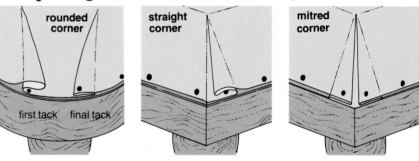

The front corners can be finished by folding in the surplus fabric in various different ways, depending on the angle of the corner. Trim away as much surplus fabric as possible from the back of pleats.
For a soft, rounded corner, pull the fabric flat over the corner and tack each side, then make the surplus fabric into a small, outwards-facing pleat on either side. Hold the underwrap of each pleat with a tack, arrange the fold of pleat neatly and tack again through all thicknesses.
On a sharp, straight corner, cut across the corner to trim away some fabric. Tack right along the front edge of the frame and push the surplus fabric into a pleat round the side.
A mitred corner Cut across the corner to trim away fabric and form the fabric into a triangular inverted pleat at the corner point.

Adding the top cover
Trim the calico close to the tacks all round the seat.
Attach the top cover in exactly the same way as the calico but, to add a neat finish to the corners, use a strong thread and a curved needle to catch stitch down the top folded edge of each pleat. If you are planning to add decorative nail heads (see Professional Touch) fold raw edge under.

a selection of
suitable fabrics

The finishing touches

Unless the fabric wraps round to the underside of the chair, the line of tacks holding the top cover in place will be visible and should be disguised by a trimming. Choose either braid or decorative nails, either of which provides an attractive finish even when there are no tack-heads to be covered.

Attach braid or gimp (upholsterers' braid) with a fabric adhesive and gimp pins, which are tacks with small coloured heads to match the gimp.

Tack down a short end of the gimp as in the diagram, then stick the gimp over this end and the row of tacks, drawing it fairly tight as you work and securing with a gimp pin at intervals. Turn in the remaining short end before completing the sticking process and hold with another gimp pin.

Decorative nails have large domed heads with a coloured, brass or antique effect finish. Placing a piece of material temporarily over the nail head to

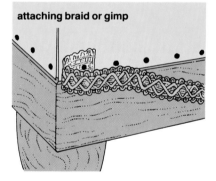

attaching braid or gimp

protect it, hammer in a nail beside each tack so that the nail head covers the smaller tack head. Either space out the nails as you would the tacks, or place them in a continuous line touching one another.

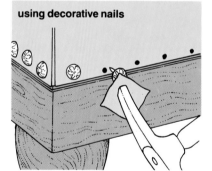

using decorative nails

The final touch, as on a drop-in seat, is to tack black cloth over the base of the frame.

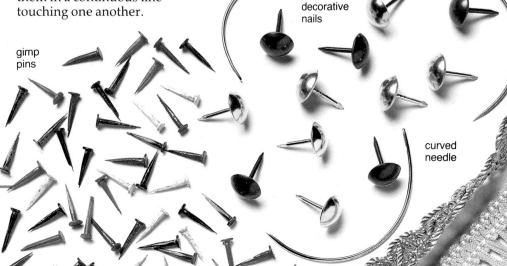

gimp pins

decorative nails

curved needle

Foam upholstery

In present day furniture production, foam and rubberized webbing have largely replaced traditional materials like horsehair and jute webbing. Readily available and clean and easy to work with, these modern materials are ideal for the home upholsterer.

Materials and methods used in upholstery remained largely unaltered for over two centuries but, with the commercial development of alternative materials, the last twenty five years or so have seen dramatic changes. Although top quality furniture is still upholstered in the traditional way, most modern furniture construction makes extensive use of foam, rubberized webbing, latex adhesives and synthetic fillings. These newer materials make upholstering stools, chairs, even simple settees, easy to tackle at home.

Upholstery foam

Initially, the cost of a foam pad for a chair seat may seem high, but there are several advantages in using one rather than traditional materials: it eliminates the need for several layers of filling or wadding; its edge gives a firm shape and feel without sewing or making edge rolls; it is clean to deal with in both installation and stripping; and it overcomes the need for springs.

Although it is slightly more expensive, you can buy foam that has been treated to become flame retardant. Even so, it is advisable to minimize fire risk by choosing natural fibre fabrics such as wool and cotton, for the top cover.

A foam pad can be placed over a base of either solid wood or rubberized webbing. If the base is solid – for example, a sheet of chipboard – drill holes about 5mm/¼in in diameter through the wood at 5cm/2in intervals. When foam is compressed by being sat upon, a large volume of air is displaced; without the holes which allow this air to escape, the pressure could burst the top cover material out of place!

Strips of calico secure foam seats in place on the frame and can also be used to compress the edges into different shapes.

Buying foam

There are three main types of foam generally available:

Latex is the original foam, made from a latex rubber, and extremely resilient. Latex foam may be referred to by trade names such as Pincore or Dunlopillo; it is the best quality foam available – firm, comfortable and durable – but the most expensive.

Polyether foam, sometimes referred to as synthetic rubber, is more reasonable in cost, more readily available and – with recent advances in the industry – is of a quality ideal for upholstery. Always ensure that the density of the foam you purchase is right for upholstery; lighter foam (often sold as 'craft foam') will give your upholstery the right look but the wrong feel and it will not last well.

Chipfoam, sometimes known as Polyfoam, is a heavy, dense type of foam made from thousands of foam chips bonded together by an adhesive. It has a multi-coloured, speckled appearance. Being so dense, it is ideal used as a base layer with normal upholstery foam on top. Although rather firm, it can be used alone in seats subjected to heavy wear.

Rubberized webbing

Use this to form a base for a seat, or a support for a back cushion, on a skeleton frame. Pirelli webbing is the best known of the elasticated webbings which, as they give when sat on, have often replaced springs.

This webbing does not fray and is very economical to use. The only tools required to attach it are a hammer, scissors and some upholstery tacks. Patented clips are available for furniture with a groove or mortice in the frame. They are squeezed on to the end of the webbing with a vice, then slid into position.

Wire clips made specifically for attaching webbing to metal-framed furniture are also available.

Cutting and shaping foam

Cutting A serrated bread knife or very sharp craft knife are all you need to cut the foam. Draw lines to mark intended cuts and place one half of the piece of foam (or the area you are retaining) on a firm surface so that the cut will be made close to the edge of that surface. Cut with firm strokes of the knife, not attempting to force the blade, and you will find an accurate cut is easily achieved.

Shaping If you can't obtain the shape you require by cutting a foam

Below: Use lightweight foam, shaping it to fit, on a chair back or back panel. Apply in the same way as for a seat, but complete the back with a panel of top fabric rather than a black undercloth. On the style shown, the seat fabric wraps round to be secured to the underside of the seat.

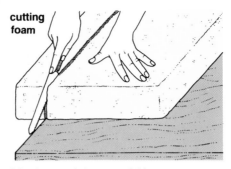

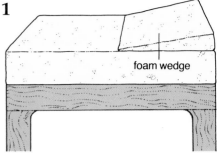

block – or if this would be uneconomical – stick foam shapes together with a foam or latex adhesive such as Dunlop or Bostik. Be sure to use the correct adhesive specifically recommended for the type of synthetic or rubber foam you are using, as the wrong one could 'melt' the foam. Following the adhesive manufacturers' instructions, simply stick the required shapes together.

1 So that the front edges of chairs and cushions are firm enough to give good support to the backs of the knees, it is advisable to glue an extra wedge of foam to the top front area of the cushion. This is compressed by the top cover to a firm, even shape.

Preparing a webbing base

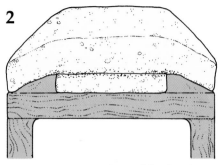

2

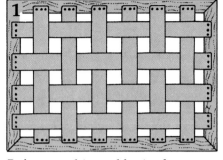

1

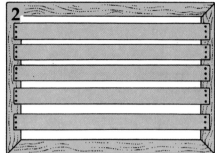

2

2 To give a seat a domed look, place a smaller piece of foam immediately beneath the main cushion as shown.
To soften hard edges of a foam block, place a layer of synthetic wadding on top, cut slightly larger than the foam. Cut away excess at corners and trim level with foam around lower edge.

Before attaching rubberized webbing, round off the inside edges of the frame if necessary, as any sharp edges will wear through it.
1 When uncovered foam is being placed directly on top of rubber webbing to form the seat of a chair, stool or settee (or the lid of a box or ottoman), the webbing must be interwoven to lie in both directions. When the webbing is to support a fabric-covered cushion, as on the

seat and back of some fireside chairs, it only needs to run in one direction, either lengthwise or crosswise.
2 Wherever possible, position crosswise webbing so that as many strands as possible are concentrated at the back of the seat where the maximum load occurs. Ideally, the spaces between the webs should be no greater than the width of the webbing used.

Simple seat upholstered with foam

The value of antique furniture would be reduced by re-upholstering with anything but the appropriate traditional materials, but foam and rubber webbing are ideal for modern chair seats and stools.

You will need
Chair or stool with fixed or drop-in seat, stripped down to frame
Rubberized webbing to span frame in both directions at 10cm/4in intervals
15mm/⅝in upholstery tacks and hammer
5–8cm/2–3in deep foam of suitable quality cut to exact size of frame
Latex/foam adhesive
5cm/2in wide calico strips
Lightweight synthetic wadding to cover foam (optional)
Top cover fabric, preferably flame-retardant
Black fabric to finish base (optional)

Attaching the webbing
Rubberized webbing is positioned and applied in much the same way as woven webbing (see page 200) but the correct tension is achieved only by careful measuring.
Attach one end of webbing to the centre back of the frame with a single row of tacks at least 5mm/¼in in from the end. It is important to

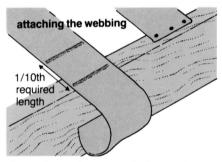

attaching the webbing

1/10th required length

drive the tacks in vertically as the heads of any knocked in at an angle may cut into the cords of the webbing and cause it to split.
Lay the unstretched webbing from front to back of chair frame and mark the required length. Measure this length, deduct one tenth of the measurement and mark a second, shorter length.
Stretching the webbing until the second mark lies in the centre of the opposite side of the frame, secure with tacks. Cut off surplus webbing at least 5mm/¼in away from tacks. Attach further strips of webbing spaced evenly over the chair at approximately 10cm/4in intervals, in the same way. Interweaving the ends, attach strips across the chair.

Adding a foam seat
Cut 5cm/2in wide strips of calico to approximately half the length of

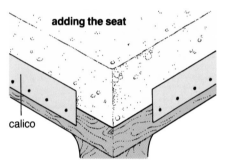

adding the seat

calico

each side of the foam. Using the appropriate adhesive, stick each calico strip centrally along one side of the foam so that half the width of calico extends below lower edge.
Place the foam in position on the seat frame and tack the calico strips to the frame sides to hold foam securely. If necessary, add a thin layer of wadding over the foam, cutting away excess at corners and trimming level with foam around lower edge, as described earlier.
Completing the seat Add a top cover by placing fabric right side up centrally over the seat. Pulling it taut, but without compressing the foam, tack in place, folding the fabric into neat pleats at corners as given for stuffed-over seats (see page 206).
Complete the underside with black cloth as on a drop-in seat (see page 198).

Loose covers: planning and cutting patterns

Add years of extra life to dull or shabby chairs and settees with new loose covers made in a smart and stylish fabric. Start by making pattern pieces from old material to help you calculate fabric requirements and to make cutting out virtually foolproof.

Well-fitted loose covers can transform the oddest collection of chairs, sofas, footstools and pouffes into a co-ordinated suite at comparatively little cost. They are an extremely practical alternative to re-upholstering old furniture or buying new, and since they can be removed for washing or dry-cleaning, they keep their good looks for a long time.

Loose covers are not at all difficult to make, although it is better to start with a simple piece of upholstered furniture such as a chair without arms or a pouffe and master the basic techniques.

No special tools or equipment are needed – a swing-needle sewing machine is useful to zigzag stitch seam edges, but not strictly necessary. It is worth buying T-pins (sold for macramé), especially if you will be working with large areas of heavy fabric, as they are easier to handle than small dressmaking pins.

The covers can be fitted to the furniture with simple cased drawstrings, zips, press stud tape or Velcro.

Furniture must be sound and in good condition and should be repaired if necessary before you start. Repairs, especially those to webbing and padding, can change the surface shape of

the furniture considerably and the new covers will no longer fit as smoothly as they should.

See pages 90-93 for details of making up gusseted covers for any box cushions that lie separately on the seat or against the back.

Careful planning

Before cutting the pattern, consider your piece of furniture carefully and plan the position of seams, deciding whether they are to be as few and as unobtrusive as possible or more conspicuous to act as design features.

Contrasting piping sewn in the seam defines the chair shape and adds extra interest but unless this is to be a feature, it is generally better to avoid any unnecessary seams. The seat piece, for example, can often be cut in

Left: With a valanced loose cover, the older chair, left, would look just as pretty as its modern counterpart.

one with the front gusset, especially if a loose box cushion is to sit on top. On many chairs, the inside back fabric curves over to seam with the outside back piece along the outer top edge. However, on furniture with deep scrolled backs, the inside back fabric should be taken right around the curve so that the seam will lie at the base of the scroll. The same applies to inside arm pieces.

Also plan the best method of attaching the cover to the chair, and whether any zips or other fastenings will be required.

Unless you are planning to finish the lower edge with a skirt or valance, a drawstring threaded through a channelled hem will hold the lower edge of a loose cover in place underneath the chair and retain a snug fit. If your chair has feet or legs right in the corners, you will need to cut away some of the extra hem allowance to fit around these.

Fastenings One zip is usually sufficient – it should be long enough to extend from the base to above the level of the arm – but two may be necessary on large items. Press stud tape or Velcro can be used on small furniture or loose cushions.

Choosing fabrics

The traditional fabrics for loose covers are linen/union, a tough blend of linen and cotton, or chintz, a lighter weight cotton fabric usually with a printed design and often with a glazed surface.

Linen/union is the more hardwearing of the two, but chintz is easier to handle. Many other furnishing fabrics can be used provided they are closely woven and suitably heavyweight to take the wear and tear of constant use. Check before you buy, too, for colour fastness and shrinkage and, if unsure, shrink the fabric before making up.

Avoid velvets, knitted, stretch or looped pile fabrics and plain satin finish fabrics which will crease in use and show every mark.

For economy, choose either plain or textured weaves or small repeat patterns without a nap, so that pattern shapes can be dovetailed neatly together to avoid waste. The least

a selection of fabrics

economical and most awkward designs are those with large motifs which need to be placed centrally on various sections of the furniture, wasting some of the surrounding area of fabric.

However the extra expense will be justified if a large motif or even a border print is carefully positioned for maximum effect.

Using piping

Piping is traditionally used in loose covers to highlight any seams which emphasise the interesting sculptural shapes of the furniture underneath. It is not difficult to include when stitching seams and as the piping cord can often be covered by off-cuts of the main fabric (although you may need to allow extra fabric), it costs very little in time or money to add this professional-looking finishing touch. You can, of course, cover the piping in a contrasting colour or in a plain colour chosen to match a printed fabric for extra effect. When choosing a separate fabric for piping, consider texture, weight, finish and durability, as well as colour, and avoid bulky fabrics with a pronounced weave.

213

Making patterns

Professional loose cover makers work without a pattern, cutting directly from the furnishing fabric even on the most complicated furniture shapes. However, by making a pattern first you can estimate exact requirements before buying fabric and also arrange the placing of motifs with the least wastage, especially if you are making covers for several items at once.

As paper will not 'give' sufficiently around the more complicated curved areas, cut patterns from fabric such as old sheets, discarded curtains, lining or cheap calico. If the furniture already has loose covers that need replacing, these can be taken apart and used as the patterns. Make sure, though, that any tears or large holes are patched or roughly repaired first so that the pattern keeps its shape, and that the old covers fit the chair correctly, altering them if necessary.

Estimating fabric quantities

It does help to decide in advance which fabric you intend buying, so that you know the fabric width and

Making patterns for a simple chair

Remove any loose seat cushions and draw a chalk line down the exact centre of the chair, on both back and front.

Inside back Cut a piece of the pattern-making fabric about 15cm/6in wider and 20cm/8in longer than the widest and longest measurements of the inside back. Fold the fabric in half lengthwise and pin the fold to the chalk line with T-pins, positioning top edge 2.5cm/1in over the line at which inside back and outside back will meet. Anchor the doubled fabric to the chair near the top and outside edges with T-pins and trim the fabric to the shape of the top and sides of the chair allowing 2.5cm/1in on each edge for seams. Trim the lower edge to allow about 10cm/4in for the tuck-in and seam.

Seat top Make the pattern to fit the seat area in the same way as for the inside back, but adding the tuck-in and seam allowance to the back edge and 2.5cm/1in allowance to remaining edges.

Outside back and front gusset These, too, are made in the same way but add 10cm/4in allowance to the lower edge on each piece to form the hem and cord channel for drawing up on underside of chair.

Side gussets The side piece and the shaped side gusset illustrated can be cut in one piece if this will not be too wasteful of fabric. Pin a single layer of fabric to the side of the chair leaving 10cm/4in on the lower edge for hem and channel allowance and 2.5cm/1in to all other edges for seams and trim to fit. Reverse pattern piece(s) by turning over when cutting the final fabric for the opposite side of the chair.

Patterns for an armchair

Make the inside back, outside back and outer side gussets as before, but flaring out the side seam allowance on the inside back tuck-in area to 10cm/4in at the base.

Seat top Make as before, allowing as well as the back tuck-in, a tuck-in allowance along each side tapering from 10cm/4in at the back edge to 2.5cm/1in at the front.

The front gussets Make the central gusset as before but also make a pattern in single fabric of one of the arm front gussets, adding the same allowances of 2.5cm/1in for top and sides but 10cm/4in for lower edge.

The inside arms Pin the fabric over one arm adding the normal seam allowance on all sides except along the edge lying over the seat and trim. This should have a 10cm/4in allowance at the back tapering to 2.5cm/1in at the front.

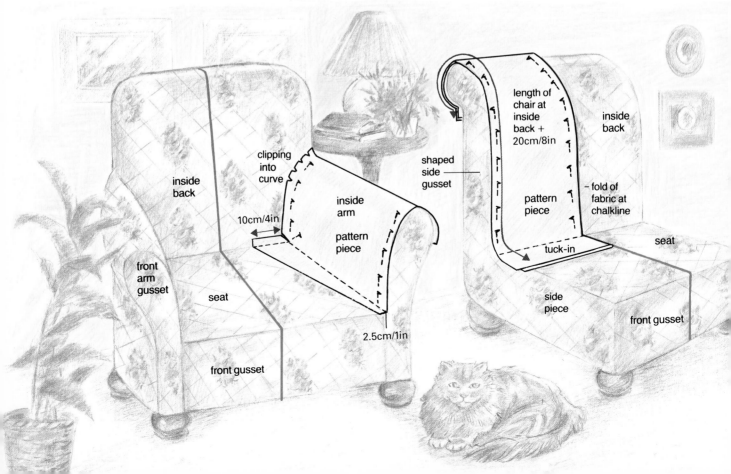

whether any pattern matching must be allowed for.

With very simple items such as footstools – and with more complex things as you gain experience – you will be able to calculate fabric requirements simply by measuring the surfaces to be covered and adding allowances for seams, hems and pattern matching. However, making a pattern simplifies fabric estimation, no matter how many pattern pieces you have and how awkward their shape. Simply mark out on the floor an area the width of your fabric (probably 120cm/48in) and lay out the pattern pieces you have made within this area, reversing sections where necessary to include both left and right hand sides of the article. Remember to make patterns for any separate box cushions and to allow extra fabric for cutting 6cm/2½in wide bias strips for piping. The length of floor area taken up by the pattern pieces will be the length of fabric you need to buy.

Below: Making and fitting a fabric pattern first helps you to visualise how the finished loose cover will look.

Patterns for a settee

Loose covers for a settee are made in almost exactly the same way as for a chair, the only real difference being the width of the seat and back pieces. These sections generally require more than one width of fabric and should be made up before you start the other seams. It is important to place designs centrally, and generally the best way to do this is to have a whole width of fabric in the centre and to add to it on either side as shown, rather than having a centre seam. In this case, measure half the width of your fabric minus a seam allowance from the centre line, draw a second line over the settee at this point and make patterns for each section as for a chair. Remember to add a seam allowance to the straight inside edge of each outer back section.

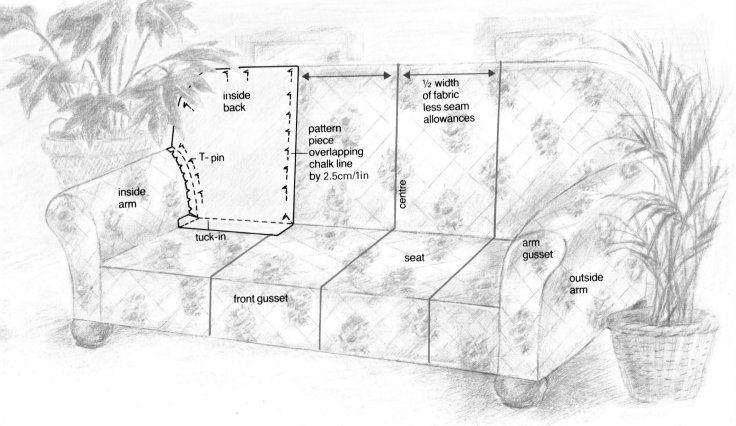

Loose covers: fitting and making up

Cutting out and making up loose covers requires only basic sewing skills and a common-sense approach. Having made a pattern and chosen a practical and attractive fabric, it is surprisingly easy to complete professional-looking and perfectly fitting covers.

The secret of professional-looking loose covers is a perfect fit.

To achieve a smooth fit, pin each seam while the cut-out cover pieces are in position on the chair. Place the fabric pieces right side down on the chair, so that you are working with the cover inside out, and simply remove the cover as you stitch each pinned seam. However, check that older chairs are still quite symmetrical before working in this way: if they are not, the cover will not fit properly when turned the right way out as this also reverses left and right hand sides. In this case, lay the fabric right side up on the chair, pin and mark positions for seamlines, remove and, before stitching, re-pin with right sides facing. You will also have to re-pin seams if inserting piping.

The finished covers should fit smoothly and firmly but not too tightly. They will stretch slightly in use and probably shrink a little in washing. (A useful tip is to put washed covers back on the chairs while slightly damp – they will stretch over the chairs more easily than if bone-dry and will probably not need ironing. This is particularly true of linen/union fabric.)

Attaching loose covers

The lower edge of loose covers can be secured in place in several different ways, depending on the type of furniture. The simplest method, used on solid foam furniture and items with no legs or where the legs of a chair are set within the perimeter of the frame, is with a cord drawstring threaded through the channelled hem.

Where the legs of the furniture are flush with the outer edges of the chair frame, the hem must be shaped to fit around them, then wrapped underneath, and can be held by a drawstring, Velcro or screw-in press studs.

With Sew 'n' stick Velcro, the self-adhesive half can be stuck to the underside of the wooden frame and the corresponding half sewn to the wrong side of the cover edge. Ordinary Velcro must be attached to the wood with small upholstery tacks.

Screw-in press studs designed for loose covers can also be used on a wooden frame. Attach the screw-in halves at the corners and spaced evenly along the frame at about 10cm/4in intervals, and sew the corresponding halves to the cover.

If you prefer to finish the lower edge with a valance or frill (explained in the next chapter), the lower hem allowance can be omitted and the cover held in place with tapes sewn into the seam allowance at the top of the valance. The tapes are positioned in pairs at the corners and tied around the legs.

You will need

T-pins and dressmaking pins
Pattern pieces cut from old material
Main fabric as estimated from
  measuring pattern
Strong sewing thread to match
Piping cord (optional)

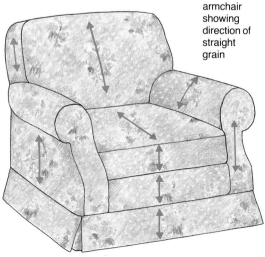

armchair showing direction of straight grain

Heavy-duty zip(s), press stud tape
  or Velcro fastening as necessary
  for openings on covers and
  cushions
Drawstring cord, Sew 'n' stick
  Velcro *or* screw-in press studs to
  attach covers
Loose cover pins
Self-adhesive labels (optional)

Cutting out

Mark the right side of each pattern piece with its position (inside back, etc), the direction of the straight

grain as in the diagram and whether it is a left or right hand piece.
Lay out the fabric. With a boldly patterned fabric, or one with a border print, it may help to work with a single thickness so that pieces can be cut with motifs centralised or well positioned; otherwise fabric may be doubled. Lay out the pattern pieces, making sure that the grain is running true on each piece and that the fabric design will be the right way up when positioned on the chair. If

cutting from single fabric, remember to reverse pieces where necessary to cut a left and right hand section. Cut out all pieces – not forgetting cushion covers and being sure to add all necessary turnings.
If you feel there is any chance of muddling sections or forgetting which is the top edge or the right side of the fabric, write the name of each section on a self-adhesive label and, as you remove the pattern pieces, stick a label on the wrong

Above: Beautifully-fitted covers can transform a well-worn piece of furniture. Piped edges and a pleated valance combine to add a professional touch to this bright, fresh-looking settee cover.

side close to the top edge on each fabric piece.
If piping is required, measure each seam to be piped and cut bias strips of fabric approximately 6cm/2½in wide from spare – or contrasting – fabric to cover this length of piping cord.

Making up loose covers

Pin each seam with the cover positioned on the chair and with both layers together, clip into the seam allowance at intervals, removing small triangular notches of fabric. Line up the notches to match exactly the same points when re-pinning the fabric off the chair, and when stitching.

Remove the pinned sections from the chair to stitch, trim and neaten each seam before adding the next section. This helps to prevent undue fraying while you work and also saves a mammoth zigzagging or overcasting job at the end. The finished seams should be trimmed to about 2cm/¾in.

As each seam is marked by pinning, place any piping required along the seamline, repinning as necessary, before stitching. See page 165 for details of joining bias strips and page 87 for covering piping cord and inserting it.

Begin by joining the inner back to the outer back. Trim and neaten the seam and press it open. Position the fabric on the chair again and hold the seamline in place along the chair edge with T-pins.

Also join the top of the front gusset to the front edge of the seat cover, neaten the seam and press open.

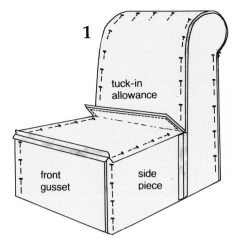

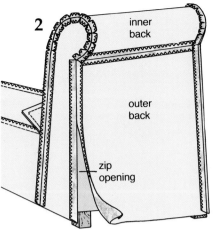

Chairs without arms

1 Join the side pieces to side gussets, neaten the seam and press open.

Assembling the cover Position all sections of the cover on the chair. Pin the side gusset piece to both sections of the back and to the seat cover, making sure that the tuck-in allowance will fit in the space down the back of the seat. Check that seams lie exactly along the edges of the chair where possible. When all sections fit smoothly over the chair and with the tuck-in sticking out, trim seam allowances to within 2.5cm/1in of the pin line and notch them for matching up.

Remove the cover from the chair, and, with notches matching, stitch the back edge of the seat cover to the base of the inside back, pivoting the stitching around the needle at the corners to continue sewing along the sides of the tuck-in allowance. Clip into the seam allowance at the ends of the stitching line and fold the tuck-in allowance out of the way to stitch the side gussets in place, matching notches and remembering to leave part of one back seam open for a zip fastener, if required. Trim the seams to 2cm/¾in, neaten and press towards gusset.

2 Replace cover on chair to check fit, and mark position of zip ends.

Completing the loose cover

Insert any fastenings required in one of the corner seams, making sure that they reach the level of the base edge of the chair but without extending into the hem allowance.

For a simple drawstring hem, press a 1cm/½in turning and then a 2cm/¾in turning to the wrong side of the cover all round the lower edge. Machine stitch close to the turned-in edge of hem to form the channel, leaving a small gap for inserting the drawstring, unless there is an opening in one corner beneath a fastening. Thread a drawstring (a piece of piping cord will do) through the channel of the hem, place the cover over the chair, and pull the drawstring up to hold the hem on the underside of the chair. Tie ends securely and tuck them inside the edges of the cover.

To fit a drawstring hem around the feet or legs of a chair, place the

cover on the chair, pulling it well down all around the base. Feeling for the position of each leg, clip vertically into the hem allowance on both sides of each leg up to 2cm/¾in below the base of the frame. Cut away the rectangle of excess fabric around each leg, insert a line of stay stitching level with the frame base and clip diagonally up to this as

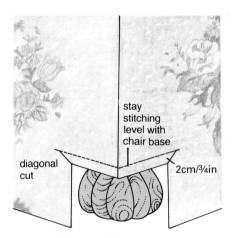

shown. When all four corners are trimmed in this way, remove the cover from the chair and turn up a 2cm/¾in hem to fit around each corner.

Turn in and stitch the side edges. Finish the lower edges with a channelled hem as before, place the cover on the chair and thread the cord through each side section in

218

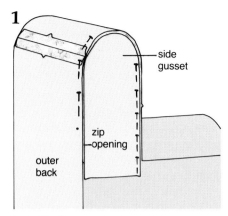

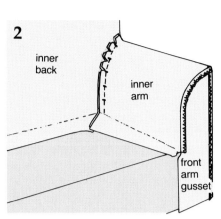

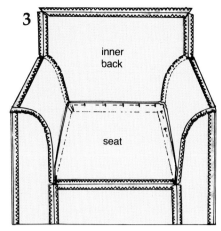

Armchairs

1 Pin the side gussets to inner and outer back sections. If you are inserting a zip in the cover, measure its length from the base upwards and leave one of the back corner seams open to accommodate it (it should reach a point about halfway between the top of the arm and the top of the chair). When each pinned section fits smoothly over the back of the chair, trim seam allowances to within 2.5cm/1in of the pin line and notch them for matching up; mark top of opening, if used. Remove the cover from the chair and, with right sides together and matching notches, stitch the seams. Trim the seam allowances to 2cm/ ¾in, overcast and press towards

the gusset. Replace on chair. Make up each arm section in turn by first joining inside arm and side-piece and then adding front gusset, fitting and pinning it in place. Press the first seam open, the curved arm seam towards gusset and the straight gusset seam open.
2 Place the arm covers on the chair and pin to back section and side gusset, easing around any curves by clipping into the seam allowance and re-pinning as often as necessary to achieve a smooth fit. Stitch the sections together, remembering to leave the zip opening if required.
Pin all sections, including the front gusset/seat cover piece in position on the chair. Remove to join the

sides of the front gusset to the front arm gussets. Neaten these seams and press open.
3 Replace the cover on the chair and pin together the seams between the seat and the inner arm and back sections. These do not require tight fitting because they will be tucked in, but they may need trimming and adjusting slightly so that the fabric edges lie together. Stitch these seams, trim and neaten all round the raw edges.

Settees

Cover in the same way as an armchair but first joining widths of fabric to make up the back, seat and front sections as described in making patterns (see page 215).

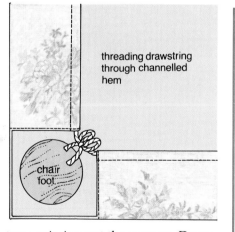

turn, missing out the corners. Draw up and tie as before.
If you are planning to add a flounce or valance to your cover, omit the drawstring.

PROFESSIONAL TOUCH

Useful aids for fitting

Various types of pins sold specifically for loose covers are available in many haberdashery departments. Use these at the base of scroll arms or backs, or wherever the fabric needs to be anchored close to the chair.
The corkscrew type of pin is screwed through the fabric of the cover into the padded upholstery of the furniture and only the small transparent button will show. The double-pronged type is simply pushed into the padding so that the short metal

bar – which is barely noticeable in use – lies on the right side of the fabric.
A useful tip to prevent covers riding out around the seat of an armchair is to push rolled newspaper down into the tuck-in area. This will form itself to the shape of the seat and help to anchor the cover.

clockwise: T-pins, double-pronged pins, screw-in press stud and corkscrew pins

Loose cover variations

Don't let furniture with padded curves or awkward-looking shapes deter you from making loose covers: these apparently problem areas are usually quite easy to cope with. And adding a valance improves furniture proportions and disguises ugly legs.

Chairs and settees suitable for loose covers come in all shapes and sizes. However, the method of cutting fabric pattern pieces directly over the furniture to be covered enables you to cope with even the most complicated-looking shapes. Follow the instructions for basic styles of chair and settee given on pages 212-215 and 216-219, incorporating the guidelines in this chapter for wing sides, scroll arms or curved backs as necessary. You will then be able to tackle almost any style of loose cover, with or without a valance.

Loose cover valances

A decorative valance can add the finishing touch to a tailored loose

Below: A beautifully printed, crisp, glazed cotton fabric adds style to a settee. Apricot binding outlines the knife pleated valance.

cover. Use one to improve the overall proportions of a piece of furniture, to disguise an unsightly gap between the base of a chair or settee and the floor, or to hide legs that are not particularly attractive. There are several different styles of valance to choose from, bearing in mind the shape and style of your furniture and the type of room scheme it is to co-ordinate with.

The simplest valance to make is a gathered strip of fabric stitched to the lower edge of the cover to form a frill. This is ideal for bedroom or cottage/country-style furniture and works well with soft or reasonably light-weight fabrics which drape easily, but is not suitable for heavy, bulky fabrics.

For elegant or sharply modern styles of furniture, choose a straight ungathered valance adding a mock pleat at each corner to prevent puckering. This is the most economical style of valance to make, requiring the least fabric, but make up with care for a smartly tailored look.

The plainness of a straight valance can be softened by the addition of a braid trim or fringing, or by shaping the lower edge into scallops.

A box-pleated valance can be an unusual and very smart alternative. It is a little more time-consuming to make since you must calculate the number and width of pleats to fit the dimensions of each side of your chair and it also takes up a larger amount of fabric. However, it looks very stylish and avoiding the 'frilly' effect of a gathered valance or the plainness of a straight style, will blend with almost any room scheme.

There are many more design possibilities including inverted pleats, knife pleats and ruffles, and all styles can have a decorative trimming.

Measuring up for a valance

As it is a straight strip of fabric, there is no need to make a fabric pattern for the valance unless you wish to use it to visualize the finished effect.

On items such as chairs with short wooden legs, try to align the top edge of the valance with the lower edge of the seat base, as long as the proportions look right. Otherwise, with the main pattern pieces in position on the chair or settee, mark the desired height for the valance with a horizontal chalk line drawn all round the chair, measuring up from the floor at intervals to ensure an even depth.

Trim the lower edge of the loose cover to 2cm/¾in below the base of seat or the chalk line.

To calculate depth of valance strip measure from chalk line to 1cm/½in above floor (to allow clearance) and add 2cm/¾in for the top seam and 5cm/2in for the hem (unless binding the edge).

The length of the strip varies according to the style, but is based on the length of chalkline (distance around seat base).

Making a frilled valance

To calculate the length of the valance strip, measure all round the chair or settee along chalk line or around seat base and add at least half as much again to this length to allow for fullness. Cut enough fabric strips of the required depth including hems to make up this length, and join pieces with narrow flat or French seams. Turn up and stitch a 5cm/2in hem so that the finished valance will clear the floor. If the furniture base is square, fold the fabric into quarters and mark each fold with a small notch cut into the top edge of the fabric. The notches mark the four corners of the chair. If the chair is rectangular,

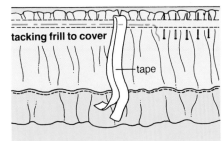

tacking frill to cover

tape

work out the relative proportions of the different sides and fold so that you will have the same amount of fullness on each side. Notch to mark corners in the same way. Insert two lines of gathering stitches between each of the notches, close to seamline 2cm/¾in down from top edge, then draw up each section in turn to fit.

Tacking frill to cover

With right sides together, pin and tack the frill to the lower edge of the otherwise finished cover from one side of the opening to the other, taking care to match notches to corners and distributing gathers evenly.

Cut four lengths of cord or tape for anchoring the cover to the chair, fold each in half and tack one to each corner with the folded edge over the valance seamline. Stitch valance to cover, catching in tapes. Remove tacking and neaten raw edges to complete.

Making a box-pleated valance

Calculate the height of the valance strip as for a gathered style. Cut and join strips to make a piece three times the length around chair plus seam allowances for the two ends which butt together at any back zip opening or at a back corner.

Turn in and stitch hems along lower edge and short ends, mitring the two outer corners.

Fold and press pleats of equal size, starting from the centre front. Tack them in place along the top and bottom edges.

With right sides together, and catching in ties as in gathered valance, pin, tack and stitch the pleated valance to the cover, ensuring that the pleating looks symmetrical along each side.

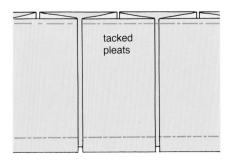

tacked pleats

Making a tailored valance

Calculate height of valance strip as above. On this style of valance, separate strips running along each side of the chair or settee meet at the corners, forming mock pleats. Measure each side of the piece of furniture separately and cut valance strips to fit, adding 4cm/1½in for side hems to each strip. If more than one piece of fabric is needed to make up the length of a valance strip, add seam allowances as necessary and join pieces with narrow French seams, matching patterns where possible.

Cut a square of fabric to the same depth as the valance strip for backing each corner 'pleat'.

Turn in and stitch a double 1cm/½in hem along short side edges of each strip and on the two vertical sides of square pleat backing pieces. Turn up and stitch a 5cm/2in hem along

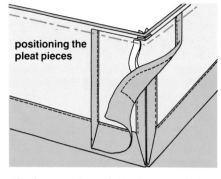

the lower edge of all pieces, mitring the corners on the main strips.

Trim about 1cm/½in from the top edge of each pleat backing piece to prevent it hanging below valance. With right sides together, pin and tack the valance strips to the lower edge of the cover, butting ends together at corners.

Place pleat pieces in position centrally over each corner join, right

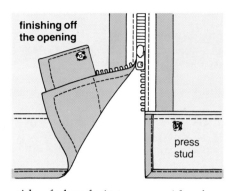

side of pleat facing wrong side of valance and top edges level. Adding tapes or cords at the corners as for the gathered frill, tack and stitch valance to cover.

Finishing off the opening

At the zip opening corner, stitch only half the pleat piece in with one side of the valance and sew a press stud or piece of Velcro to the other half to close the corner.

Coping with curves

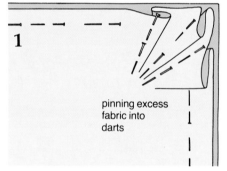

Because you are working with fabric directly on the piece of furniture, it is not difficult to tailor a loose cover to fit apparently awkward shapes such as deep padding on curved backs or scroll arms.

Curved backs

When the inside back piece curves over the padded back of a chair or settee to meet the outside back piece, with no side gussets in between, make unstitched darts or small pleats to dispose of the extra

Left: Piped wings, panelled scroll arms and an unusual valance add the professional touch to a chair cover. As loose covers are easy to clean and to replace when worn or outdated, many top-quality manufacturers offer chairs and settees upholstered only in calico leaving the choice of cover fabric entirely up to you.

Making loose covers for wing chairs

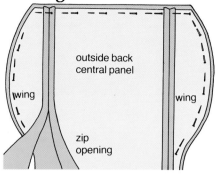

These are made in basically the same way as for other armchairs but with the addition of the wing sections.

To make the pattern, cut three separate pieces for the outside back – a central panel and two added wings – so that the zip fastener can be inserted into one of the seams between wing and panel. Cut the inside back in one piece including

wings, taking care to anchor the fabric well down into the crease where the wing joins the main part of the chair. If insufficient fabric is allowed here, the cover will pull away from the chair, losing the definite shape of the inside of the wing.

To make up, start by joining the outside back to the two wing sections, leaving a zip opening from bottom edge upwards in one of the seams.

Join the outside back to the inside back around the top and sides and then proceed as for an ordinary armchair.

When the finished cover is fitted on to the chair, anchor it in the inner wing crease with a line of double-pronged loose cover pins.

Right: Removing covers for cleaning.

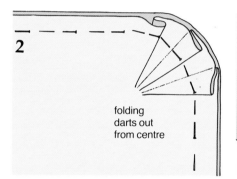

fullness of fabric created at corners. Position the relevant fabric pieces on the chair and pin the centre top edges and all straightforward areas together, keeping the grain straight. Smooth the fabric over the chair, with the excess accumulating at corners.
1 Keeping the effect symmetrical, divide the excess fabric into several small darts where necessary and pin.
2 Trim seam allowance to an even 2cm/1in all round, folding darts outwards from centre.
Stitch seam between outer and inner back pieces, catching down base of darts.

Curved scroll arms
An attractive way of dealing with the very full, curved arms found on some chairs is to gather or pleat the front edges of the arm covers behind a piping-edged, flat front panel. Allow extra fabric on the front edges of the inner and outer arm cover pieces, to wrap over the arm edge around the curve to the flat front of the arm. Join the inner and outer arm pieces and use T-pins to anchor them firmly to the chair, with seam correctly positioned and *right side out.*
1 By hand, run a line of large gathering stitches around the top front edge beginning and ending just below the start of the curve. Draw up tightly, distributing the gathers evenly in tiny pleats around the curve of the arm.
Cut a shaped front panel (usually keyhole-shaped) to fit the front of

the arm inside the padded curve, adding 2.5cm/1in turnings around the top and sides and usual hem allowance at base.
2 Pin, tack and stitch the piping to right side of panel along the seamline around top and sides, using a piping foot to stitch as close as possible to the cord. Turn the raw edges over to the wrong side so that piping protrudes around edge, clipping the curves to enable the seam to lay flat. Tack the turnings to hold them in place, position the panel on the front of the arm and pin in place.
3 Taking care not to take the stitches through to the upholstery of the chair, tack the panel to gathered edge of cover, enclosing raw edges. Remove cover from chair and topstitch the panel to the gathered section, stitching just inside the line of piping. Trim and neaten as usual.

223

PART 8

Garden ideas

These final chapters contain suggestions for re-covering deck-chairs and director's chairs and instructions on how to make a hammock together with ideas for quilted covers and cushions for added comfort. Children will love the teepee and space capsule, which makes use of appliqué, stencilling and fabric painting and can be used successfully indoors and out.

All the seating projects are made from tough fabrics such as canvas which will withstand occasionally being left out of doors in sun and rain and are strong enough to take the weight of an adult. To help repel dirt and moisture, spray the material with a fabric protector such as Scotchguard. Unfortunately all dyes will fade ultimately if the fabric is left in bright sunlight but you can delay this by making sure your garden furniture is left in the shade when not in use.

The heavier types of canvas used to make the hammock or deckchair are best sewn on a machine using heavyweight needles, size 110/18. Choose a heavy-duty polyester thread and a stitch size of 2.5-3mm/⅛in. Work a double row of machine stitches for extra strength where necessary.

Re-furbishing canvas chairs for house and garden

When the canvas on a deck-chair or director's chair has worn through but the wooden frame is still perfectly sound, simply replace the canvas to give the chair a completely new lease of life. Add a quilted cover to make a deck-chair really luxurious.

Deck-chairs and director's chairs were designed for use in the garden or conservatory but nowadays both have found their way into the home as inexpensive and versatile seating. Whether used indoors or out, the chair canvas is likely to need replacing long before the frame wears out, and this is simple and inexpensive to do.

Traditional deck-chair canvas is tough, durable and less likely to rot if left out in a shed during the winter. It is available in a variety of widths including a narrow width that will fit any standard deckchair. If you wish to match the chairs to the room décor, however, any strong, non-stretch furnishing fabric could be used although it is unlikely to last as long. Add extra comfort to a deck-chair, by making a detachable quilted top-cover. Either quilt in simple straight lines or make the most of your needlecraft skills and quilt around the pattern on a suitable printed, patchwork or appliquéd fabric.

Re-covering a director's chair

Although all director's chairs are made to much the same basic construction with a separate canvas back and seat, on some the back is fixed, whereas on others it can be pivoted to a comfortable angle, and the method of attaching the back canvas varies accordingly.

You will need
Canvas or suitable tough fabric
Flat-headed tacks about 16mm/⅝in long
Suitable strong thread

Measuring up
Estimate the amount of new canvas needed by measuring the old back and seat fabric whilst still on the chair. Allow sufficient canvas to wrap around the wooden struts or to make casings in the same way as on the existing covers.

If attaching with tacks, add 1cm/½in for turning fabric to the wrong side before hammering in the tacks, and if making casings, allow for the size of casings that are on the existing cover plus 1cm/½in at each end for neatening.

Allow for a 1cm/½in and 1cm/½in double hem to neaten long edges of the back and seat which run across the width of chair unless you are able to make use of selvedges, in which case a 1cm/½in single hem is sufficient.

Removing the old covers
While doing this, take careful note of how everything is attached and in what order washers, bolts, etc, will fit back together.

The seat may have been attached with large headed tacks or staples. The latter are likely to be the industrial type with pre-glued ends – the glue melts as the staples are driven into the wood – and cannot be replaced with the average home or office staple gun.

Mark the position of the seat fabric edges by drawing pencil lines on to the wood, then use a blunt chisel or similar tool to ease out the old tacks or staples. If a staple is particularly difficult to remove, don't risk

Left: Paint the frame a cheerful colour before adding smart, new canvas to transform an old deck-chair or director's chair into stylish seating.

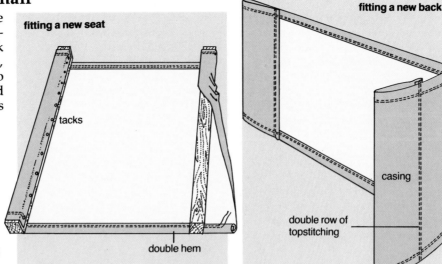

ruining the wood by forcing it, but cut away the fabric with a sharp craft knife and hammer the staple further into the wood until it lies flush with the surface. Remove the old seat canvas carefully, trying to keep it in one piece if possible as it can then be used as a pattern for the new seat.

The canvas back on some styles of director's chair can simply be lifted off. On others, you will first have to undo the appropriate nuts and bolts to remove the wooden back struts from the chair frame to release the fabric. Either slip the struts out of the fabric casing or, if the fabric is attached by tacks or staples, remove in the same way as the seat.

Fitting the new seat
Cut out the rectangle of fabric as measured, including hem allowances. On both long edges, which will lie unattached across the seat, turn a double hem (1cm/½in twice) to the wrong side and machine stitch, using a strong thread and a heavy-duty needle. Run a second row of stitching close to the first for extra strength. If you have a selvedge on one or both sides of the piece of fabric, a small single hem will be sufficient.

Turn 1cm/½in to the wrong side along each short edge. Lay the chair on its side and place one folded edge of fabric along the pencil line marked on the side bar. Hammer a tack into the centre of the fabric, close to the folded edge. Working outwards from this tack, insert three more on either side, spacing

them out evenly so that the outer tacks lie close to the corners of the fabric.
Stretch fabric across chair and attach opposite edge in the same way.

Fitting the new back
Neaten the long edges in the same was as on the seat.

If the old cover had a casing at each side to slip over side struts, turn 1cm/½in to the wrong side on each short edge, then fold the fabric over a second time to form a casing of the required size to take the strut. Hold down the edge with a double row of topstitching placed close together. Repeat on the opposite side.

If the old cover was tacked or stapled in position, turn 1cm/½in to the wrong side along each short edge of the fabric and wrap each of these edges around the back struts to lie on the inside edge of the strut. Working outwards from the centre tack each time and inserting five tacks each side, tack in place.

To replace any bolts that hold the back strut to the chair, pierce the fabric over the original hole with sharply pointed scissors then cut a small hole in the fabric.

Replace the canvas back and struts in the chair frame and secure with the nuts and bolts.

On the simpler style of chair back, just slip a cover with casings at each end over the back struts of the chair. Before attaching, topstitch across the top of each casing if you do not want the tip of the back struts to be visible.

Re-covering a deck-chair

Make any necessary repairs to the frame – or paint or stain it a bright new colour – between removing the old canvas and attaching the new.

You will need

Approximately 1.30m/51in of deck-chair canvas 40–43cm/16–17in wide
14 flat-headed tacks about 16mm/⅝in long

Measuring up

As most deck-chairs are made to a standard size, some manufacturers pre-package cut lengths of deck-chair canvas and may also include the necessary tacks to attach it. These pre-cut deck-chair lengths are about 129cm/51in long – measure your deck-chair to check that this would be sufficient before buying. The easiest way to estimate the required amount of canvas, whether buying as a kit or by the yard, is to remove the old cover (see below), lay it out flat and measure it. Allow for a 1cm/½in turning at each end of the required length. If the old cover no longer exists, measure the required length of canvas by wrapping a tape measure around the top bar and allowing it to drop in a comfortable-looking curve before wrapping over to the underside of the bottom bar. Add 2cm/1in turnings to this length. The width of deck-chair canvas sold on a roll does vary slightly but any width between 40cm/15½in and 43cm/17in will fit the top bar of a standard deck-chair.

Removing the old cover

Tacked canvas covers Lay the deck-chair flat on the ground, face down. The canvas is usually attached to the top and bottom bars by flat-headed tacks. Gently ease them out

Random quilted deck-chair covers

Design a quilted cover, made from a bright washable fabric and polyester wadding, to lay over a deck-chair for added comfort. Attached with ties, it is easily removed for washing and storage.

Before you begin, read page 128 for instructions for quilting fabric in straight lines. If you are using a boldly printed or appliquéd fabric as shown here, try quilting round the pattern shapes for an unusual effect.

You will need

To fit a standard deck-chair
1.6m/1¾yd of 120cm/48in wide washable furnishing fabric
1.6m/1¾yd of 8oz weight polyester wadding at least 55cm/22in wide
Matching thread
5m/5½yd binding 2.5cm/1in wide

Preparing the fabric

Cut the fabric into two pieces, each 160cm × 55cm/63in × 22in.

Place the two pieces of fabric wrong side facing with the length of wadding sandwiched between. Trim the wadding to the same width as the fabric. Starting at the centre and working outwards, secure all three layers together with horizontal and vertical lines of tacking, about 15cm/6in apart.

Below: Quilt around printed motifs to highlight a bold design.

with an old blunt chisel or similar tool and remove the canvas, trying to keep it in one piece so that it can be used as a size guide.

Stitched canvas cover Some covers are stitched at each end of the fabric to form a casing and slotted on to the wood before the chair is assembled in the factory.

In this case, the old cover must be cut away and the original method of attaching ignored.

Fitting a new cover

Turn 1cm/½in to the wrong side on the top and bottom edges of the fabric and press well.

Lay the fabric flat on the ground, right side downwards, and place the deck-chair frame right side down on top. Wrap the end of the fabric around the top bar of the frame, so that the turned-under edge lies along the underside of the top bar.

Centre the fabric on the bar and then hammer a tack through the middle of the fabric turning into the wooden bar. Working outwards from this centre tack, hammer in three evenly-spaced tacks on either side. Place the last tack on each side just inside the outer edge of fabric. Try to avoid hammering tacks into holes left by the previous tacks as they will not grip.

Wrap the fabric around the bottom bar of the frame, placing the fabric turned-under edge on the underside of the bar. With most widths of canvas the bottom bar is slightly too narrow for the fabric to be spread flat, in which case fold under the necessary amount of fabric, dividing the excess amount evenly between the two sides.

Tack down the canvas in the same way as on the top bar.

DESIGN EXTRA

Making up

Machine stitch the quilting, either in squares or following the pattern shapes, but always working from the centre outwards to minimise puckering. Trim the quilted fabric to 132cm × 41cm/52in × 16½in. Machine stitch all round the outer edges, 1cm/½in from the edge, then trim away the wadding only from within this 1cm/½in wide strip cutting as close to the stitching as possible. Neaten all round the edge of the cover with bias binding (see page 163).

To make the ties, use pretty ribbons or cut eight 18cm/7in lengths of bias binding, fold each in half lengthways, wrong sides facing, and turn in the short raw ends. Edge stitch around the three open edges to hold together. Pin four ties to one side of the quilted cover, positioning them on the two long side edges, 2cm/¾in from each corner. Machine or hand stitch one end of each tie securely to the edge of the cover, so that the ties protrude over the edge.

Lay the quilted cover over the deck-chair with each end overhanging the horizontal bars. Pin the remaining four ties to the edges of the cover so that each one corresponds to one of the first ties, forming pairs that will tie together to hold the cover in place. Remove the cover and securely stitch ties in position.

easy to make attractive deck-chair covers using basic appliqué, patchwork and quilting techniques

A canvas hammock for lazy summer days

Enjoy lying in the summer sunshine, gently rocking in this comfortable canvas hammock with its tie-on pillow. It is simple and quick to make and ideal for the garden and the practical carrying bag makes it easy to take on holiday or store when not in use.

Make this simple canvas hammock in less than an evening and it will provide you with endless hours of comfort while dozing, reading or just enjoying the fresh air on a sunny summer's day.

A tough fabric such as canvas, wooden dowel, metal rings and ropes are all you need to make the hammock. A little carpentry is involved – cutting the dowel to the right length and drilling a hole through each end – but this is so simple that even a total beginner will find it fun to do.

Of course you do need to have either suitable trees or a stable structure from which to hang the hammock.

Alternatively, you could make or buy a wooden hammock frame.

The handy drawstring bag complete with a shoulder strap makes light work of carrying the hammock around on outings and provides neat storage during the winter. The other accessory you may wish to make is a pillow that ties on to the hammock.

Choosing materials

The fabric of a hammock is put under a great deal of strain and must, therefore, be very strong. Use a deck-chair weight canvas as this will be strong enough without being too bulky to fit under the foot of a domestic sewing machine.

Above: Use a tough canvas for the hammock, but the pillow can be made from any pretty furnishing fabric.

If in doubt about your sewing machine being able to cope with a particular thickness of canvas, buy a small amount first and test it. You need to be able to sew easily through three layers of the canvas, and to cope with up to five layers at times. Use either an extra length of the same canvas or any tough fabric to make the drawstring bag for carrying and storing the hammock. Although the pillow cover could also be in matching canvas, a softer, more easily washable fabric is preferable.

A strong rope is of the utmost importance. To be on the safe side, buy a 5mm/⅜in thick plaited nylon rope which has a breaking strain of 936lbs – well in excess of the weight of the heaviest adult. Specialist shops such as ship's chandlers or climbing equipment suppliers stock this rope and also the steel rings you will need. As nylon plaited rope quickly unravels once cut, hold a lighted match to each cut end for a second or so, until the nylon fibres have just melted and fused themselves together.

The canvas hammock

Use a heavy-duty machine needle (size 100/16) for stitching canvas and make sure that all knots are correctly and securely tied.

You will need

2.50m/2¾yd strong canvas at least 82cm/32¼in wide
176cm/69½in wooden dowel 3.5cm/1¼in in diameter
4.60m/5yd strong nylon rope plus extra rope (about 14m/15yd) to tie hammock to trees – see below
Two steel rings 3cm/1¼in diameter×5mm/¼in thickness
Matching strong sewing thread

Preparing the hammock

Cut one piece of canvas 247cm/97½in long×82cm/32¼in wide. Turn a double hem (1.5cm/⅝in and 1.5cm/⅝in) to the wrong side down

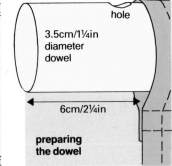

preparing the hammock

8.5cm/3⅜in

76cm/30in

channel for dowel

hole

3.5cm/1¼in diameter dowel

6cm/2¼in

preparing the dowel

both long edges and stitch in place. Turn 1cm/½in to the wrong side on both short ends and stitch.
To make a channel for the dowel turn a further 8.5cm/3½in to the wrong side on each short end and stitch down 5mm/⅜in and 1.5cm/⅝in from the edge.
Preparing the dowel Cut the dowel into two 88cm/34¾in lengths and make a pencil mark 6cm/2¼in in

from each end on both pieces. With an electric or hand drill, make a hole straight through the dowel on each pencil mark. The hole must be large enough to pass one thickness of the rope through. Slide a length of dowel into the casing at each end of the hammock fabric, positioning the dowel so that an equal amount protrudes at each end.

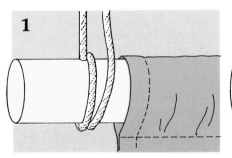

Adding the rope Cut two 230cm/90in lengths of rope and slip a steel ring on to each one.
Slot the ends of one piece of rope down through the holes in one piece of dowel, pulling a 40cm/16in length of rope through each hole. Knot each end of the rope in the following way.

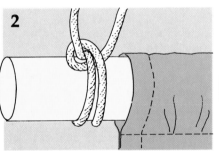

1 Pass the shorter, leading end of the rope round the dowel 1½ times to meet the main length of rope at the top of the dowel.
2 Pass the leading end behind the main rope and then under both wraps of the rope against the dowel. Pull tight.

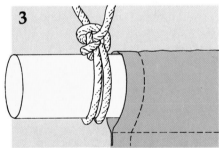

3 Pass the leading end across in front of the main rope, round behind it, then out to the front between the main rope and leading end. Pull tight. This completes the knot.
Attach the other length of rope to the opposite dowel in the same way.

Hanging the hammock

Assuming that the hammock is to hang between two trees, ideally spaced about 4m/4½yd apart, cut two 6m/7yd lengths of rope. This length of rope is sufficient for tying the hammock to average sized trees, but adjust as necessary.
Slot one length of rope through each steel ring and adjust the ropes so that the steel ring is exactly in the middle of each length.
Allow the hammock to sag slightly between the trees, rather than pulling it absolutely taut.
At each end of the hammock, wrap the two thicknesses of rope twice

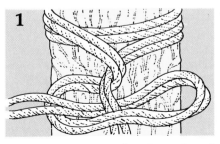

around the tree trunk or branch and tie with a knot (a round turn and two half hitches) in the following way.
1 Wrap the leading end of the rope (which is double thickness) right around the main rope (also double thickness) and then pass the

leading end in front of the main end, round behind, and out over the leading end.
2 Once again pass the leading end in front of the main end, round behind, and out between the leading and main ends to secure.

The tie-on pillow

Use either the same canvas as the hammock for the pillow covering or, for more comfort, choose a co-ordinating, plain or printed, lighter weight fabric.

You will need
30cm/12in×55cm/22in oblong cushion pad (or make your own to size)

70cm/¾yd of 60cm/23in wide canvas or lightweight fabric – or 35cm/13½in of 120cm/48in wide fabric

2m/2yd ribbon about 16mm/⅝in wide for ties

Matching sewing thread

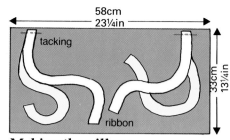

Making the pillow
Cut two pieces of fabric each 33cm×58cm/13¼in×23¼in and four 50cm/18in lengths of ribbon. Place two pieces of ribbon in each top corner of one piece of the fabric so that the ribbon ends lie across the seamline, as in the diagram. Tack the ribbon ends in place.
Place the two fabric pieces together,

right sides facing, and tack all round. Taking a 1.5cm/⅝in seam and leaving a gap on the bottom long side of the pillow cover sufficiently wide to insert the cushion pad, sew round, catching in the ribbon ends.
Remove the tacking and turn the pillow cover through to the right side with the ties protruding from the seam along the top. Press well, insert the cushion pad and hand sew the opening to close.
Lay the pillow inside the hammock, centring it along one of the shorter ends with the ties to the top. Tie the ribbons around the protruding dowel to secure.

Carrying or storage bag

This handy drawstring bag, complete with a shoulder carrying strap, keeps hammock and ropes together in one neat parcel for easy carrying around during the summer and safe storage during the winter.

You will need
1.3m/51½in strong fabric, at least 70cm/27½in wide

1m/40in thin cord for drawstring
Matching sewing thread

Cutting out
Cut out one piece of fabric 93cm×53cm/36¼in×21in for the body of the bag, one strip 53cm×10.5cm/21in×4¼in for the top of the bag and one strip 103cm×10cm/40in×4in for the

long shoulder strap.
Drawing round a suitably sized plate or dish, cut two circles 19cm/7½in diameter for the base of the bag which is made in a double thickness of fabric for extra strength.
Note: The bag is designed for neat storage of the hammock rope and dowels only.

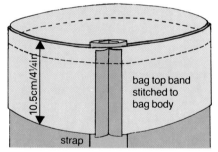

bag top band stitched to bag body

strap

Making up
Fold the large piece of fabric (the bag body) right sides facing and tack the long edges together. Stitch together, taking a 1.5cm/⅝in seam. Press seam open and turn right side out.
Fold the strap piece in half along its length, right sides facing, and sew the long edges together with a 1cm/½in seam. Turn through to the right side and press.
Tack the ends of the strap to the right side of the bag body, level with the bag edges and positioned over the seam.
Lay the two circles of fabric *wrong* sides facing and stitch together all round 1cm/½in in from the edge. From now on, treat the two circles

as one – the double thickness of fabric gives extra strength to the base of the bag.
With right sides facing and snipping into the seam allowance, pin the lower edge of the bag body to the circular base.
Tack and stitch taking a 1.5cm/⅝in seam, catching strap end into the seam. Stitch again 1cm/½in from the edges where the strap is enclosed in the seam to give added security. Turn through to the right side.
Fold the strip of fabric for the top band of the bag right sides facing and stitch the two short edges together with a 1.5cm/⅝in seam. Press seam open.
With right sides together slip the

bag top band over the bag body, lining up seam lines, and pin the edges together. Catching in the strap end, tack and stitch with a 1.5cm/⅝in seam, then stitch again over the strap end, 1cm/½in from the edges, for added strength.
On the raw edge of the top strip, turn 5mm/⅜in and then 1.5cm/⅝in to the wrong side and press. Stitch close to the edge to form a casing, leaving a small gap between the beginning and end of stitching. Ease the length of cord through the casing leaving the two protruding ends an equal length.
Zigzag all raw edges to neaten. Place the rolled up hammock and rope in the bag, pull up the cord ends and tie to close the bag.

Above: Both the teepee and the space capsule are washable and easy to put up either indoors or out in the garden on a dry day.

A colourful teepee or a super space capsule

Small Red Indians, both braves and squaws, will have hours of fun playing inside this stunning teepee.
Or send a would-be astronaut over the moon with excitement by making the silver space capsule.

These two super play tents are based on the traditional wigwam or teepee shape and are simply made from four triangular panels. Make the most of modern sewing aids such as fold-over braid, fabric paints, and bonding material for easy iron-on appliqué, and they take little time to make.

Any tough cotton fabric can be used. The Milium backing of some thermal linings gives a lovely silvery effect for the space capsule and ordinary curtain lining, now available in a wide range of colours, is inexpensive but has enough body to be the main part of the teepee.
Use up colourful scraps of cotton backed with Bondaweb to make appliqué motifs or use your artistic skills to add decorative touches with fabric paints, sealing them with a heated iron.

233

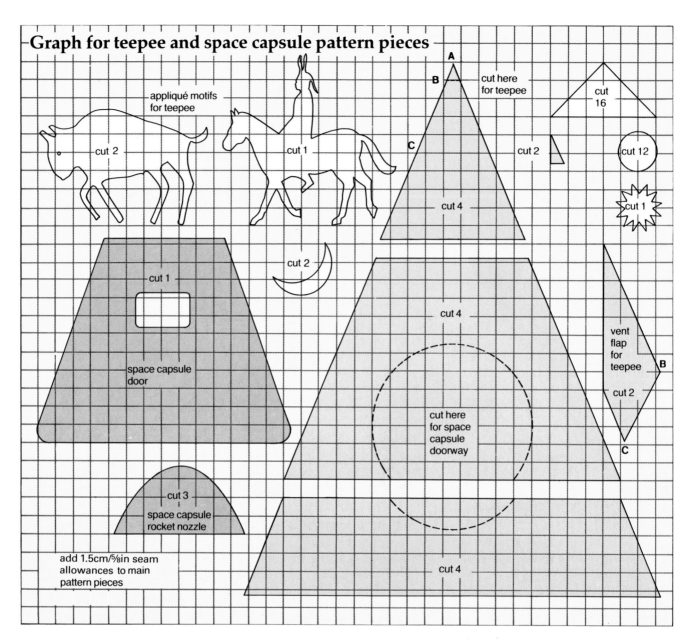

Graph for teepee and space capsule pattern pieces

appliqué motifs for teepee

cut 2

cut 1

A
B
cut here for teepee

cut 16

C

cut 2

cut 12

cut 4

cut 1

cut 2

cut 1

cut 1
space capsule door

cut 4

vent flap for teepee
B

cut 2

C

cut here for space capsule doorway

cut 3
space capsule rocket nozzle

add 1.5cm/⅝in seam allowances to main pattern pieces

cut 4

cut 4

back and side view of teepee showing appliqué motifs

The teepee

Curtain lining is ideal for the teepee. If you prefer to use fabric paint rather than appliqué to decorate the teepee, omit the appropriate fabrics and the Bondaweb.

You will need

3.5m/3⅞yd dark red cotton 90cm/ 36in wide or 2.6m/2⅞yd 120cm/ 48in fabric
3.5m/3⅞yd cream or beige cotton or calico 90cm/36in wide or 2.6m/ 2⅞yd 120cm/48in fabric
1.8m/2yd scarlet, 70cm/¾yd green and 20cm/8in yellow fabric for appliqué motifs, or colourful scraps
4m/4⅜yd each of red and yellow ric-rac braid
Vilene Bondaweb

4 garden canes each 1.90m/6ft long
3.5m/3¾yd red straight tape
1.8m/2yd red fold-over braid
Pattern paper

Cutting out

Enlarge the pattern pieces from the grid on to squared paper to make patterns. Adding 1.5cm/⅝in seam allowances all round each piece, cut four top and four bottom sections from dark red cotton, four middle sections, two vent flaps and two small triangles from beige and 16 appliqué triangles from red. For the appliqué, back the appropriate area of fabric with Bondaweb and cut out one Indian and two bison from green, 12 circles from red and a sun and moon from yellow, without any seam allowance.

234

Making up

1

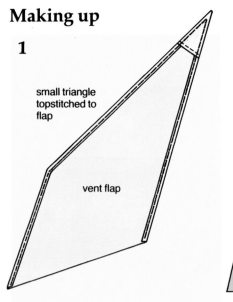

small triangle topstitched to flap

vent flap

2

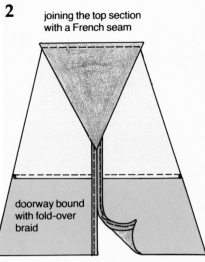

joining the top section with a French seam

doorway bound with fold-over braid

adding the decoration

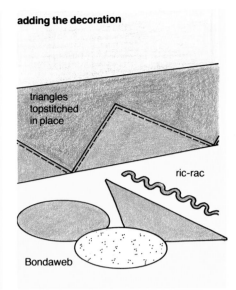

triangles topstitched in place

ric-rac

Bondaweb

1 Turn in and machine stitch a narrow double hem (5mm/¼in and 1cm/⅜in) on the short edge of the smallest triangles and all round the vent flaps, except along the edge B-C. Turn under and press 1.5cm/⅝in on remaining raw edges of the triangles. Position a small triangle on the sharp point of each vent flap, wrong sides together, and topstitch along the two long edges of the triangle to make a pocket.
Using French seams (5mm/¼in and 1cm/⅜in) join three sets of top, middle and bottom sections together to make three triangular side panels. On the fourth set of pieces, join only the middle and bottom sections. Cut down the

centre of these to make the doorway, lay a strip of fold-over braid over cut edges and topstitch.
2 Lay the two bound edges butting together, wrong side up, and place the top section wrong side down on top. Pin and tack, then stitch together with a French seam to make the fourth, front panel.
On each of the four panels, turn and stitch a narrow double hem to the wrong side along narrow cut-off tip of top triangle and along wide bottom edge.

Adding the decoration
Press a narrow turning to the wrong side all round each red triangle and tack four appliqué pyramids to the

bottom section of each panel as in the illustration. Topstitch each one in place.
Sew a row of red ric-rac 2cm/1in below seam joining bottom and middle sections. Add a row of yellow ric-rac 2cm/1in below this. On the front panel, stitch two evenly spaced rows of red straight binding down the middle section on either side of the doorway, turning in short ends to neaten.
Following the manufacturer's instructions, peel off the backing paper from the Bondaweb-backed motifs and iron the motifs into place on the side and back panels. Zigzag stitch round each one or oversew by hand for extra durability.

Completing the teepee

1

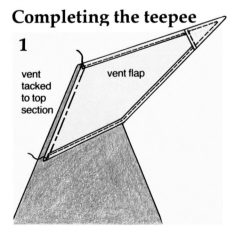

vent tacked to top section

vent flap

2

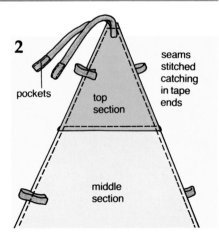

pockets

top section

middle section

seams stitched catching in tape ends

1 With right sides together, pin and tack the B-C edge of the vent flaps at the top of the side edges on the front panel.
Taking 5mm/¼in seams and with *wrong* sides facing, join the four side

panels together. Refold so that right sides are together and tack 1cm/⅜in in as if making a French seam.
2 Cut 12×5cm/2in lengths of tape and fold each in half as a loop. Tack the short ends of three tape loops, evenly spaced out, to each tacked seamline. Stitch the seam catching in the tape ends.
Fold a 52cm/21in length of tape in half and stitch the fold to the top edge of the back panel. Turn in each end of the tape 1cm/½in then 5cm/2in and stitch down the sides to make a pocket. Sew on six 15cm/6in lengths of tape as door ties.
Remove all tackings and press well.
To erect the teepee, slip a pole through the three loops on each side seam and let the end protrude

through the top. Stand the teepee up and slip the ends of the two forward-sloping poles into the pockets on the vent flaps; tie the tapes tightly around the four poles where they cross.

Space capsule

Lettering stencils are available from most stationer's but if you cannot buy one, make your own from a piece of stiff card.

You will need

4.5m/4⅞yd silvery Milium curtain lining 120cm/48in wide
1m/1yd square of matt black fabric
1.5m/1⅝yd red bias binding
1.5m/1⅝yd fold-over braid
30cm/11¼in Velcro
20cm/8in transparent pvc (optional)
Lettering stencil or card
Red fabric crayon or paint such as Dylon Colorfun
120cm/48in straight tape
Curly cable (optional)
4 garden canes 1.6m/1¾yd long

Making the pattern and cutting out

enlarge the pattern pieces from the diagram on page 234 on to squared paper. Cut off a 1.5m/1¾yd length of Milium (curtain lining) which will be used for the base sections. Cut four middle sections, one door and three rocket nozzles from the remaining Milium and four top sections from black fabric, adding 1.5cm/⅝in seam allowances.

Below: Young children will enjoy acting out imaginative games inside the exciting space capsule.

Making up the space capsule

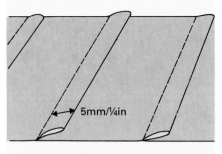

making the pintucks

5mm/¼in

pintucks folded across the width of 1.5m length of fabric

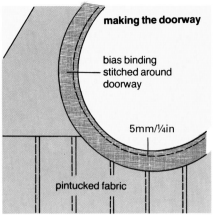

making the doorway

bias binding stitched around doorway

5mm/¼in

pintucked fabric

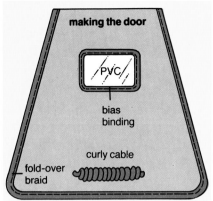

making the door

PVC

bias binding

curly cable

fold-over braid

Make pintucks across the width of the 1.5m/1¾yd length of Milium by pressing folds (wrong sides together) across the width at 6cm/2¼in intervals. Edge stitch each fold 5mm/¼in in, press, then cut four base sections from the pin tucked fabric, adding 1.5cm/⅝in seam allowances all round.

Join a top and bottom section to each middle section to make four panels and zigzag seams to neaten. Turn under and stitch a double hem (5mm/¼in and 1cm/⅜in) along the bottom edge of each side. Make a

tailor's tack where seamlines cross at point A on each panel.

Making the doorway Choose one panel to be the front of the space capsule and cut out a doorway as indicated by the dotted line on the pattern piece. Tack bias binding around the edge of the doorway, right sides together, and stitch 5mm/¼in in. Press bias binding to wrong side of fabric and topstitch down.

Making the door Tack the fold-over braid around the curved edge of the door piece and topstitch through all

layers to hold. Cut out a window as indicated on pattern, press bias binding in half lengthwise, fold over the raw edge and topstitch it in place. Cut a piece of transparent pvc 2cm/1in larger all round than the window, fasten it behind the window with adhesive tape, and topstitch with large stitches round the window from the right side to secure.

Stitch down the ends of a length of braid or curly cable to make a door handle.

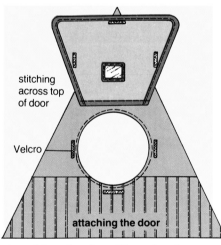

stitching across top of door

Velcro

attaching the door

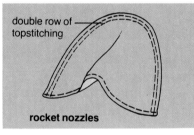

double row of topstitching

rocket nozzles

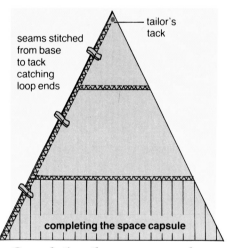

tailor's tack

seams stitched from base to tack catching loop ends

completing the space capsule

Attaching the door Place the door right side down on the front panel as in the diagram and stitch across top 1cm/½in from door edge. Fold door down over doorway and make a second row of stitching 1.5cm/⅝in from the top so the raw edge is enclosed.

Stitch a 10cm/4in length of Velcro to each side and lower edge of wrong side of door, and sew the corresponding halves around the doorway so that the door will lie flat when closed.

The rocket nozzles Stitch a narrow double hem on the straight edge of each nozzle piece. Press a 1.5cm/⅝in turning to the wrong side around the curved edge. Pin and tack a nozzle to the centre of each panel so that the two sides of the nozzle are almost parallel. Machine stitch with a double row of topstitching.

Adding decoration

Make little peephole windows in various sizes and positions on the panels, in the same way as on door. Using a letter stencil or working freehand, add a name and suitable space slogans (see illustration or make up your own) in fabric paint or crayon. Follow instructions to seal fabric paint by ironing.

Completing the space capsule With right sides facing, tack the four panels together, adding three tape loops to each side seam (as for the teepee, but do not make French seams). Stitch seams from base to tailor's tack on each side then zigzag stitch raw edges to neaten. Turn right side out, remove any tacking and press well, then slip a pole through each set of loops to meet at the centre top.

Index

Acknowledgments

The artwork was drawn by the following artists:
Lindsay Blow, Sharon Finmark, Eugene Fleury,
Susanna Lisle, Dawn Mason, Colin Salmon,
Sue Sharples, Jill Shipley and Sara Silcock.
The photographs on the following pages are by
courtesy of: Camera Press 27, 63, 65, 100, 101,
142, 144, 172; Coloroll 49; Curtain Net Advisory
Bureau 15, 16, 20, 66; Derwent Upholstery 222;
Designers' Guild 169; Dulux 76; Laura Ashley
52, 71, 123, 129, 132; Mayfair 21; Osborne & Little
210; Rufflette 22, 23, 30, 41; Sanderson 17, 42, 102,
125, 137, 217; Swish Products 47, 51, 57.
The remaining photographs were taken by the
following photographers: Jan Baldwin, Tom
Belshaw, Jon Bouchier, Alan Bramley, Allan
Grainger, Clive Helm, Monique le Luhandre,
Liz McAulay, Spike Powell, John Suett and
Jerry Tubby.